Latin American Cinema

Latin American Cinema

Essays on Modernity, Gender and National Identity

Edited by LISA SHAW *and*
STEPHANIE DENNISON

McFarland & Company, Inc., Publishers
Jefferson, North Carolina, and London

ISBN 0-7864-2004-9 (softcover : 50# alkaline paper)

LIBRARY OF CONGRESS CATALOGUING-IN-PUBLICATION DATA

British Library cataloguing data are available

Cover photograph: Walter Venencio in *Mataron a Venancio Flores*
(Juan C. Rodríguez Castro, 1982) (courtesy Cinemateca Uruguaya)

Manufactured in the United States of America

McFarland & Company, Inc., Publishers
Box 611, Jefferson, North Carolina 28640
www.mcfarlandpub.com

For Fernando and Alex

Acknowledgments

The editors and contributors would like to thank the following filmmakers, institutions, colleagues, and friends for their help and support in bringing this volume to fruition: Carlos Ameglio, Diego Arsuaga, Jose Pedro Barran, Alicia Casas de Barran, Mariela Besuievski, The British Academy, Álvaro Buela, Manuel Martínez Carril, Juan C. Rodríguez Castro, Cinemateca Brasileira (São Paulo), Cinemateca do MAM (Rio de Janeiro), Eduardo Correa, Department of Spanish and Portuguese of the University of California, Los Angeles, Pablo Dotta, Escola de Comunicações e Artes of the University of São Paulo, Mónica Lettieri, Eudora Loh, the Margaret Herrick Library of the Academy of Motion Picture Arts and Sciences, Robert J. Miles, Norma Rivera and her staff at the Filmoteca de Lima, Clarisa Pardina, Rob Rix, Roberto Rodríguez Saona, Victoria Ruétalo, Claire Taylor, Michael Chanan, the University of Leeds. We would also like to thank the British Academy for funding the conference Latin America Cinema: Theory and Praxis, which provided the stimulus for this volume.

The titles of films cited in this book are given in the original Spanish or Portuguese, with an English translation provided by the authors in parentheses the first time the title appears in a given chapter. Subsequently the title is given in Spanish or Portuguese alone within each chapter. Where films have been exhibited abroad under a translated title, the latter is given in italics, also in parenthesis.

Citations from screenplays have been translated by the authors into English. Quotations from secondary sources written in Spanish or Portuguese are provided in English translation, as indicated in the endnote references.

Contents

Introduction: Reflections on Modernity, Gender, and Nation in the Latin American Context

Lisa Shaw and *Stephanie Dennison*

This collection of essays is a response to the increased academic interest in Latin American cinema in recent years, which has been inspired partly by the many cinematic revivals that have been taking place in the region since the 1990s (see chapters 1 and 7) but is also a result of student-led demand for a film studies component in Spanish, Portuguese, and Latin American Studies programs. Scholarly publications still tend to concentrate on the arthouse, revolutionary projects of the 1960s and 1970s for which Latin American cinema is perhaps best known abroad: Glauber Rocha's *Aesthetics of Hunger/Tri-continental Cinema*; Julio García Espinosa's *Imperfect Cinema*, and Fernando Solanas's and Octavio Getino's Third Cinema. While some aspects of the region's revolutionary cinema are discussed in this volume (an early film by the so-called godfather of Brazilian Cinema Novo, Nelson Pereira dos Santos, in chapter 4, and Cuban Third Cinema in chapter 8), the focus of most chapters lies elsewhere, including commercially successful filmmaking in Latin America (e.g., the work of Argentine director María Luisa Bemberg in chapter 5 and the Brazilian Bruno Barreto in chapter 6) and the lesser-known cinema industries of Uruguay (chapter 7) and Peru (chapter 2). In collecting the essays, we have attempted to provide diverse coverage, both historically (the volume covers films produced throughout the 20th century and into the 21st) and geographically.

Modernity and Globalization

Uneven processes of development characterized Latin American countries throughout the 20th century, and continue to do so in an increasingly globalized new millennium. Cultural theorists often refer to the "other" or "peripheral" experience of modernity in Latin America, where the modern and the premodern continue to coexist. Néstor García Canclini, for example, has contrasted the advanced state of cultural modernity in the region with the relatively underdeveloped socioeconomic and political modernity.[1]

Although the moving image arrived in Latin America very soon after its emergence in Europe and the United States, this event did not coincide, as it did elsewhere, with other technological advances and the social changes associated with modern life. Images from abroad contradicted the realities of Latin American spectators, but nevertheless fostered aspirations to modernity.[2] Attitudes to modernity, and by extension to the cinema, perhaps the most pervasive sign of the new, have shaped the process of nation building across Latin America, as examined in the context of Peru in chapter 2. As Sarah Barrow concludes: "Peru's filmmakers moved from having a clear, if somewhat functional role within the inward-looking nationalist modernization agenda of General Velasco, to the promise of a broader cultural one under President Fujimori."

In recent years, creative possibilities have been opened up by economic and cultural globalization, a feature of late modernity that has given rise to new markets and increasingly important additional sources of income. As Sarah Barrow writes in relation to Peru, in chapter 2: "With very limited national investment, and the narrowing of the internal market, the only way forward in terms of funding in recent years has tended to be via international coproduction arrangements." Nowhere has the strategy of international cooperation proved more successful than in Brazil, where agreements between Motion Pictures Association member companies and certain Brazilian producers have been responsible for films such as *Carandiru* (2003), distributed by Columbia, the most successful Brazilian film in terms of box office receipts since the so-called *retomada* or renaissance of national film production in the mid–1990s. In chapter 1, Randal Johnson illustrates how when released properly, with an adequate marketing budget, Brazilian films frequently outperform North American movies being screened at the same time, as was the case with *Carandiru* and *Cidade de Deus* (*City of God*, 2002). The latter benefited from worldwide distribution courtesy of Lumière. Since the crisis of the Brazilian film industry in the early 1990s, the most successful home-grown productions have repeatedly proved to be those distributed by the MPA member companies Columbia, Warner, and Fox.

In spite of such reasons for optimism, within the context of neoliberal globalization, the products, not least films themselves, of Western Europe and above all North America continue to swamp the Latin American market.[3] As Randal Johnson concludes in relation to Brazilian cinema since its "re-birth" in the mid–1990s: "The one thing that has remained constant is the foreign occupation of the domestic market, with all of its implications.... State support continues to be necessary if Brazil is to continue to have a diverse national cinema, although it is not clear precisely what form that support should or will take."

The "nationality" of films based on international collaboration is being increasingly called into question. Chapter 3 outlines the debate surrounding the cultural specificity of the films Luis Buñuel made in Mexico, and in particular assesses the criticism of one of the last films he made there, *El ángel exterminador* (*The Exterminating Angel*, 1962). Considering the film a performance of the imagined border, Robert J. Miles regards it as a proposition of the mysterious and the interstitial, as symptomatic of the struggle to "cross the line," or, alternatively, the inevitability of inhabiting the margin. Countering the preponderant idea that the film represents a return to the critics' idealized notion of the director's European form with its apparently straightforward surrealism, Miles argues that *El ángel exterminador* is a philosophical work and Buñuel's first truly (post) modern film. Subsuming gender, class, and sexuality, the film critiques modernity's self-conscious preoccupation with exclusion and inclusion, and, by extension, those attempts to categorize or nationalize and fix the director and his films.

Gender and Sexuality

Jean Franco has observed that "the use of the body, the foregrounding of the precariousness of gender identity, [and] the emphasis on performance is very much part of contemporary sensibility."[4] The three chapters in the section on gender and sexuality, while discussing aesthetically very different films, reflect this sensibility. As with many films produced throughout the world, most Latin American cinema has tended only to bring women in from the margins when they symbolically represent the national (e.g., Alison Fraunhar's discussion of the allegorical role of the Afro-Cuban woman in chapter 8) or when they provide a love interest or sexual titillation (for examples of such a treatment, see chapters 6 and 9).

In this sense, one of Nelson Pereira dos Santos's lesser known early features, *Boca de Ouro* (Gold Mouth, 1962), can be said to buck a trend. In the first chapter of this section, Ismail Xavier discusses this film, which is an adaptation of a play of the same name by Nelson Rodrigues (1912–1980), the writer whose work has most often been adapted for the cinema in Brazil to date. Xavier argues that dos Santos made some shrewd choices with regard to camera work and lighting, adding characters and slightly changing the ending of the original play, in order to produce an ideologically more left-wing film.

Dos Santos seeks in his film version to cast the poor, and in particular women, in a sympathetic light, in an adaptation that Xavier describes as being "marked by an absence of moral judgment and less dependent on the traditional stereotype of Brazilians as weak fatalists who are obsessed with easy money, and who reject any work ethic." Xavier argues that focus is shifted in dos Santos's adaptation from the hypermasculine Boca de Ouro, to Guigui, the female lead. The role of Guigui forms the basis of Xavier's argument in this chapter, namely that she can liberate herself from the legacy left by her violent, macho ex-lover, thus altering the intention of Rodrigues's play, which was to condemn characters who are not absolutely pure. Although he stops short of using the term, Xavier, in what is a lesson in close textual analysis, suggests that dos Santos produced a feminist rereading of Rodrigues's morally conservative play.

Continuing with the subject of feminist rereadings, Claire Taylor in chapter 5 discusses the work of Argentine director María Luisa Bemberg, focusing on the issues of performativity and citation in two of her most acclaimed films, *Camila* (1984) and *Yo la peor de todas* (*I, The Worst of All*, 1990). *Camila* is set in the 19th century during the violent and oppressive Rosas regime and is based on the real-life experiences of Camila O'Gorman, a wealthy young Argentine woman who shocked society by eloping with her priest and confessor. The film simultaneously installs and questions the melodramatic mode in which it functions. This is an interesting aesthetic choice, given that melodrama is not only a genre closely associated with Latin American film production, and in particular, the Golden Age of Mexican cinema, but is also traditionally seen as "ideologically suspect." It was, for example, a genre that Latin America's revolutionary cinematic movements of the 1960s and 1970s had in mind when criticizing domestic film production's reliance on Hollywood models.[5] In terms of citation, reference is made to Buñuel: the film reworks the objectivization of the female protagonist in *Belle de jour* by showing Camila defying societal controls and refusing to be the passive object of desire. *I, The Worst of All* portrays another transgressive female, a 17th-century Mexican nun, Sor Juana Inés de la Cruz. Taylor observes that "the configuration of gender given in this film challenges any notion of a preexisting gendered essence, instead revealing the role-playing and assumption of codes intrinsic to the production of gender." Taylor concludes that in both films the protagonists "rework existing gender codes in order to fashion a tentative space for self-affirmation."

David William Foster has written that

> if the codes of sexuality ... were not so unstable — not so inherently ambiguous and internally contradictory — it would not be necessary for society to concern itself so much with vigilance, enforcement, correction, and chastisement for noncompliance.[6]

Just as Bemberg's characters struggle to find sexual expression in a climate of patriarchal oppression (colonial Mexico, and the dictatorship of Rosas and by extension, of the 1970s), so too do the protagonists of the two films discussed in chapter 6. This chapter is the second to deal with the adaptation of Nelson Rodrigues's work for the screen, and again the focus is clearly on issues of gender and the portrayal of sexuality. Stephanie Dennison compares two very different adaptations of Rodrigues's most successful play, *O beijo no asfalto* (Kiss on the Asphalt), and in particular the ways in which both films treat the issue of homosexuality. In the play and film versions, a married man, Arandir, kisses a dying stranger on the street at his behest, and is persecuted by the press and society at large for being a homosexual. In the first film, Flávio Tambellini's little-known pseudoexpressionist *O beijo* (1965), the issue is clearly avoided, but what is made implicit is sufficient to give an ironically more conservative treatment of homosexuality than that offered by the "reactionary" playwright himself. In the second film version, the box office hit *O beijo no asfalto* (1980), director Bruno Barreto cleverly plays with definitions of masculinity and the Brazilian cinemagoer's understanding of sexuality on the screen. Released at the height of the success of *pornochanchada*, the homegrown, soft-core porn comedies, ironically condoned by the dictatorship, it mixes scenes of erotica and sexual violence in a deliberate ploy to reveal the confusion and hypocrisy of Brazilian society at the hands of both the pornographer and the censor. Dennison argues that, despite Barreto's good intentions, Rodrigues's murdering homosexual (the father-in-law who kills Arandir in the closing scenes) is sufficiently grotesque as to convince homophobes in the audience that they were right after all.

Nation and Identity

Across Latin America domestic film production has often been seen as a central component of the national project, and has traditionally played a key role in the creation of an "imagined community," to use Benedict Anderson's famous phrase.[7] Renato Ortiz and Carlos Monsiváis have argued that the mass media as a whole were instrumental in consolidating national identity in the region.[8] The search for a sense of self has remained a favorite theme of Latin American movies, as Keith Richards illustrates in relation to Uruguayan film in chapter 7. Although Argentina is one of a number of countries that have provided increasingly essential funding for coproductions, Uruguay continues to portray itself on screen in relation to its more powerful neighbor. Richards writes that, "the second half of the 20th century saw enormous changes in national identity (the mere definition of which has become increasingly problematized) and social imaginary on a global level.... These seismic changes have caused fissures in the nation's self-perception that require urgent attention. This is hardly simplified by the current situation of postmodern or postnational flux, and the effects of globalized imagery upon previously stable notions of allegiance, belonging, and identity."

In their quest to capture a perceived national essence, Latin American filmmakers have repeatedly turned to allegory, particularly when free speech has been curtailed. The avant-garde Cinema Novo movement in Brazil, for example, drew on allegorical images of the nation during the most repressive years of the military dictatorship after 1968. In chapter 8, Alison Fraunhar analyzes how representations of the Afro-Cuban woman or *mulata* in four key films of the Cuban Third Cinema movement relate to national identity. She explores the way in which race and gender function in these films to both support and disrupt notions of Cuban identity. The issue of how a nation may be imagined, in this case from the exterior, is taken up again in chapter 9, where Lisa Shaw and Maite Conde consider Hollywood's depictions of Brazil from the silent era to the "Good Neighbor" period of the 1930s and early 1940s. They argue that Brazil's cinematic image in the United States, originally reduced to the bloodthirsty inhabitants of the country's jungles and sexually liberated city dwellers, was tamed and civilized in the 1930s and 1940s to comply with the imperatives of Pan-Americanism, and North America's geopolitical and commercial motivations. Perhaps more surprisingly, the stereotypical portrayal of Brazil, most famously personified by the living caricature of Carmen Miranda, when projected back to Latin America, was appropriated by Brazilian filmmakers themselves, often with an ironic slant, and equally used to promote their nation's commercial potential.

Latin American cultural forms, not least film, have perennially been involved in complex negotiations with foreign models and the demands of "Westernization," giving rise to what has been called cultural *mesti-*

zaje/*mestiçagem* (literally "racial mixing" in Spanish and Portuguese respectively), or cultural hybridity. With the advent of modernity this process intensified, and as López says, "we could argue that the cinema was one of the principal tools through which the desire for and imitation of the foreign became paradoxically identified as a national characteristic shared by many Latin American nations."[9]

Organization of the Book

The book is organized, then, around the paradigms of modernity, gender, and nation. The first three chapters deal with the impact of modernity and globalization on both the cinema industry and screen images of Latin America, and they relate to current debates as well as providing a historical perspective. In the second section on gender and sexuality, the three filmmakers upon whom the chapters concentrate bring questions of gender to the forefront of their work, whether through the discussion of sexual transgression, adapting literary work with a view to increasing the role of the female characters, or deliberately dealing with sexuality in order to both challenge the status quo and cash in on displays of nudity. The major focus of the final section is nation and identity, and the chapters consider, respectively, the viability of a national cinema in certain Latin American countries, the role of race and gender in nation building, and the filmic processes through which identities are constructed.

Although the chapters that make up this volume have been organized into three discrete sections, it is not our intention to suggest that they do not engage with other issues. Robert J. Miles's chapter, for example, calls into question the whole concept of a film's "nationality," and Alison Fraunhar's chapter on the allegorization of Afro-Cuban woman as nation clearly relates to questions of gender identity. This book attempts to reflect the fact that Latin American cinematic production continues to be characterized by its creative and multifarious responses to hegemonizing artistic forces and by its critical and innovative engagement with transnational currents and global trends.

Endnotes

1. Néstor García Canclini, *Hybrid Cultures: Strategies for Entering and Leaving Modernity* (Minneapolis and London: University of Minnesota Press, 1995).
2. Ana M. López, "'A Train of Shadows': Early Cinema and Modernity in Latin America," in Vivian Schelling (ed.), *Through the Kaleidoscope: The Experience of Modernity in Latin America* (London and New York: Verso, 2000), pp. 148–176.

8 Introduction

3. Vivian Schelling, "Introduction: Reflections on the Experience of Modernity in Latin America," pp. 1–33 (p. 27), Ibid.

4. Jean Franco, "From the Margins to the Center: Recent Trends in Feminist Theory in the United States and Latin America," in Elizabeth Dore (ed.), *Gender Politics in Latin America: Debates in Theory and Practice* (New York: Monthly Review Press, 1997), pp. 196–208 (p. 199).

5. In her revisionist choice Bemberg preempted a tendency also found in film criticism: see, for example, Christine Gledhill (ed.), *Home is Where the Heart is: Studies in Melodrama and the Women's Film* (London: BFI, 1987), and Ana M López, "Tears and Desire: Women and Melodrama in the 'Old' Mexican Cinema," in John King, Ana M López, and Manuel Alvarado (eds.), *Mediating Two Worlds: Cinematic Encounters in the Americas* (London: BFI, 1993), pp. 147–163.

6. David William Foster, *Gender and Society in Contemporary Brazilian Cinema* (Austin: University of Texas Press, 1999), pp. 10–11.

7. Benedict Anderson, *Imagined Communities: Reflections on the Origin and Spread of Nationalism* (London and New York: Verso, 1983).

8. Renato Ortiz, *A moderna tradição brasileira* (São Paulo: Brasiliense, 1988), and Carlos Monsiváis, *Contratexto*, 3 (July 1988).

9. Ana M. López, "'A Train of Shadows,'" p. 167.

PART I

Modernity and Globalization

1

TV Globo, the MPA, and Contemporary Brazilian Cinema

Randal Johnson

Introduction

"Os eleitos: o público brasileiro redescobre o cinema nacional" ("The Chosen: The Brazilian Public Rediscovers National Cinema"). Thus says the cover of the June 2003 issue of *Monet*, the programming magazine of Brazil's cable television provider NET. The caption accompanies a photograph of Hector Babenco, Carlos Diegues, and Fernando Meirelles, directors of *Carandiru* (2003), *Deus é brasileiro* (*God Is Brazilian*, 2003), and *Cidade de Deus* (*City of God*, 2002), respectively. Released in August 2002, *Cidade de Deus*, which was codirected by Kátia Lund, deals in very graphic terms with urban violence, using a cinematic language that draws from advertising and video clips. With a largely unknown and nonprofessional cast of actors, the film exceeded all of its producers' expectations, becoming the most successful film since the reemergence of Brazilian cinema in the mid–1990s. It was the first film in many years to dislodge children's stars Xuxa and Os Trapalhões from the top of the charts. It eventually attracted more than 3 million spectators in Brazil alone and secured distribution around the globe. It also provoked a great deal of controversy, sparking a series of debates and polemics concerning its representation of violence.

Some eight months later, in April 2003, Hector Babenco's much anticipated *Carandiru*, based on Dráuzio Varella's best-selling *Estação Carandiru* (1999),[1] a nonfiction work about one of the country's most infamous prisons, broke box office records, attracting more spectators during its first

Buscapé (Alexandre Rodrigues, left) learns about photography from a newspaper editor (Gustavo Engracia) in *Cidade de Deus* (Fernando Meirelles and Kátia Lund, 2002) (courtesy 02 Filmes).

weekend than any other film —foreign or Brazilian — had yet attracted that year.[2] By mid–May, *Carandiru* had surpassed *Cidade de Deus* as the most successful Brazilian film since the reemergence of Brazilian cinema in the mid–1990s, with more than 4.5 million spectators in its first two months of exhibition. The film also provoked a measure of controversy, although nothing compared to that of *Cidade de Deus*. The two films have much in common, not the least of which is their graphic representation of violence. Diegues's *Deus é brasileiro*, which was released in February 2003, completes the trio. Although not quite as successful as the other two, it drew more than 1.6 million spectators in its initial run (Table 1.3). These films reveal what Brazilian filmmakers have been saying for years, that the Brazilian public wants to see well-made films that deal with issues that have something to say about their own reality.

The undeniable success of these and other films does not solve some of Brazilian cinema's long-standing problems; for example, a market occupied by a foreign power, the insufficient number of movie theaters in the country, distribution and exhibition bottlenecks, the instability of sources of film production financing, and excessive dependence on the state. Nor does it efface the political and ideological cleavages that characterize Brazil's field of cinematic production. As filmmaker Eduardo Escorel has noted, "the outcome of the ideological struggle for the existence of Brazilian cinema is still undefined."[3]

Buscapé (Alexandre Rodrigues) takes time out from the violence of the *favela* in *Cidade de Deus* (Fernando Meirelles and Kátia Lund, 2002) (courtesy 02 Filmes).

Not long after *Carandiru*'s release, a polemic broke out when one of "the chosen," Carlos Diegues, gave an interview in which he harshly criticized the direction of government film policy under President Luiz Inácio Lula da Silva, accusing it of *dirigismo*, that is, of attempting to shape the content of cultural products in accordance with its political objectives. Different sectors and figures of the cinematic field rushed to take sides in support of, or in opposition to, Diegues's opinions. This polemic will be contextualized and discussed below. At this point suffice to say that what was at stake in this polemic — besides a certain model of film production financing, and, by extension, a certain model of production — was a form of symbolic power: the ability to shape government film policy in accordance with the professional interests of those involved.

Polemics have also emerged concerning modes of representation, politics, and film aesthetics, in particular, although by no means exclusively, in relation to *Cidade de Deus*. One critic, anachronistically counterposing Meirelles's film with those of Cinema Novo icon Glauber Rocha, characterized *Cidade de Deus* as embodying a "cosmetics of violence" as opposed to a Glauberian "aesthetics of violence."[4] In an interview published in *Monet*, Fernando Meirelles acknowledges that his film caused hundreds of articles and debates to be generated, but "if you ask some journalistic film critics, they will tell you that it is just a film made to sell popcorn. It's amazing how dialectics ruins people's minds. They are unable to conceive of entertainment, emotion, and reflection in the same package. They always think in an exclusive and antagonistic way: it's either art or entertainment. It's sad."[5] Delving into the terrain of the politically correct, at stake in this and similar polemics is a certain aesthetic (or political) model of cinematic discourse.

In this chapter I will use these two events— the success and controversy of recent films and polemics concerning government film policy — to discuss some of the achievements, conflicts, and tensions that have traversed the Brazilian field of cinematic production since the reemergence of Brazilian cinema in the mid–1990s after the crisis caused by former president Fernando Collor de Mello's scorched-earth policy toward state support of culture earlier in the decade.[6] Such tensions come to the fore paradigmatically in polemics wherein different agents clash over definitions that have an impact on the very structure of the field and their position in it. The polemics reveal, in an important moment of transition, the underlying dynamics of the field in which a homology exists between debates over models of production and debates over aesthetic models. In the final analysis, these debates form part a struggle over the diverse forms of economic and symbolic capital that are at stake in the field. In order to contextualize these polemics, I will first outline the theoretical or methodological framework that guides my discussion.

Framework

Any field of cultural production is traversed by tensions, conflicts, and contradictions deriving from its very structure, based on the relations between positions that participants, or agents, occupy in the field, and thus on the distribution of the diverse forms of capital at stake. This is particularly true in the case of fields of cinematic production in countries like Brazil, where film industries are shaped by multiple economic, ideological, social, and cultural exigencies that are compounded by U.S. domination of local film markets and the consequent need for diverse forms of state support. In addition to long-standing tensions between commercial and cultural (or artistic, or political) modes of cinematic discourse, conflicts also emerge concerning such things as government film policy, which has a determinant impact on production models and, indeed, on the very survival of most national industries.[7]

With his groundbreaking work in the sociology of practice, the late Pierre Bourdieu offers an important conceptual framework and analytical tools for disentangling some of these tensions. The notion of field — a structured space with its own laws of functioning and its own relations of force — is particularly useful for charting opposing positions between agents. Such agents may include directors, producers (who are often also directors), distributors, exhibitors, critics, certain government officials or agencies, and so forth.

Both economic and symbolic capital is at stake in the field of cinematic production. In terms of Brazilian cinema qua film industry, the primary stake is obviously economic capital, based on the number of spectators attracted and the return on investments, which can potentially lead to the accumulation of profits on a transnational scale. However, given the fact that Brazilian cinema, like most "national" cinemas, has only limited access to its own market and is thus largely dependent on the state, the market per se is perhaps somewhat less important than it might otherwise be, because market success does not necessarily affect the ability of directors and producers to make subsequent films. The international success of *Cidade de Deus*, however, reveals the truism that capital begets capital, because director Fernando Meirelles received multiple offers to make films both in Brazil and abroad. Had the film been a commercial failure that might not have occurred.

This fact results in a number of distortions. First, "independent" filmmakers, who generally subscribe to an auteur model of production, are in fact dependent on the state.[8] Second, for many filmmakers, the most significant "market" involves competition not for spectators or advantageous release dates, but rather for the right to make films based on the ability to participate in government-sponsored production financing programs, whether the state role is direct, as it was in Brazil prior to 1991, or indirect, as it has been since that time. This "market" constitutes one of the initial steps of the production process. Third, perhaps for ideological reasons or because of what Bourdieu might call a "logic of resentment," some Brazilian filmmakers resist making concessions to audience preferences and insist on a politically correct auteur stance, while at the same time demanding public funding of their film projects. An antimarket mentality thus combines with a statist view of cinematic entitlements to recreate and perpetuate the kind of situation that led, in the late 1980s, to a loss of social legitimacy for public investments in the film industry. In a post to the CinemaBrasil listserv, filmmaker Romeu di Sessa quite correctly outlines the dilemma: "We cannot imagine that the government will guarantee Brazilian film production ad infinitum without a clear objective and commitment to create a Brazilian market; if we don't do that, we will be condemning ourselves to eternal adolescence."[9]

Symbolic capital, which refers, in Bourdieu's analytical framework, to degree of accumulated prestige, celebrity, consecration, or honor and is founded on a dialectics of knowledge (*connaissance*) and recognition (*reconnaissance*), is equally important, and perhaps more important than it might otherwise be. It too has multiple dimensions. Put in extremely simple (and simplistic) terms, the possession of a significant degree of symbolic capital, garnered through critical, although not necessarily commercial, success, also makes it easier for a director to make additional films in a situation where market success is not determinant. Symbolic capital can, under certain circumstances, be converted into economic capital and vice versa.

In "The Field of Cultural Production" Bourdieu discusses this field as an "economic world reversed" based on a "winner loses" logic, since economic success (e.g., a best-seller) may well signal a barrier to specific consecration and the accumulation of symbolic capital in the field. In other words, short-term consecration, based on success in the marketplace, does not guarantee long-term consecration. Indeed, it may well work against such consecration, which is based on specific forms of symbolic capital. One might think, in this regard, of the difference between films starring Xuxa and those directed by Júlio Bressane. Xuxa's films are commercial successes that are likely to be soon forgotten, whereas Bressane forms part of Brazil's cinematic canon, with diverse forms of national and international legitimization (e.g., recognition by *Cahiers du Cinéma*).

This difference can also be understood in terms of Bourdieu's distinction between two subfields within the field of cultural production, the field of restricted production, and the field of large-scale production.[10] The dominant principle of hierarchization of the subfield of large-scale production, that is, commercial production or production for a broad audience, involves economic capital, or success in the marketplace.

In the subfield of restricted production, on the other hand, the stakes of competition between agents are largely symbolic, involving prestige and critical consecration. Economic profit is normally disavowed, and the hierarchy of authority is based on different forms of symbolic profit. The assuming of a position in this subfield constitutes, in Bourdieu's words, "production for producers," or production for those who share the producer's aesthetic disposition and who possess a similar degree of cultural capital. Júlio Bressane again serves as a pertinent example. His films appeal to a small but specialized and cinematically sophisticated audience that understands and appreciates his unconventional filmic discourse, which is generally unappreciated or not understood by a broader audience. The symbolic power of the subfield of restricted production depends on a network of critics, film historians, art house circuits, cultural centers, cinemathèques, and so forth. The very logic of this subfield, based on disavowal of the market, makes it more conducive to formal experimentation and innovation than might be possible in the subfield of large-scale production.[11]

Through their interventions, be they journalist or academic, critics also play a crucial role in the field. Edward Said has argued that differing critical and cultural perspectives are "competitors for authority" that attempt not only to earn a place for themselves but to displace others.[12] In a more rigorous formulation, Bourdieu wrote:

> Every critical affirmation contains, on the one hand, a recognition of the value of the work which occasions it ... and on the other hand an affirmation of its own legitimacy. All critics declare not only their judgment of the work but also their claim to the right to talk about it and judge it. In short, they take part in a struggle for the monopoly of legitimate discourse about the work of art, and consequently in the production of the value of the work of art.[13]

The legitimacy and authority of a specific critical interpretation, in other words, derive at least in part from the legitimacy and authority of those who propagate it. Identification with the presumably most advanced forms of aesthetic discourse — those produced in the subfield of restricted production — reinforces the critic's belief in the validity and superiority of his or her own position in the field, despite a frequently professed disinterestedness. There is, as Bourdieu has said, an interest in disinterestedness.

Given the fact that government film policy is crucial for the industry's survival, the state also has a determinate impact on the cinematic field, and with it diverse forms of political capital also come into play. The structure of government support for the film industry has changed dramatically since the 1980s. Struggles over the shape of government film policy, and those over models of production, are homologous with struggles for control of the diverse forms of capital that circulate in the field as well as with struggles over the legitimate discourse about the work of art in the field of criticism.

Collapse and Reemergence

In early 1990, shortly after taking office as Brazil's first democratically elected president in 30 years,[14] Fernando Collor de Mello terminated, in the name of a neoliberal economic agenda, a federal cultural policy that had developed somewhat irregularly since the 1930s. The film industry was particularly hard hit, because it had become almost entirely dependent on the state for production financing. Since the creation of the Instituto

Nacional de Cinema (INC) in 1966 and the Empresa Brasileira de Cinema (Embrafilme) in 1969, the state's role had evolved from that of regulator of market forces (through a modest but essential screen quota) to active agent and productive force in the industry, especially through its various programs of film production financing (low-interest loans, advances on distribution, and coproduction with private companies).[15] Suddenly finding itself without support, production collapsed and Brazilian cinema virtually disappeared from the domestic film market.

Brazilian cinema attracted only slightly more than 36,000 spectators in 1992, with three films released. This is a far cry from its most successful year ever, 1978, when it attracted 61.8 million spectators and 29.2 percent of the market. It achieved its largest market share, 30.8 percent, in 1980, with 50.6 million spectators, 11 million less than it had two years earlier.[16] The years 1978 to 1980 also represented the apex of Brazil's production levels, averaging 100 films per year. This was the period when Embrafilme, under the direction of Roberto Farias, was engaged in the coproduction of Brazilian films and had an active national distribution agency, which also ceased to exist in 1990. During this period the compulsory exhibition quota was at its strongest, increasing from 133 to 140 days per year between 1978 and 1980, thus theoretically guaranteeing Brazilian cinema 38 percent of screen time in the country.[17]

After the bottom dropped out in the wake of Collor's disastrous action, Brazilian cinema faced the daunting task of rebuilding itself and reoccupying the portion of its own market that it had lost with the collapse. By the early 2000s it had made some progress in doing so. In 2002, Brazilian cinema attracted 7.4 million spectators, a number that was surpassed in the first half of 2003.[18] This is still a long way from the late seventies and early eighties, but it is an obvious improvement over the 36,093 spectators of 1992 (Table 1.1).

A combination of factors has contributed to its reemergence. Numerous critics have correctly remarked on the great diversity of themes and styles in recent Brazilian cinema, including animation, children's films, historical dramas, historical farces, comedies of manners, romantic comedies, urban dramas, literary adaptations, neo-*cangaceiro* or social bandit films, political thrillers, neo-noir detective films, documentaries, and experimental films. On one level, this diversity is the natural result of production in a film industry that has long been characterized more by atomization rather than concentration (e.g., there are many small producers rather than a few large ones). On another level, however, it represents attempts by filmmakers to explore diverse ways of reestablishing communication with the Brazilian public.

Although veteran filmmakers such as Hector Babenco, Eduardo

Table 1.1. Brazilian Films Released/Number
of Spectators, 1992–2002

Year	Films Released	Spectators
1992	3	36,093
1993	4	69,290
1994	7	292,036
1995	12	2,966,239
1996	22	1,227,220
1997	22	2,401,959
1998	26	3,608,279
1999	32	5,194,058
2000	44	7,207,654
2001	31	7,198,257
2002	30	7,361,293

Sources: *Filme B, Database Brasil 2000; Database Brasil 2001; VI: 266, 16 December 2002.*

Coutinho, Carlos Diegues, and Nelson Pereira dos Santos have continued to make important films, perhaps more important has been the emergence of a new generation of filmmakers who have brought new aesthetic approaches to Brazilian cinema, often influenced by the language of video clips and advertising.[19] Among directors who made their first features since 1990 are Tata Amaral (*Um céu de estrelas* [*A Starry Sky*], 1997), Beto Brant (*Os matadores* [*Belly Up*], 1997), Carla Camurati (*Carlota Joaquina, Princesa do Brasil* [*Carlota Joaquina, Brazilian Princess*], 1995), José Henrique Fonseca (*O homem do ano,* [*The Man of the Year*], 2003), Jorge Furtado (*Houve uma vez dois verões,* [*Two Summers*, 2002), Monique Gardenberg (*Jenipapo,* [*The Interview*], 1996), Fernando Meirelles (*Menino maluquinho 2* [*The Nutty, Nutty Boy 2*], 1998), Mara Mourão (*Alô?!,* [*Hello?!*], 1998), Walter Salles Jr. (*A grande arte,* [*Exposure*], 1991), Andrucha Waddington (*Gêmeas* [*Twins*], 1999), and Sandra Werneck (*Pequeno dicionário amoroso* [*Little Book of Love*], 1997), not to mention numerous talented filmmakers who have directed outstanding short films but have yet to make feature-length films. These filmmakers have by and large broken free of the aesthetic and ideological legacy of Cinema Novo, and they have charted new directions for Brazilian cinema in consonance with the personal, political, and social issues confronting contemporary Brazil.

The number of films produced has increased from near zero to around 30 per year, which is not far from production figures in the 1980s.[20] At the same time, the exhibition sector has started rebuilding from its own collapse in the 1980s and 1990s, increasing from a low of slightly over 1,033 theaters nationwide in 1995 to more than 1,635 at the end of 2002. Although that is still an unacceptably small number for a country of 170 million people, the sector's expansion is a positive sign for the Brazilian film market, and expectations are that it will continue to grow.[21] Most important for the revitalization of Brazilian cinema, however, are a reformulated government film policy and the exploration of new forms of cooperation with some of its traditional antagonists, notably Globo Filmes (the film division of the powerful Globo television network), and foreign film distributors.

Government Support Reconfigured

Like most film industries outside of the United States, Brazilian cinema is largely dependent on the state for production financing and protectionist measures designed to guarantee a certain presence in the domestic film market, which has long been occupied by Hollywood. If Brazil is to have a cinema, the question is not *whether* the state should support the film industry, but *how* it should do so. After the 1991 implosion of the Embrafilme/Concine model — direct government investment in coproductions, bolstered by compulsory exhibition laws and other forms of support — the post–Collor administrations have preferred indirect investments through tax incentives and write-offs.

The Rouanet law (1991) offered, for the first time in Brazil's history, a tax credit for investments in the cultural field. More importantly, the audiovisual law (1993) allowed public and private businesses and corporations to invest a portion of their income tax in audiovisual projects, thus offering the (often remote) possibility of making a profit at no risk, because funds invested would otherwise be paid to the federal government. In addition, the law permits foreign film distributors in the country to invest up to 70 percent of their income taxes in national film production. The idea behind the Audiovisual Law was to foster productive relationships between the film industry and the private sector and, by extension, to encourage success in the marketplace. The ultimate goal of the policy was for the industry to attain self-sustainability. Funds raised under the provisions of these two laws have at least partially financed almost all Brazilian films since 1993.

As indicated above, since the implementation of these two laws, Brazilian cinema has expanded its share of its own market, but it is still far from reaching the objective of becoming a self-sufficient cultural industry. Production has increased considerably since the early 1990s, but that in itself does little to address the major problem: American cinema's occupation of the Brazilian market, based on unequal relations of economic and symbolic power, as well as such practices as block booking and intensive lobbying efforts in defense of its interests. When released properly, with an adequate marketing budget, Brazilian films frequently out-perform American films being screened at the same time (e.g., the three films mentioned at the outset: *Cidade de Deus, Carandiru,* and *Deus é brasileiro*). Nonetheless, most films remain confined to one of the arthouse circuits (such as the Espaço and Estação groups), if indeed they are commercially released at all. This explains, in part, why so few films have surpassed the mark of 100,000 spectators (Table 1.3).

Although crucial for the reemergence of Brazilian cinema, the two laws are not perfect, and they have introduced additional distortions into the process. Hector Babenco, for example, suggests that under the tax incentive policy one must generally serve as producer and director at the same time, or, somewhat more colorfully, be "both the whore and the pimp."[22] He further notes, somewhat facetiously, that most of Brazilian cinema is based on three elements: a screenplay, which allows for the project's approval under the law, a fundraiser (*captador*), and Adhemar de Oliveira, of the Espaço arthouse circuit. Although the circuit does what it can, it cannot exhibit all Brazilian films, and it makes little sense to make an expensive production that will be shown in just a few movie theaters. Unfortunately, that is precisely the situation. The government does nothing that will affect or challenge the interests of the American film industry in Brazil's domestic market, while little can be done to place Brazilian films in the American market.[23]

At the same time, access to funds potentially available under the Rouanet and Audiovisual laws is not equal; some filmmakers have more capital of social relations than others. There have been numerous cases of filmmakers whose projects have been approved but who have been unable to raise the necessary funds within the stipulated time limit. The press has given ample coverage to other cases in which funds were raised, but the proposed film was not completed, or in which accounts of expenditures did not satisfy government auditors. Furthermore, many film industry professionals have expressed serious concerns that decisions concerning availability of production financing often seem to be made by marketing directors of corporations, whose interests lie with promoting their own company rather than with the development and diversity of Brazilian cinema.

Largely because of the limitations of the production-financing scheme provided by the two above-mentioned laws, in September 2001, Brazil's president, Fernando Henrique Cardoso, signed a *Medida Provisória* (Provisional Measure) establishing a new government policy toward the film industry.[24] The centerpiece of this policy was the creation of a new government film agency, the Agência Nacional de Cinema (Ancine). Designed to regulate the distribution and exhibition market in the country as well as to foment the development of the film industry, Ancine was to be subordinated initially to the office of the presidency and subsequently transferred to the Ministry of Development, Industry, and Commerce.

New Partners?

The creation of Ancine, which was still being structured when Fernando Henrique Cardoso left office, was clearly designed to take Brazilian cinema a step closer to its desired stability. Its implications and the debates surrounding its creation illustrate in exemplary fashion the often tense, and certainly complex, relations between Brazilian cinema and Hollywood. Attempting to overcome some of structural problems that have long hindered the development and stability of the national film industry, the measure runs head-on into Hollywood's financial stake in the Brazilian film market by creating a new tax on foreign film distributors' profit remittances.

In a press release issued in 2001 in response to public reports concerning the possible shift in Brazil's film policy, the Rio de Janeiro office of the Motion Pictures Association asserted that it did not oppose financial contributions to the development of the Brazilian audiovisual industry. It believed, however, that incentives for voluntary investment in coproductions between Brazilian and foreign companies would be preferable to obligatory fiscal contributions such as those being proposed in the new law. It pointed out that MPA companies had been engaged in the coproduction or distribution of Brazilian films for some time, with significant success. In the first half of 2001, the number of spectators for Brazilian cinema had increased 7 percent over the previous year. According to the MPA, the increase was due almost entirely to films that were coproduced or distributed by MPA companies. The press release noted further that all of the Brazilian films that had enjoyed a modicum of success in the United States in the previous five years were either coproduced or distributed by MPA companies, and two of the three Brazilian films that were nominated for Academy Awards in the 1990s had the participation of MPA firms.

Table 1.2 lists the Brazilian productions that had coproduction or distribution support from MPA member companies between 1996 and 2003. It is of course not surprising that most of these films are more market oriented than some of the other significant productions during the same period.

Table 1.2. MPA Member Companies' Participation in Brazilian Cinema, 1996–2003

Year	Title	Director	Company	Co-P	Dist
1996	*O que é isso, companheiro?*	Bruno Barreto	Columbia	X	X
	Quem matou Pixote?	José Joffily	Columbia	X	X
	Tieta do agreste	Carlos Diegues	Columbia	X	X
1997	*Guerra de Canudos*	Sérgio Rezende	Columbia	X	X
	Buena sorte	Tânia Lamarca	Columbia	X	X
	For all — o trampolim da vitória	Luiz Carlos Lacerda and Buza Ferraz	Columbia	X	X
	O noviço rebelde	Tizuka Yamasaki	Columbia		X
1998	*As aventuras de Zico*	Antônio Carlos Fontoura	Columbia		X
	Coração iluminado	Hector Babenco	Columbia	X	X
	Simão, o fantasma trapalhão	Ronald Teixeira	Columbia		X
1999	*Bossa nova*	Bruno Barreto	Columbia	X	X
	Castelo ra-tim-bum	Cao Hamburguer	Columbia	X	X
	Gêmeas	Andrucha Waddington	Columbia		X
	O caminho dos sonhos	Lucas Amberg	UIP		X
	Orfeu	Carlos Diegues	Warner		X
	Xuxa requebra	Tizuka Yamasaki	Fox		X
	Zoando na tv	José Alvarenga	Columbia		X
2000	*Auto da compadecida*	Guel Arraes	Columbia		X
	Eu, tu, eles	Andrucha Waddington	Columbia	X	X
	O dia da caça	Alberto Graça	UIP		X
	Oriundi	Ricardo Bravo	Warner		X
	Tolerância	Carlos Gerbase	Columbia	X	X
	Um anjo trapalhão	Alexandre Boury	Fox		X
	Villa-Lobos, uma vida de paixão	Zelito Viana	UIP		X
	Xuxa popstar	Tizuka Yamasaki	Warner		X
2001	*Amores possíveis*	Sandra Werneck	Fox		X
	O bicho de sete cabeças	Laís Bodansky	Columbia		X
	Bufo & Spallanzani	Flávio Tambellini	Warner		X
	Caramuru, a invenção do Brasil	Guel Arraes	Columbia	X	X
	Condenado à liberdade	Emiliano Ribeiro	UIP		X
	A hora marcada	Marcelo Taranto	UIP		X
	A partilha	Daniel Filho	Columbia	X	X
	O xangô de Baker Street	Miguel Faria	Columbia	X	X
	Xuxa e os duendes	Paulo Sérgio Almeida	Warner		X
2002	*Avassaladoras*	Mara Mourão	Fox		X

Table 1.2. MPA Member Companies' (continued)

Houve uma vez dois verões	Jorge Furtado	Columbia	X	X
Xuxa e os duendes 2	Paulo Sérgio Almeida	Warner		X
2003 *1972*	José Emílio Rondeau	BVI	X	X
Caminho das nuvens	Vicente Amorim	BVI	X	X
Carandiru	Hector Babenco	Columbia	X	X
*Casseta e planeta**	Lula Buarque de Hollanda	Warner	X	X
Cristina quer casar	Luiz Villaça	Fox	X	X
Desmundo	Alain Fresnot	Columbia	X	X
Deus é brasileiro	Carlos Diegues	Columbia	X	X
A dona da história	Daniel Filho	BVI	X	X
O homem do ano	José Henrique Fonseca	Warner		X
O homem que copiava	Jorge Furtado	Columbia	X	X
*Ilha rá-tim-bum**	Eliana Fonseca	Warner	X	X
*Lisbela e o prisioneiro**	Guel Arraes	Fox	X	X
*Pelé**	Aníbal Massaini Neto	UIP	X	X
*O redentor**	Fernanda & Cláudio Torres	Warner	X	X

Source: Motion Picture Association. Note: Films marked with an asterisk (*) were in production in July 2003.

One should note that most of the MPA companies' participation came under the provisions of the Audiovisual Law, but in some cases (e.g., *Carandiru*) the distributor invested a considerable amount of money outside of those provisions for distribution publicity. In at least one case, an MPA distributor entered into a multipicture coproduction and distribution agreement with a Brazilian producer.[25] One should also note that participation in Brazilian films under the terms of the Audiovisual Law is optional, not obligatory.[26]

Market Success

The information in Table 1.2 becomes even more significant when compared with Table 3, which lists the most successful Brazilian films since the crisis of the early 1990s. Films distributed by MPA member companies Columbia, Warner and Fox dominate the top half of the table.

A number of things besides the MPA presence warrant attention in this list. First, despite the fact that films with adult themes and graphic depictions of violence — *Carandiru* and *Cidade de Deus* — top the list, comedy is the clear winner when it comes to audience preferences. Seven of the top 10 and 13 of the top 20 films are comedies. Of those, 9 are clearly directed at a children's or adolescent audience. Superstar Xuxa accounts

Table 1.3. The Top 50 Brazilian Films, 1994–2003 (June) (Numbers of Spectators)

Title	Director	Distributor	Year	Spectators
1 *Carandiru*	Hector Babenco	Columbia	2003	4,556,533
2 *Cidade de Deus*	Fernando Meirelles	Lumière	2002	3,317,372
3 *Xuxa e os duendes*	Paulo S. de Almeida and Rogério Gomes	Warner	2001	2,657,091
4 *Xuxa popstar*	Tizuka Yamasaki	Warner	2000	2,394,326
5 *Xuxa e os duendes 2*	Paulo. S. de Almeida and Rogério Gomes	Warner	2002	2,301,152
6 *O auto da compadecida*	Guel Arraes	Columbia	2000	2,157,166
7 *Xuxa requebra*	Tizuka Yamasaki	Fox	1999	2,074,461
8 *Simão, o fantasma trapalhão*	Paulo Aragão	Columbia	1998	1,658,136
9 *Deus é brasileiro*	Carlos Diegues	Columbia	2003	1,626,634
10 *Central do Brasil*	Walter Salles Jr.	Riofilme/SR	1998	1,593,967
11 *O noviço rebelde*	Tizuka Yamasaki	Columbia/Art	1997	1,501,035
12 *A partilha*	Daniel Filho	Columbia	2001	1,449,411
13 *Carlota Joaquina*	Carla Camurati	Elimar	1995	1,286,000
14 *O quatrilho*	Fábio Barreto	S. Ribeiro	1995	1,117,154
15 *Orfeu*	Carlos Diegues	Warner	1999	961,961
16 *Zoando na tv*	José Alvarenga	Columbia	1999	911,394
17 *Tainá— uma aventura no Amazonas*	Tânia Lamarca	Art/MAM	2001	853,210
18 *O trapalhão e a luz azul*	Paulo Aragão	Lumière	1999	771,831
19 *Castelo rá-tim-bum*	Cao Hamburger	Columbia	1999	725,329
20 *Eu, tu, eles*	Andrucha Waddington	Columbia	2000	695,682
21 *Guerra de Canudos*	Sérgio Rezende	Columbia	1997	655,016
22 *Bossa nova*	Bruno Barreto	Columbia	2000	520,614
23 *Tieta do agreste*	Carlos Diegues	Columbia	1996	511,954
24 *Pequeno dicionário amoroso*	Sandra Werneck	RioF/Lum	1997	402,430
25 *Bicho de sete cabeças*	Laís Bodansky	Columbia	2001	401,565
26 *Menino maluquinho*	Helvécio Ratton	RioF/SR	1995	397,023
27 *Amores possíveis*	Sandra Werneck	Fox	2001	396,224
28 *O xangô de Baker Street*	Miguel Faria	Columbia	2001	366,353
29 *O que é isso, companheiro?*	Bruno Barreto	Columbia	1997	321,450
30 *Abril despedaçado*	Walter Salles Jr.	Lumière	2002	314,329
31 *Avassaladoras*	Mara Mourão	Fox	2002	284,260
32 *Todos os corações do mundo*	Murilo Salles	S. Ribeiro	1996	265,017
33 *Caramuru*	Guel Arraes	Columbia	2001	246,023
34 *O homem que copiava*	Jorge Furtado	Columbia	2003	236,474
35 *O grilo feliz*	Walbercy Ribas	Hoyts	2001	216,611

Table 1.3. The Top 50 Brazilian Films (continued)

36 *Menino maluquinho 2*	Fernando Meirelles	RioF/SR	1998	213,336
37 *Surf adventures*	Arthur Fontes	Lumière	2002	200,853
38 *Memórias póstumas*	André Klotzel	Lumière	2001	186,380
39 *Mauá— o imperador do rei*	Sérgio Rezende	RioF/BVI	1999	185,107
40 *Copacabana*	Carla Camurati	Elimar	2001	178,090
41 *Navalha na carne*	Neville d'Almeida	S. Ribeiro	1997	170,929
42 *Super colosso— o filme*	Luís Ferré	Paris	1995	154,762
43 *Como ser solteiro*	Rosane Svartman	RioF/SR	1998	150,778
44 *A paixão de Jacobina*	Fábio Barreto	Playarte	2002	145,321
45 *Lavoura arcaica*	Luiz F. Carvalho	Riofilme	2001	141,321
46 *O cangaceiro*	Anibal Massaini Neto	S. Ribeiro	1997	140,932
47 *Villa-Lobos*	Zelito Viana	RioF/UIP	2000	138,032
48 *Anahy de las misiones*	Sérgio Silva	S. Ribeiro	1997	131,000
49 *Janela da alma*	Walter Carvalho	Copacabana	2002	130,683
50 *Lamarca*	Sérgio Rezende	Riofilme	1994	123,683

Sources: *Filme B*, Edição especial (November 2002), *Filme B*, 294 (June 30, 2003).[27]

for four films (*Xuxa e os duendes* [Xuxa and the Elves], *Xuxa popstar*, *Xuxa e os duendes 2* [Xuxa and the Elves 2], and *Xuxa requebra* [Xuxa Gets Down]), all of which are in the top 7, while Renato Aragão (former leader of Os Trapalhões comedy team, long box office leaders in Brazil) has three films among the top 25 (*Simão, O fantasma trapalhão* [Simão, the Ghost Trapalhão], *O noviço rebelde* [*The Rebel Monk*], and *O trapalhão e a luz azul* [The Trapalhão and the Blue Light]).

Xuxa and Renato Aragão also point to the importance of television for success in the film market, for they both have close and long-standing relationships with the Globo television network. Several of the other successful comedies also have roots in TV Globo: Guel Arraes's *O auto da compadecida* (*A Dog's Will*), based on Ariana Suassuna's play of the same name, was reedited for the cinema after being successfully screened on TV Globo; Daniel Filho's *A partilha* (*The Inheritance*, 2001) features well-known Globo actresses and the director himself has long been closely associated with TV Globo[28]; *Zoando na tv* (Messing about on TV, 1999) features Globo star Angélica; and Cao Hamburger's *Castelo rá-tim-bum* (Rá-Tim-Bum Castle, 1999) is a cinematic version of a popular children's series. The only children's films that stand apart from TV Globo are Tânia Lamarca's *Tainá— uma aventura no Amazonas* (Tainá— An Adventure in the Amazon, 2001), and Helvécio Ratton's *Menino maluquinho* (*The Nutty, Nutty Boy*, 1994), based on Ziraldo's popular children's book.

The casts of other films, such as *Deus é brasileiro, Orfeu* (1999), *Guerra de Canudos* (*Battle of Canudos*, 1997), *Pequeno dicionário amoroso, Eu, tu, eles* (*Me, You Them*, 2001), *Bossa nova* (2000), *Tieta do agreste* (*Tieta*, 1996), and *Avassaladoras* (*Overwhelming Women*, 2002), also draw heavily from popular Globo actors. This is not surprising, because the Brazilian "star system," which has largely developed since the mid–1970s, is associated less with the film industry than with television, and particularly with the Globo network and its major product, the popular *telenovela* or soap opera. Because of the cinema's subordinate position in the field of cultural production, starting in the 1970s many film producers began to make concerted attempts to hang on to television's coattails in their quest for commercial success in very a competitive film market.[29] Those attempts have obviously continued in various forms until today.

The Globo presence is even more pervasive than the mere use of its actors in many of the most popular films. In 1997, Globo created its film division, Globo Filmes, much to the dismay of many sectors of the industry who feared its economic power. That power is evident in the above list: all of the top 10 films—and numerous others on the list—had the participation of Globo Filmes.[30] Although not considered an "independent" producer under the terms of the audiovisual law, and thus unable to participate directly in its tax incentive programs of film financing, Globo has developed productive relationships with production companies which *are* entitled to raise funds under the law. At the same time, Globo Filmes has established good working relations with several of the MPA member companies, which were responsible for the distribution of 8 of the top 10, and 18 of the top 25, films on the above list.

It should be clear from this brief description that the currently dominant (but not necessarily hegemonic) model of film production in Brazil involves the association of independent producers, Globo Filmes, and foreign film distributors under the terms of the Audiovisual Law.

Not surprisingly, opinion in Brazilian film circles is divided about this arrangement. Director Jorge Furtado, whose *O homem que copiava* (The Man Who Copied, 2003) was coproduced and distributed by Columbia, argues that the success of such films as *Cidade de Deus, Carandiru,* and *Deus é brasileiro* is due not only to their undeniable quality, but also to their partnership with television through Globo Filmes, and he believes that such arrangements should be broadened.[31] Others are not so optimistic. In the July 2003 issue of the *Revista de Cinema*, director Aluízio Abranches (*Um copo de cólera* [*A Glass of Rage*, 1999], *As três Marias* [*The Three Marias*, 2002]) says the following: "One of the obstacles facing Brazilian cinema is the duo Globo-Columbia. If you are not associated with this duo, you have few chances for success. The biggest problem is thus exhibition and distribution.... The public only goes where Globo Filmes is involved."[32] Given the absence of a national distributor along the lines of Embrafilme, films without such support have a much more difficult time finding adequate distribution outlets and thus reaching a significant audience beyond the art house circuit, even though many of them are among the most important films of the last decade.

Despite the fact that many excellent films *are* on the top-50 list, there is no necessary correlation between box office success and cinematic quality. Not on the above list are such important films as Tata Amaral's *Um céu de estrelas*, Karim Ainouz's *Madame Satã* (2002), Sérgio Bianchi's *Cronicamente inviável* (*Chronically Unfeasible*, 2000), Beto Brant's *Os matadores* and *O invasor* (*The Trespasser*, 2001) (which many critics consider the best film of the reemergence),[33] Lírio Ferreira and Paulo Caldas's *Baile perfumado* (*Perfumed Ball*, 1997), Ugo Georgetti's *Sábado* (Saturday), José Joffily's *Dois perdidos numa noite suja* (*Two Lost in a Dirty Night*, 2002), André Klotzel's *Memórias póstumas* (*Posthumous Memories*, 2001), Walter Lima Jr.'s *A ostra e o vento* (*The Oyster and the Wind*, 1997), Fernando Meirelles's *Domésticas* (*Maids*, 2000) Domingos de Oliveira's *Amores* (Love Affairs) and *Separações* (Separations), Walter Salles Jr.'s *Terra estrangeira* (*Foreign Land*, 1995), and Nelson Pereira dos Santos's *A terceira margem do rio* (*The Third Bank of the River*, 1994), just to mention a few. Also missing from the list are the films of Júlio Bressane and outstanding documentaries such as Eduardo Coutinho's *Santo forte* (*The Mighty Spirit*, 1999) and *Edifício Master* (2002), and José Padilha's *Ônibus 174* (*Bus 174*, 2002).

Polemics 1: Social Counterparts

On January 1, 2003, Luiz Inácio Lula da Silva was sworn in as Brazil's president. His choice of singer/songwriter Gilberto Gil as Minister of Culture was not met with great enthusiasm in the film industry, which had hoped for someone with greater political influence and experience in the field. The appointment of filmmaker Orlando Senna as head of the ministry's audiovisual division was taken as a positive sign, but during the first half of 2003 the industry was waiting anxiously to see the precise shape of the new government's film policy. Reports surfaced that some sectors of the administration saw Ancine as unnecessary and that changes were on the way. In the meantime, the government extended the audiovisual law, which was to expire in 2003, until the end of 2006, guaranteeing at least temporary continuation of a policy that had led to the reemergence of Brazilian cinema.

Within the general context described above, as well as in the general atmosphere of uncertainty about the new government's intentions, on May 3, 2003, the Rio de Janeiro daily *O globo* published an interview with Carlos Diegues occasioned by what journalist Arnaldo Bloch describes, in his introduction, as "strong indignation" among directors and producers concerning criteria for investments in the cultural field under the administration of Luiz Inácio Lula da Silva.[34] With the government's approval, state enterprises Furnas Centrais Elétricas and Eletrobrás had announced that future investments in culture would be made in accordance with new guidelines favoring projects that would democratize access to culture, contribute to the decentralization of cultural production, valorize national traditions and identities, and include low-income communities in some way. This "social counterpart" should both provide the target public access to cultural goods and contribute to community development through the creation of jobs in low-income communities or training in the production of popular culture.[35]

In the interview, Diegues expresses deep concern over the direction of government film policy, which he sees as threatening the "extraordinary evolution toward a self-sustainable national cinema, which was precisely the objective of the Audiovisual Law starting in 1994," by imposing ideological and political perspectives on films in a way that not even the military dictatorship had dared to do. Diegues accuses the administration of wanting, in authoritarian fashion, to centralize decisions concerning film production financing according to the designs of the powerful Secretary of Communication, Luiz Gushiken. He sees such impositions on individual freedom of creation as a Zhdanovian move within the heart of a democratic government, "an attempt to revive the old idea of culture as an arm of political struggle, as an instrument of the struggle for power."

On the question of "social counterparts," Diegues argues: "the counterpart is the work itself! Its ability to entertain, to move and excite people, to make them think, to bring them together, promoting their spiritual progress, their identification with others." Rather than politically oriented social counterparts, Diegues calls on the government to work in the area of the industry's infrastructure, increasing the number of theaters in the country and supporting the development and exploration of new technologies in filmmaking.

Diegues closes the interview by suggesting that Brazilian cinema is on the right track and that the Brazilian people are again beginning to be proud of their cinema, just as they have gained a renewed self-esteem through the election of Lula to the presidency. He notes— referring specifically to MPA companies— that potential partners are beginning to see Brazilian cinema as a profitable area for investments. He warns, however, that with the new guidelines, Brazilian cinema may once again be the victim of the myth of Sisyphus; every time it is close to success, it rolls back down the mountain in what Diegues sees as a chronic, self-destructive tendency.

After the publication of Diegues's interview, numerous film industry professionals endorsed his comments while others publicly disagreed. In a widely circulated "dissonant note," Eduardo Escorel suggests that Diegues's argument seems to presuppose the unconditional defense of a model of film production based on the policy of fiscal incentives, although there is no evidence that the model had led Brazilian cinema anywhere close to self-sufficiency or independence from government support.[36] It was thus inevitable, Escorel suggests, that the new government would seek to redefine the terms of such support, and doing so does not necessarily infringe on artistic freedom. Escorel asks if the government is not just "indicating its willingness to assume its responsibility for the use of public funds?" He recalls that the administration of Fernando Henrique Cardoso had been severely criticized for its "omission" in this regard, leaving investment decisions in the hands of the marketing departments of corporations or forcing producers to lobby ministers of state or politicians to obtain support for financing.

Escorel suggests that Diegues is overreacting. "Who is opposed," he asks, "to the democratization of access to culture? Who opposes the geographical decentralization of the projects financed? Who can deny the need for 'social inclusion' or the 'promotion of citizenship' and the 'development of low-income communities?' Who is against the 'strengthening of national identity'?" The questions Escorel raises have to do with the appropriate use of public funds in a country marked by extreme social inequality. In his view, the government has the "need, right, and duty to evaluate the artistic and cultural merit of proposals for financing."

Escorel notes further that, by and large, the Brazilian people do not go to the movies. He thus finds it somewhat inappropriate to invoke, in their name, "privileges to which the vast majority of Brazilians do not have access." He concludes that the true focus should not be on the specific terms of government programs of film financing, but rather on the structural issues— unfair terms of competition with foreign films, Brazilian cinema's preferential access to its own market, the outsourcing of television production, and so forth — that could in fact lead to the development of a self-sustaining national film industry.

Because of the outcry and ensuing controversy over the new financing criteria, and thus over what was perceived to be a new cultural policy direction on the part of Lula's government, Minister of Culture Gilberto Gil and

Secretary of Communication Luiz Gushiken met in Rio de Janeiro with Diegues, producer Luiz Carlos Barreto, and other like-minded representatives of the film industry. In the meeting the decision was made to rescind the new directives and to give responsibility for developing financing criteria to the Ministry of Culture. That, however, did not end the controversy. Two days later, on May 8, 49 film industry professionals, including Escorel, Beto Brant, Eduardo Coutinho, Fernando Meirelles, Jorge Furtado, and Nelson Pereira dos Santos, released the following public declaration:

Public Declaration
We, the film producers and directors who have signed below, inform public opinion, governmental organs and the press that, despite media reports, the group of filmmakers that met in Rio de Janeiro on May 6 with ministers Gilberto Gil and Luiz Gushiken do not speak for the totality of Brazilian filmmakers.
   We would like to emphasize the following basic points:
   (a) On social counterparts:
        We are in favor of having fiscal incentives for cultural production distributed in a manner that is attuned to a more just distribution of cultural goods in our country.
        We believe that the policy can be outlined quickly between producers and governmental organs based on collaboration, and not unilaterally.
   (b) On the concession of public resources as practiced during the last few years:
        We request a more democratic, decentralized and totally transparent access to the cultural funding granted by state enterprises and an end to the privilege of small groups who have received a disproportionate share of such resources in the last few years.
   (c) Representation and dialogue:
        We request that the dialogue between the Minister of Culture, the Secretariat of Communication, the state enterprises, and filmmakers take place through the industry's official associations and organizations throughout Brazil and not in a personalistic manner.

   With its concern with representation (they "do not speak" for all of us, "the privilege of small groups," "in a personalistic manner"), this statement represents a collective stance in opposition to those seen to have an inordinate amount of influence in government policy and in decisions concerning film production financing. Its call for discussions to take place through the sector's official associations and organizations (e.g., the Brazilian Association of Documentary Filmmakers; ABD) also seeks to create a structure for negotiation in which its signatories' interests will best be represented.

The stakes in this debate are clear. Although couched, in both cases, in political terms (*authoritarianism, freedom, representation*), the polemic involves a struggle over symbolic power, or rather, the power to influence the direction of government policy, to gain greater access to production financing, and, ultimately, to achieve viability in the field. As a filmmaker who has repeatedly obtained financing under the terms of the Audiovisual Law, and who depends on that financing to make additional films, Diegues was concerned that the directives would make things more difficult, particularly if decisions on criteria were moved from the Ministry of Culture to the Secretariat of Communication. His stance was thus defensive, an effort to maintain the status quo. On the other hand, other sectors, perhaps imbued with a logic of resentment or perhaps staking out a political position in support of the Lula administration, would like to see things become easier for them. Put another way, on one side are those who have taken an entrepreneurial stance toward film industry development; and on the other, those who would rather have some kind of collective bargaining through professional organizations. The reality is that both sides depend on the state for the ability to make films, which explains why such a policy matter is of such import. Both have symbolic and material interests at stake.

The recent polemic echoes earlier debates that took place in the 1970s concerning a reorientation of state policy that led to Embrafilme's coproduction of a select number of films. The reorientation in policy gave rise to a dichotomy between cultural and commercial views of the state role. On the cultural side were filmmakers who felt that the state should support films based on their cultural importance, regardless of commercial potential. On the other side were those who thought that the state should have a more entrepreneurial role, investing in a small number of films leading to capital accumulation in the industry rather than in a larger number of films by "independent'" filmmakers.[37] The recent polemic also echoes the "cinemão" (literally, big cinema) versus "cineminha" (little cinema) debate of the 1980s (relatively expensive films, such as those produced by Luiz Carlos and Lucy Barreto, and less expensive independent or auteur films).

Polemics 2: Aesthetics and Cosmetics

Although a false dichotomy, the cultural versus commercial divide continues to thrive in Brazilian film circles, and, to at least a certain extent, it is one of the underlying cleavages of the polemic described above.[38] In late May 2003, for example, a symposium held in Rio de Janeiro, "O cinema como expressão cultural" (Cinema as a Cultural Expression), posited just such an dichotomy, proposing, among other things, a discussion of the opposition between the "culture industry and culture" and "strategies against the reduction of the cinema to strictly commercial criteria." Eduardo Escorel, who was one of the symposium's invited participants, warned against falling into a kind of Manichaeanism that sees "culture" as essentially positive and "commerce" as essentially negative. The reality of the situation is that the major challenge facing Brazilian cinema since the crisis of the early 1990s is to reestablish a solid presence in the Brazilian market. Escorel was right on the mark when he suggested: "Rejecting commercial criteria implies accepting our relegation to a ghetto, or, put another way, it means passively accepting our exclusion from our own market."[39]

The cultural/commercial divide is seen clearly in critical reactions to certain films, particularly those of a cultural impact or import that goes beyond their status as what *Variety* or the MPA would call "product." Polemics rarely if ever erupt over the films of Xuxa or Renato Aragão, but reaction to some of the more successful, culturally "serious" films has sometimes been very harsh. For example, Gilberto Vasconcelos denounced Walter Salles Jr.'s award-winning *Central do Brasil* (*Central Station*, 1998) as an expression of globalized, neoliberal standards dictated by Hollywood and as "a publicity icon of the FHC [Fernando Henrique Cardoso] era," suggesting that "we would be better off watching a documentary about the Central Bank."[40] Vasconcelos's remarks are symptomatic of a certain current within Brazilian film criticism (and among some "independent" filmmakers) who prefer ideological purity to successful communication with the audience, an attitude that contributes to the continued marginalization of Brazilian cinema in its own film market. In the 1970s, Carlos Diegues referred to such criticism as "ideological patrols."

More recently, critic Ivana Bentes provoked a heated discussion when she denounced recent production for not living up to the social and cinematic vision of Glauber Rocha and the Cinema Novo movement. When *Cidade de Deus* was released in August 2002, for example, she was one of a number of critics who took issue with certain aspects of Meirelles's film. In an article titled "*Cidade de Deus* Promotes Tourism in Hell," Bentes took aim at *Cidade de Deus* and other contemporary cultural expressions that in her view depict violence as pure spectacle for the viewing pleasure of a voyeuristic middle class.[41] Using as models the ethical cinematic portraits of documentarist Eduardo Coutinho, the ironic black humor of films such as *O invasor*, and the inevitable, but somewhat more distant, Cinema Novo, she is particularly critical of the film's supposed "decontextualization": "Here the favela (slum) is totally isolated from the rest of the city, as an autonomous territory. At no time can one suppose that drug trafficking develops and sustains itself (guns, money, police protection) because it has a base outside of the favela. This outside does not exist in the film." Numerous critics disagreed, and the ensuing polemic almost certainly contributed in some way to the film's success.

Bentes's critique has roots in a polemical exchange that had taken place the year before. In an article published in Rio de Janeiro's *Jornal do Brasil* in 2001, Bentes draws a contrast between Cinema Novo and Brazilian cinema of the 1990s, focusing particularly on contemporary representations of what she calls Cinema Novo's "territories of poverty," that is, the *sertão* or backlands, urban slums, and poor suburbs.[42] According to Bentes, Rocha had asked crucial ethical and aesthetic questions concerning the representation of poverty, the disinherited, and the excluded and had proposed, in his seminal manifesto, "An Aesthetic of Hunger" (1965), an aesthetic of violence capable of creating 'an intolerable and unbearable [situation] … a kind of aesthetic apocalypse that forces the spectator to abandon his immobility' (at least that is the theory; in practice things did not quite work that way).

Bentes argues that certain tendencies of Brazilian cinema in the 1990s, with their "tenuous political perspective and rare aesthetic experimentation," transform Cinema Novo's "territories of poverty" into "exotic gardens" or historical museums. She is particularly hard on Sérgio Rezende's *Guerra de Canudos* and Walter Salles Jr.'s *Central do Brasil*. In the former, with its historical reconstruction, told through the eyes of its heroine, "a lucid and ambitious northeastern Scarlett O'Hara," Rocha's violent and mystical *sertão* has become a "stage and museum … a 'folk-world' ready to be consumed by any audience." *Central do Brasil*, on the other hand, presents a romanticized *sertão*, an "idealized return to the roots," a "territory of conciliation and pacification,' offering a 'melancholic and conciliatory 'happy ending' that is distant from Rocha's utopian gesture toward transcendence and freedom."

Two days later, on July 10, *Guerra de Canudos*'s producer, Mariza Leão, responded to Bentes's analysis.[43] She agrees with Bentes that neither *Guerra de Canudos* nor *Central do Brasil* intended to create an intolerable situation for the spectator; rather, they wanted to "establish a strong relationship with him, without underestimating his intelligence and critical capacity." They did not seek the kind of conflict that Bentes values in Rocha; rather, what they did that was "unbearable" for some critics was attract the Brazilian public and compete head to head with foreign films in the Brazilian market. The two films, in the producer's words, "sought to bring light and comprehension to themes that are very dear to the country, at the same time that they brought millions of Brazilians into their reflections about Brazil."

Mariza Leão goes much further in her commentary on Bentes's critique, but the essential can already be seen in the preceding paragraph. While Bentes makes aesthetic and political demands on contemporary films, based on a model from the 1960s, Leão's focus is on communication with the public and the expansion of Brazilian cinema's space in its own market in a very different context. This exchange represents paradigmatically the difference between the logic of the subfield of restricted production, where the stakes, as indicated above, involve symbolic capital, and the subfield of large-scale production, where they involve, first and foremost, economic capital.[44] As indicated above, in the final analysis polemics involving aesthetics and modes of representation, which are common in any field of cinematic production, constitute struggles over the authority to determine the legitimate form of cinematic discourse, and they are homologous with, but not identical to, struggles over models and modes of production.

Concluding remarks

It makes little sense in the early 21st century, to expect Brazilian cinema to conform to the political idealism or the film aesthetics of the 1960s. Brazilian society has changed since then, as has Brazilian cinema. The one thing that has remained constant is the foreign occupation of the domestic market, with all of its implications. Although, as indicated above, cooperation has increased between MPA member companies and certain Brazilian producers, this has taken place largely at no cost to the foreign film distributor. State support continues to be necessary if Brazil is to continue to have a diverse national cinema, although it is not clear precisely what form that support should or will take. Given the considerable infrastructural challenges that have not been addressed seriously, it seems clear a policy focused exclusively on the supply side (i.e., production) without increased attention to the demand side (i.e., distribution and exhibition) will do little to change the underlying situation that maintains Brazilian cinema in a disadvantageous position it its own market. No matter what government policy of support and protection is in place, it will not be effective if Brazilian films do not continue to strengthen their relationship with the Brazilian public, fostering in them the habit of seeing Brazilian films.

Endnotes

1. Dráuzio Varella, *Estação Carandiru* (São Paulo: Companhia das Letras, 1999).
2. *Filme B*, 6:283 (April 14, 2003).
3. Eduardo Escorel, "Quadrilha — Não há cinema sem consumo." Communication presented at the symposium on *O Cinema como Expressão Cultural*, Centro Cultural Banco do Brasil, Rio de Janeiro. May 27–29, 2003. Available at *www.criticos.com.br* (consulted August 1, 2003, our translation).
4. See Ivana Bentes, "'Cosmética da fome' marca cinema do país," *Jornal do Brasil* (July 8, 2001) and "*Cidade de Deus* promove turismo no inferno," *O estado de São Paulo* (August 31, 2002).
5. Alberto Nogueira and Shirley Paradizo, "Casamento reatado." *Monet* 3 (June 2003), pp. 46–51.
6. For a brief discussion of the crisis, see Randal Johnson, "The Rise and Fall of Brazilian Cinema, 1960–1990," *Iris: A Journal of Theory of Image and Sound*, 13 (Summer 1991), pp. 97–124. Reprinted in Randal Johnson and Robert Stam (eds.), *Brazilian Cinema*. Expanded edition (New York: Columbia University Press, 1995), pp. 362–386; Randal Johnson, "Departing from *Central Station*: Notes on the Reemergence of Brazilian Cinema," *The Brazil e-Journal* (a publication of the Brazilian Embassy in Washington, DC, http://www.brasilemb.org/) (Spring 2000).
7. In reality, the commercial/cultural divide is a false dichotomy, because all films have a certain cultural content and are inevitably directed, explicitly or implicitly, at certain sectors of the market, if not the market as a whole.
8. On the notion of the subsidy-dependent "independent" filmmaker, see Jean-Claude Bernardet, "A crise do cinema brasileiro e o plano Collor"; *Folha de São Paulo* (Letras F-3) (June 23, 1990) and Johnson, "The Rise and Fall of Brazilian Cinema."
9. Consulted on December 8, 1997.
10. It is important to recognize that while Bourdieu's distinction refers, in the broadest sense, to the difference between "high art" and "mass culture," it is nonetheless useful for understanding the dynamics of the contemporary field of cinematic production in Brazil.
11. For a brief discussion of these two subfields, see the introduction to Randal Johnson (ed.), *The Field of Cultural Production: Essays on Art and Literature* (Cambridge, UK: Polity Press, 1993).
12. Edward W Said, "Opponents, Audiences, Constituencies," in Hal Foster (ed.), *The Anti-Aesthetic: Essays on Post-Modern Culture* (Port Townsend, WA: Bay Press, 1983), p 139.
13. Pierre Bourdieu, "The Field of Cultural Production, or: The Economic World Reversed." Tr. Richard Nice, *Poetics*, 12 (1983), pp. 311–356. Reprinted in Johnson (ed.), *The Field of Cultural Production*, pp. 29–73.
14. João Goulart was Brazil's last democratic president prior to the military coup d'état of 1964. However, he was not elected to the presidency. Rather, he was Jânio's vice president, and he became president after Jânio resigned.
15. For an overview of the evolution of government film policy since the 1930s, see Randal Johnson, *The Film Industry in Brazil: Culture and the State* (Pittsburgh: University of Pittsburgh Press, 1987).
16. The precipitous decline in the Brazilian film market, in terms of numbers of spectators, began in 1975, coinciding with the consolidation of television as the preferred form of domestic entertainment — with almost 15 million television sets in Brazilian households — as well as with the introduction of the videocassette recorder in the Brazilian market.
17. "Theoretically" because the screen quota was never fully and effectively enforced.
18. *Filme B*, 292 (June 16, 2003).
19. Among the "veterans" who have contributed to the reemergence are Hector Babenco (*Coração iluminado* [*Foolish Heart*], 1998; *Carandiru*, 2003), Sylvio Back (*Yndio do Brasil* [*Our Indians*], 1995; *Cruz e Sousa, o poeta do desterro* [*Cruz e Sousa, the Wilderness Poet*], 1999), Bruno Barreto (*O que é isso, companheiro?* [*Four Days in September*], 1997; *Bossa nova*, 1999),

Fábio Barreto (*O quatrilho*, 1995; *A paixão de Jacobina* [The Passion of Jacobina], 2002), Sérgio Bianchi (*A causa secreta* [*The Secret Cause*], 1994; *Cronicamente inviável*, 1999), Júlio Bressane (*Miramar*, 1997; *Dias de Nietzche em Turim* [*Days of Nietzche in Turin*], 2002), Eduardo Coutinho, 1999; *Edifício Master*, 2002), Carlos Diegues (*Orfeu*, 1999; *Deus é brasileiro*, 2002/3), Lúcia Murat (*Brava gente brasileira* [*Brave New Land*], 2001), and Nelson Pereira dos Santos (*A terceira margem do rio*, 1995; *Cinema de lágrimas* [*Cinema of Tears*], 1995).

20. In absolute terms, production figures were higher in the 1980s, but a large number of films produced were hard-core pornography. Indeed, between 1981 and 1988, almost 70 percent of the films made in Brazil were pornographic. The current level of production is on a par with nonpornographic production in the 1980s. See Johnson, "The Rise and Fall of Brazilian Cinema," p. 363.

21. *Filme B*, 290 (June 2, 2003).

22. Cited in Lúcia Nagib (ed.), *O Cinema da Retomada: Depoimentos de 90 cineastas dos anos 90* (São Paulo: Editora 34, 2002), p. 81.

23. Ibid.

24. Despite the "provisional" in the name, at that time *Medidas Provisórias* were not, in fact, provisional; they immediately became law.

25. The agreement between Warner and Conspiração involves the coproduction and distribution of four features: Flávio Tambellini's *Bufo & Spallanzani* (2001), José Henrique Fonseca's *O homem do ano* (2003), Cláudio Torres's *Redentor* (Redeemer)(in production, 2003), and Lula Buarque de Hollanda's *Casseta e planeta — o filme* (Casseta e Planeta, The Film, in production, 2003). See "Pacote une Conspiração e Warner," *Jornal do Brasil* (November 30, 2000), Caderno B, p. 52.

26. It is also worth noting that the Rio de Janeiro office of the MPA, headed by Steve Solot, has sponsored screenwriting workshops, a screenwriting contest, and a tour of Latin American films to university campuses across the United States. One of the winners of the screenwriting contest was Bráulio Mantovani's *Cidade de Deus*.

27. The table was compiled by combining data from *Filme B*, 294 (June 30, 2003) with a table of the top 50 films of the reemergence published in the special anniversary issue of November 2002. Babenco's *Carandiru* and Furtado's *O homem que copiava* were still being shown at the end of June 2003, and another film almost certain to find a place on the list, *Didi — O cupido trapalhão* (Didi, the Cupid Trapalhão), was released at the end of June. Numbers thus may not be entirely accurate.

28. Daniel Filho is Artistic Director of Globo Filmes.

29. The most successful Brazilian film ever, Bruno Barreto's *Dona Flor e seus dois maridos* (*Dona Flor and Her Two Husbands*), is exemplary in this regard. When released in 1976, it was accompanied by an extensive television advertising campaign promoting actress Sônia Braga, who had recently starred in a popular Globo *telenovela*.

30. *Filme B*, Edição Especial (November 2002).

31. Jorge Furtado, "Cultura em cheque, com ch mesmo," *CineWeb* (May 5, 2003). [*http://www.cineweb.com.br/claquete/default.asp?idclaquete=224*]

32. *Revista de Cinema* iv:39 (July 2003), p. 33

33. A survey of 40 critics undertaken by the *Revista de Cinema* lists the following as the best films of the retomada: *O invasor*, *Cidade de Deus*, *Central do Brasil*, *Baile perfumado*, *Santo forte*, *Um céu de estrelas*, *Lavoura arcaica* (*To the Left of the Father*), *Bicho de sete cabeças* (*Brainstorm*), *Cronicamente inviável*, *Ônibus 174*, *Madame Satã*, *A ostra e o vento*, *Terra estrangeira*, *Edifício Master*, *Estorvo* (*Turbulence*), *Notícias de uma guerra particular* (*News of a Private War*), *Carlota Joaquina*, *Alma corsária* (*Buccaneer Soul*), *Amores*, and *O viajante* (The Traveler). Only 5 of these 20 films are on the box office top 50 list. See Maria do Rosário Caetano, "O Invasor' é eleito o melhor da retomada," *Revista de Cinema* 3:34 (February 2003), pp. 51–53. Note: *Carandiru*, *Deus é brasileiro*, and *O homem que copiava* had not been released when this survey was taken.

34. Arnaldo Bloch, "A cultura está sob intervenção," *O Globo* (March 3, 2003) [interview with Carlos Diegues].

35. Eletrobrás, "Política de Apoio da Eletrobrás a Projetos Culturais" (2003). See also Mariângela Gallucci, Roberta Pennafort and Wilson Tosta, "Artistas protestam contra 'dirigismo' e PT intervém," *O Estado de São Paulo* (May 5, 2003).

36. Eduardo Escorel, "Nota Dissonante," Post to *CinemaBrazil* listserv (May 6, 2003) (our translation).

37. For a brief discussion of this dichotomy, see Johnson, *The Film Industry in Brazil*, especially chapter 6.

38. I should make it clear that I am not suggesting that all signatories of the declaration fall on one side or another of the issue. Indeed, many of them recognize the false dichotomy for what it is. Nonetheless, a divide clearly exists at some level and to some degree.

39. Escorel, "Quadrilha."

40. Gilberto Vasconcelos, "*Central do Brasil*/outra visão," *Folha de São Paulo* (February 12, 1999).

41. Bentes, "*Cidade de Deus* promove turismo no inferno."

42. Bentes, "'Cosmética da fome' marca cinema do país."

43. Mariza Leão, "Condenados em nome de Glauber?" *Jornal do Brasil* (July 10, 2001).

44. Ivan Bentes responded rather ferociously to Mariza Leão in the *Jornal do Brasil* (July 29, 2001).

2

Images of Peru: A National Cinema in Crisis

Sarah Barrow

A brief look at the major trends in the history of the national cinema of Peru suggests that the relationship between the development of the moving image and the onset of modernity in that country has always been awkward. Many have argued that the advent of cinema coincided in most parts of the world with the decades when modernity was already "at full throttle ... a watershed moment in which a series of sweeping changes in technology and culture created distinctive new modes of thinking about and experiencing time and space."[1] However, the reality for the majority of Latin American countries was quite different. As Ana M. López points out, it simply is not possible to link the rise of cinema in that part of the world to "previous large-scale transformations of daily experience resulting from urbanization, industrialization, rationality and the technological transformation of modern life."[2] Such developments were only just starting to emerge, so that as cinema was launched across the world, modernity in Latin America "was above all a fantasy and a profound desire."[3]

Nevertheless, the arrival of cinema in Peru was, it appears, warmly welcomed by the elite of Lima, who greeted it as the very incarnation of the modernity to which they aspired. President of the Republic Nicolás de Piérola was influenced in the reconstruction of his capital city by images of Paris brought by the world's first filmmakers, that iconic city of modern sophistication with its grand spacious boulevards and fashionable inhabitants. Peruvian film production was late in getting started compared to the rest of the world, and during Piérola's regime (1895–1899) the newsreel and documentary forms were encouraged as modes of expression ideally suited to flaunting the efforts made by the "Aristocratic Republic" as it was known, to modernize and expand its capital using funds raised from the export of its sugar, cotton, rubber, wool, and silver. Furthermore, many of the early moving images made in Peru coincided with the first aviation flights in the country, with images of Lima taken from the air filling its inhabitants with pride at such an overt display of progress.[4]

During the second decade of the 20th century, many more films were made to illustrate national ceremonies, funerals, and civic or religious occasions. Lima was the focus of these cinematic documents, with little attention being paid to the country's multiethnic heritage. Unlike in many other countries where moviegoing was most popular with the working classes, the first Peruvian cinemas were installed in the more affluent parts of the capital, where dramas and comedies from France could be enjoyed by the social elite.

Between 1919 and 1930, the 11-year period known as the Nueva Patria (New Fatherland), the country was ruled by the omnipotent President Augusto B. Leguía. Wishing to complete the project begun by Piérola, Leguía and his government wanted to see Lima further transformed into a beautiful spacious city, the utmost expression of modernity. They thus ignored the realities of hardship and fragmentation throughout the rest of the country, and the tension between nationalism and cosmopolitanism that would mark Peruvian culture during the 1920s.[5] Documentaries were made, sponsored by the state, to record the grand carnivalesque celebrations held in Lima to commemorate the centenaries of Peruvian Independence in 1921 and the end of the battles of Junin and Ayacucho in 1924, and according to national film critic and historian Ricardo Bedoya:

> Alongside films that praised and congratulated the President were those that talked about the growing status and wealth of the country, of the prosperity which would last for many years, the product of collaboration with investment and technology from overseas, particularly the United States. Cinema found itself tied to the official ideology and history of the state, promoting the message of a greater and more modern Peru.[6]

This chimes with a suggestion made by social theorist Jorge Larrain that the "power of an entertaining spectacle transmitted through images is very useful to create and maintain traditions that boost national feelings."[7] But despite this encouraging flurry of activity for documentary makers, the fact remains that as the rest of the world adjusted to the introduction of sound to the moving image medium, Peruvian filmmakers were only just grappling with their first silent features, highlighting the real lack of technological resources, investment, and experienced filmmakers in a country still struggling with the pressures of U.S.-led industrialization.

Leguía's approach to modernization was simply to block any radical change that would benefit the working classes, and to open the country to further investment by U.S. companies.[8] Ironically, however, Peru's first fiction films were in fact quietly critical of the impact of Western-led progress, and promoted instead the traditional, rural life experienced by the majority of the population, thus presenting a challenge to the very idea of a coherent national state that was at the heart of modernity. One example was *Camino de la venganza* (Path to Revenge, Luis Ugarte, 1922), a medium-length drama that recounts the story of an innocent servant girl from a mining town who is kidnapped and brought to Lima by a military captain, and is corrupted by the many distractions in the city. Conflict is established between a morally idyllic rural life where work in the fields alternates with collective gatherings for eating and dancing, and the dangers of Lima, a city replete with threat and temptation. This focus on the tension between urban and rural life was to become a recurrent theme of Peruvian cinema.

The early 1930s saw film activity virtually grind to a halt as the Peruvian economy, so dependent on the export of its raw materials to the wealthy northern countries, was devastated by the effects of the Wall Street crash in 1929. Attempts were made by a handful of key individuals to sustain production, but these projects were doomed to fail in such unstable circumstances. Later, that decade saw the establishment of a film production company that holds an important place in the history of Peruvian cinema: Amauta Films, named after the journal founded by leading Peruvian Marxist intellectual José Carlos Mariátegui, who had died in 1930, having also set up the first Socialist Party in Peru. As the government of the time became ever more repressive and intent on aggressive modernization of the country, Amauta Films made feature-length movies that offered a romantic view of traditional life in the barrios of Lima. These were popular in some areas, but competition from the United States, Italy, and Mexico in particular—countries whose film industries were actively supported by their governments— eventually contributed to the downfall of the company by the end of the 1930s.

Peruvian films made over the next few decades tended to reproduce the conventions of European or U.S. movies and were lacking in any distinctive local color or national sentiment; indigenous communities were almost completely absent from the screen. Films were amateurish and unsophisticated, production was sporadic, and investment went into the distribution and exhibition of foreign films. Many filmmakers left Peru, their films were lost, and no infrastructure was left for their successors, who had to start from scratch.

It is difficult to disagree therefore with Bedoya's view that "[T]he his-

Enrique Victoria (left) and Germán González in *Alias la gringa* (Alberto Durant, 1991) (courtesy of the Filmoteca de Lima).

tory of cinema in Peru has always been one of crisis. The instability of crisis has been the normal condition at all stages of its intermittent existence."[9] Certainly, no legacy has been left by Peru's early filmmakers, and the infrastructure and political support for a national film industry are as absent today as they were at the beginning of the 20th century. However, there is one important period that appears to be at odds with this general assessment of events. In the early 1970s, the populist military regime led by General Velasco took a long-term interest in the possibilities of cinema production to support its own modernization projects. Whereas in the past such support had been singularly self-serving and short-lived, legislation passed in 1972 provided sufficient flexibility and longevity for a range of filmmakers with varying ideological approaches to benefit and to develop a degree of continuity verging on the creation of a national film industry.

And yet just 20 years later, this protective legislation had floundered and been abolished, and by the end of 1994, President Fujimori had introduced a more market-oriented cinema law. Since then Peru's film industry has continued its steep decline. Despite much fanfare and excitement at the announcement of fresh legislation and economic support, delays in administration resulted in four "empty" years for domestic film production.[10] In the end, the majority of the resources promised by the state for this law to be upheld were allocated elsewhere, with the result that between 1997 and 2001 just 10 Peruvian feature films had been produced.[11] Thus, the nation's own film funding scheme had no money to award, and Fujimori's government collapsed suddenly amidst dramatic discoveries of widespread institutional and individual corruption.

The remainder of this chapter will investigate these two most recent attempts by the Peruvian state to address its national cinema crisis, and the circumstances leading to the failure of those interventions. It further considers the ways in which Peru's filmmakers have variously reacted and responded to the changes imposed upon them in a society steeped in many different social and economic crises. I suggest that these latest developments in fact echo the frustrating and frustrated stop-start tendencies of the history of cinema in Peru outlined above, and are inextricably linked to the approaches of successive regimes to the modernization of the country.[12]

The Cinema Law of 1972

In 1972 a protectionist cinema law was introduced by the military government of General Juan Velasco, after five years of consultation with Peru's filmmaking community. Velasco promoted himself nationally as a defender of the poor, redistributing land, and renationalizing private oil and mining companies. The motivation for the positive support given to the development of national cinema could therefore be interpreted as complementary to an overarching socialist reform program. Velasco was keen to fill national cinema screens with Peruvian images to replace the foreign ones that had dominated screens since the advent of cinema in Peru. The motivation for reclaiming Peruvian cinema screens for national directors and images of their country was in line with moves by the state to reclaim the oil fields of Talara from the International Petroleum Company and telecommunication systems from the All America Cables and Radio and ITT.[13] Christian F. Wiener has further argued that the establishment of this type of cinema law was part of a very ambitious project to intervene in the arena of mass communications, to stimulate national media production, and to convert it into an educational tool, a means of consolidating national culture and promoting the benefits of modernity.[14]

This 1972 "Legislation for the Promotion of the Film Industry," included the following five key features:

1. Exhibitors were obliged to show a short Peruvian film before every imported feature presentation, and 8 percent of the total box office for that event would be paid to the makers of the short. The result was that some 1,200 shorts were made during a 20-year period, providing a stable training ground for filmmakers, the potential for technological and personnel infrastructure to be established, and the development of financial resources to be invested into feature filmmaking.

2. Up to five Peruvian-made features would be selected each year for screening in the top cinemas of Lima. Investors, more certain of financial reward, would as a result commit to developing strategic marketing and promotions campaigns. The outcome in 1985, for example, was that a small national film called *Gregorio* (Gregory, made by the Chaski Group) enjoyed the same box-office success in Peru as several U.S. blockbusters released during that decade. Although the number of feature films produced each year in this period did not rise significantly, there was a constant flow of work for cinema crew and cast.[15]

3. A "holdover" strategy was established whereby Peruvian features would remain on release until the weekly box-office figures dipped below a specified level. This allowed for word of mouth to build, and restricted exhibitors from replacing a reasonably successful Peruvian film with a guaranteed money-spinning Hollywood blockbuster.

4. Subsidies would be available to filmmakers and investors in the form of welcome tax exemptions.

5. In addition, ticket prices were kept artificially low, controlled in much the same way as were prices for sugar and bread, to keep moviegoing accessible to as wide a range of the population as possible, thus safeguarding its status as a medium for the "masses." This factor contributed further to the success of films such as *Gregorio*, which was made with an audience from the more deprived parts of the country and the capital in mind.[16]

Protectionist legislation such as this was common to many "infant" film industries in Latin America; its general aim, according to observers such as Jorge Schnitman, was to encourage an industry threatened by foreign competition, enabling it to achieve economies of scale before moving to more independent models of operation.[17] The specific and overt aim of this legislation was to further the government's modernization program, which followed Ernest Gellner's argument that modernization entails, among other things, acquisition and mastery of technology.[18] Indeed Bedoya is clear that the practice of film production in Peru was used as an affirmation of modernity, and the cinema law was put in place primarily to ensure that national filmmakers would promote the state's ideology of revolution.[19]

Despite the advantages outlined above, some issues of concern to Peruvian filmmakers remained neglected by the legislation. The market for films was still limited to the domestic one because difficulties in finding distribution channels abroad were not fully addressed. There were insufficient funding sources, and it was increasingly hard for new, inexperienced filmmakers to gain access to credit. There was, furthermore, no guarantee that the decision to approve a film for obligatory screening would not be influenced by an increasingly intolerant political regime that was wary of any form of criticism.[20]

Nevertheless, national film production in Peru was undoubtedly stimulated during the 1970s and 1980s. The making of short films became a lucrative activity with exhibition guaranteed and investments quickly returned, especially with an exchange rate kept artificially favorable so as to assist the purchase of equipment and stock from the United States. New filmmakers thus gained more opportunities for artistic and technical experimentation and training. In particular, this era saw the rise of Peru's only internationally renowned director of recent times, Francisco Lombardi.

Meanwhile, one sector grew increasingly alienated. The owners of cinema theaters considered the law to be an unwanted imposition of films that they would not have screened given the choice. An authoritarian government was breathing life into cinema production at the expense of box-office income, leading to an unhelpful fragmentation of the national cinema project. Exhibitors even complained of having to bear increased electricity costs caused by longer screening sessions. Moreover, there was soon an unrealistic glut of shorts to be screened and it must have come as little surprise that the demise of the 1972 cinema law was welcomed, and to some extent encouraged by national cinema exhibitors.

The public also reacted negatively to the poor technical quality of many of the films of this period, especially the shorts. With the pressure mounting to produce as many films as possible, the criterion for success being quantity over quality, many production companies, to their ultimate cost, neglected to make improvements to sound and color. This was partly due to a lack of proper equipment, but was also caused by the proliferation of companies established primarily to benefit financially in the short term from the opportunities that the cinema law promised. Indeed, few of them reinvested profit in the development of a national cinema infrastructure. Furthermore, technical blunders were largely overlooked as increasingly films were rejected from the guaranteed screening and tax credit system purely for offering a critical vision of the military regime and social order, regardless of whether they were well made.

The Decline of the Cinema Law and Its Abolition in 1992

By the end of the 1980s, the cinema law had all but run its course, and its original deficiencies were clear. In addition, the reality of an acute economic crisis within the country and the breakup of the model of development promoted by Velasco's government, were reflected in the growing difficulties posed by making films in Peru. The lack of secure funds put the brake on developments and frustrated expectations. Investment in film production became, once again, a high-risk activity as cinemas began to contravene the law by refusing to show national product. The internal market weakened, and the export of films became almost impossible. Little money was left from the preceding period, and the Banco Industrial, the main bank involved in supporting film activity, now actively excluded from credit arrangements all new filmmakers, along with any more experienced directors who had no guaranteed backup resources. Hyperinflation meant that any funds acquired were in any case spent within a few days of starting shooting, and projects were either abandoned or took several years to reach the screens.

Many out-of-town cinemas, where the appeal of locally made movies had been greatest, went out of business during the 1980s and early 1990s for several reasons. Terrorism led to the imposition of curfews, regular power cuts broke into almost every screening, and ticket prices eventually had to rise beyond the reach of most people due to the devastating effects of hyperinflation, despite government efforts to keep them low.

So it was within this context that the new President, Alberto Fujimori, announced in 1992 that he intended to make important changes to the framework for national cinema.[21] With some anxiety, the Filmmakers Association of Peru reluctantly began to work with the government on representing a policy that they had started to develop during the late 1980s, one which would support the development of national cinema, but within the new economic framework, and involving representatives from the distribution and exhibition sectors. The 1972 cinema law was officially abolished in December 1992, and the Association worked with Congress for two years on a new plan.

U.S. distributors saw an opportunity meanwhile to develop a more middle-class audience which would now identify more readily with the affluent lifestyles offered by the Hollywood products than with the more somber Peruvian reality portrayed by the majority of the country's own filmmakers. These distributors became involved in the debate, and via the U.S. ambassador put pressure on a government showing signs of interest in foreign investment from the United States.

In the event, a new cinema law was passed in October 1994, by which time plans for U.S. financed and programmed multiplex cinemas in affluent areas of Lima were in place, audience demographics had inevitably shifted almost entirely to the middle classes, and national filmmaking had all but ground to a halt.

The 1994 Cinema Law and Its Impact

The key difference with regard to the new law was its objective that cinema should no longer be regarded principally as an industrial activity and overt signifier of the country's progress toward modernization, but as an important cultural activity for producers and viewers. In the text accompanying the law, President Fujimori signaled for the first time since his election what he considered ought to be the cultural policy of the state at a time of liberal democracy, declaring that: "one of the responsibilities of the state [was] to develop, disseminate, and preserve national culture, for the purpose of affirming the country's cultural identity, without seeking financial recompense."[22]

Filmmaker and lawyer José Perla Anaya, in his final speech to fellow national filmmakers after four years as president of the body set up to administer and apply the new law, gives the following summary of its development and nature:

> In October 1994, the new Peruvian cinema law 26370 was established, and was finally approved in May 1995. CONACINE was set up on January 5, 1996. Three representatives were designated from the Ministry of Education, Indecopi [the national body for the protection of intellectual property], and INC [the National Institute of Culture], and seven members elected by cinema associations.... Thus Law 26370 came into effect, with a model of incentives for production based on competitions and prizes. There was no longer to be any tax exemption nor obligatory exhibition for Peruvian films. The law's other ambitious responsibilities included the dissemination of national cinema, cinema education, the organization of film archives, and the establishment and maintenance of a cinema register.[23]

This competition-based funding model was based very loosely on similar experiments in Europe and elsewhere in Latin America. A new national film organization, CONACINE (Consejo Nacional de Cinematografía — National Film Council), was set up within the Ministry of Education to assess, administer, and award the $1.5 million per year promised by Fujimori. In theory there were to be six prizes per year for features and 48 for shorts. In practice, however, no more than half a dozen feature films and around 30 shorts have been awarded funding since 1994, partly because of the government's failure consistently to make available the promised resources. This was due in part to the fact that the Ministry of Education's limited resources have been more urgently required for basic education costs, and also because the necessary matched funding has been almost impossible to locate, especially for short films. Moreover, when compared to the annual sum of $40 million promised to Argentine filmmakers in 1995, the $1.5 million that Fujimori set aside a year earlier seems woefully inadequate.[24]

The President's announcements in 1994 aroused suspicion amongst filmmakers, who specifically attacked the abandonment of the obligatory screening aspect of the previous legislation. They also feared that the competitions would become a form of indirect censorship by the state, and there was general concern about how long the financial commitment would last. Although they admitted that there had been a need to revise the old law, and indeed a great deal of effort had been put into doing just that, the filmmakers themselves were reticent about placing their faith in a regime still lacking an overarching cultural policy, and with more pressing economic priorities. The following extract from a speech given by Nilo Pereira del Mar, filmmaker and President of the Filmmakers Association of Peru, at the first prize-giving ceremony for shorts and feature film projects in December 1996, gives some indication of the anger that was still felt by many:

As everyone knows, these last four years have been devastating for national cinema. The production of national films, which had been fairly constant since 1972, was abruptly interrupted by the abolition of the main financial incentives for the production of shorts and features. It is important to point out that when this regrettable break occurred, national cinema had reached a maturity of content and professional quality which opened up an international space thanks to prizes and screenings all over the world. Twenty years of unbelievable effort by more than 200 filmmakers over two generations were about to be sent into oblivion. Nevertheless, we persevered with our dreams. And for four years we battled tirelessly to achieve a new legal framework that would allow us to really get on with our work.[25]

Despite Perla Anaya's positive and determined attitude to make this law work, it seemed doomed from the start. At the very first prize-giving ceremony, filmmakers criticized the fact that only 7 out of the 12 available prizes had been awarded, especially as some of those who were not recipients had already been given prizes at national and international festivals for those very films now undergoing domestic assessment. Pereira del Mar questions the criteria on which the CONACINE awards were allocated a little later in the same speech:

> We sincerely hope that judgment of each film project was not based on its ideological approach, when the decision should have been based on artistic criteria. We only say this because several of the jury members have made a point of supporting freedom of expression and battling against film censorship, and it surprises us that they have rejected precisely those works whose vision is not the most sympathetic toward our reality.[26]

His criticisms continue:

> In the case of the competition for features, we are delighted that the three prizes have been awarded, as indicated by the law. However, we would have

Reynaldo Delgado (on horseback), Diego Bertie (in shorts), Gilberto Torres (pointing small shotgun) and José Luis Ruiz (in uniform) in *Bajo la piel* (Francisco Lombardi, 1996) (courtesy of the Filmoteca de Lima).

liked one of those to have been a proposal from a new director, so as to fit in with the law's objectives and ethics of promotion.[27]

Thus it appears that at least one important group of filmmakers had concerns about the interpretation and application of the new law. Pereira admits that they were aware that it was no longer appropriate simply to replicate the phenomenon of Law 19327, under which practically every work had benefited. They also believed that they needed to be shown evidence of coherence and understanding of a cinematic reality which had been paralyzed for four long and difficult years. Their most immediate concern was that the decision not to award more than 40 percent of the prizes would make the production of shorts even more challenging in the coming year.

The year 1997 was, however, more promising, with two further competitions for shorts (still only half that promised by the law), in which all 24 available prizes were awarded, and one further competition for features, in which three more projects received support. However, by 1998 funds had become extremely scarce, and by Perla Anaya's own admission, amounts owed to prize-winning companies for feature productions were mounting up.[28]

One film project that suffered tremendous setbacks, partly as a result of uncertainty caused by the "new" cinema law, was *El bien esquivo* (The Elusive Good). Augusto Tamayo's project was awarded the top prize of $188,000 (648,000 nuevos soles) in 1997, but was not released until July 2001, four years later, having received just $14,500 (50,000 nuevos soles).[29] The delay in itself is not wholly exceptional, but the unfortunate dispute in which the film's writer and director was for a long time engaged with CONACINE and the Ministry of Education, displayed some of the inherent weaknesses of the legislative system. The film took longer to make than was allowed by the contract agreed with CONACINE, primarily owing to problems with the identification of matched funding. As a result, the $14,500 received may have to be returned. And yet the film was welcomed on its release as an important cultural product according to positive reviews at the time, and achieved moderate success at the box office.

Outspoken veteran filmmaker Armando Robles Godoy is rather more emphatic in his criticism of the system. In an article in *La República*, November 22, 1998, on the state-supported film *Coraje* (Courage), completed by Alberto Durant that year, he offered a cry of protest at the state's indifference toward Peru's national cinema:

This [*Coraje*] is one of very few national films that have been made in recent years. There is almost no cinema in Peru because the government won't get on with fulfilling the very same laws that it set up. At this rate, the century and the millennium will close with the complete abolition of Peruvian cinema, a death throe that began in 1992, with the action of the Ministry of Finance and its sterile dogma of market-oriented policy.[30]

In the same article, producer Andres Malatesta continues in a similar vein:

A country without its own cinema is like a country without a face. We've demonstrated that we're ready to compete, but for a long time we've had to confront so many financial headaches. CONACINE doesn't have any money, it seems like cultural activity isn't taken seriously, it's terrible. We want clear quotas and obligatory exhibition, as we had with the 1972 cinema law that was abolished in 1992. It's incredible that in our own country we have to beg to get our films screened in our own cinemas.[31]

More recently, producer Stefan Kasper, one of the founding members of the socialist filmmaking Chaski Group, responded to an e-mail interview on the importance of national cinema in the following way:

Yes, national cinema is very important, and the state should definitely support it. Why? There is a range of ways in which cinema can contribute to the development of a country. It acts as the mirror and reflection of reality. People see themselves in their own films and need this image of themselves to help them construct their own identity. Cinema is also the image that one country projects to other countries, its way of communicating. Cinema is art and industry, and each country should develop it according to its own criteria, priorities, and interests.[32]

The Films of the 1990s

What kinds of films were eventually produced once the new cinema law was in place? To what extent is it possible to identify a distinctive style and set of thematic concerns common to Peruvian films of the 1990s? Peruvian cinema has never been greatly influenced by the major trends which made their mark elsewhere in Latin America; indeed the overtly left-wing political agenda of the pioneers of the 1960s and 1970s "new" and revolutionary cinemas of the continent has had little impact on the Peruvian scene. Commentators argue that this is not because Peruvian filmmakers themselves have no political inclination, but rather because they have been drawn into a more quietly critical or allegorical discourse owing to the need to have films approved by a government body in order to qualify either for obligatory screening or for a competitive award.[33] The few exceptions

Rosa María Olórtegui (right) and member of the Comunidad Campesina de Ccachín (left) in *La vida es una sola* (Marianne Eyde, 1993) (courtesy of the Filmoteca de Lima).

to this trend, such as Marianne Eyde's *La vida es una sola* (You Only Live Once, 1993) which dared to show less sympathy for the military than for the rural communities caught up in violence with the Shining Path rebels, suffered from a delayed release, difficulties with funding, and a negative reception from certain areas of the press.

Furthermore, the lack of economic support has meant that filmmakers have had to rely almost exclusively on box-office returns, and a desire to please rather than challenge the audience has become fundamental to ensuring continuity. Hence, a rather unremarkable approach to filmmaking has emerged, with either a focus on realist reconstructions of actual events already in the public sphere, or a ransacking of myths from the past, mixing anthropology with fetishistic mysticism and an increasingly touristic gaze. Indeed many Peruvian film critics have lamented the lack of innovation and dynamism shown by many of the nation's filmmakers.[34]

The most consistent director, and the only one to have gained sustained international recognition, is Francisco Lombardi, whose works have been appreciated for their classic dramatic structure and realist themes concerning personal and political violence. He benefited from the opportunities offered by the 1972 cinema law and gained early success at festivals with controversial feature films exploring the military and the terrorist movements, such as *La ciudad y los perros* (*The City and the Dogs*, 1985) and *La boca del lobo* (*In the Mouth of the Wolf/The Lion's Den*, 1988). During the 1990s, Lombardi made six features, none of which relied on government-sponsored prizes or subsidies, but which succeeded in attracting investment from overseas.[35]

Coproductions and Foreign Relations

With very limited national investment, and the narrowing of the internal market, the main way forward in terms of funding in recent years has been via international coproduction arrangements. Even during the 1980s, out of 37 national films, 17 were part financed by overseas capital, mainly from Europe.[36] Throughout the 1990s, Lombardi's projects built on the success of the previous decade and attracted a good level of coproduction support from Europe and other parts of Latin America, leading perhaps inevitably to a certain internationalization of subject matter, but enabling him to remain independent of the vagaries of the state system. Yet even he has seen the funds dry up as investors' attentions have been diverted to filmmakers who are backed by some sort of national infrastructure. More recently, Lombardi saw his own production infrastructure collapse when his main Peruvian producer was last year found to be implicated in the Fujimori corruption scandals.[37]

In his last speech as president of CONACINE, Perla Anaya summarized all the most recent steps that had been taken by this organization in collaboration with filmmakers' associations in an attempt to stimulate film production once more. Several of these measures acknowledge the need to participate in the global market and to develop partnerships with other countries. For example, a proposal was put to PromPeru, a government body set up to promote the country as a destination of choice for tourism and business, to put together a traveling exhibition of national cinema, and to finance trips by the makers of feature films in search of resources. Some interest was expressed at first, but the progress made has been limited. In 1997, the Filmmakers Association of Peru, with the support of CONACINE, drew up a plan to create a national film fund, with resources to be drawn from the exchange of external debt for investment in film production. This proposal, named FINPROCI, has not yet been formally approved by the government despite repeated campaigns to highlight the need for such a project. Other projects include a Peruvian Film Commission, promoting the use of Peru as a film location for overseas companies, and the Ibermedia program, a multilateral fund for film production that promotes the development of film projects by Latin American companies through awarding grants. However, despite government promises since 1997 to pay the annual quotas required for Peru to become a member of such a program, no resources have yet been forthcoming.[38]

The government of the late 1990s appears to have favored more direct and increasingly accessible means of communication technology such as television and the Internet, and the potential for national cinema to contribute to this renewed modernization project via mass communication seems remote. Moreover, although observers such as Ian Jarvie may argue that movies might still be considered as at least a way-station to acquiring and mastering the more politically useful communication technologies of television and computers, the Fujimori government demonstrated no interest in protecting its film industry even for that reason.[39]

Concluding Remarks

Despite two rounds of legislation aimed ostensibly at stimulating national cinema, the Peruvian film industry at the turn of the 21st century was again in crisis. The first intervention in 1972, with its overt links to a state modernization project, enjoyed a measure of success, but required evaluation, revision, and development both to stay in line with changing political and economic contexts, and to benefit distribution and exhibition activities as well as film production. Instead it was abolished and replaced with a funding competition which was received with some skepticism, and which in the event completely failed, mainly due to a lack of genuine interest and economic support from the Fujimori regime. In addition, potential international coproducers turned their back on Peru's filmmakers, government corruption dragged the whole country into further turmoil, and the new Toledo-led regime installed in 2001 has yet to turn its attentions seriously to developing a coherent cultural policy as it grapples with the more pressing social dilemmas of acute poverty and unrest. As a consequence, a new generation of potential film talent is being driven to seek opportunities abroad, or within the more lucrative markets of television and multimedia.[40]

Meanwhile, the filmmaking community in Peru remains somewhat divided: while some (such as Robles Godoy and Kasper, cited above) have campaigned for a system based on the one developed during the protec-

Rebeca Raez (left) and Tatiana Astengo in *El destino no tiene favoritos* (Álvaro Velarde, 2003) (courtesy of Álvaro Velarde Producciones).

tionist years of quota, subsidy and guaranteed screening, others (such as Lombardi, Salvini, Velarde) seem to have embraced, however reluctantly, the need to find ways of working within a global market dominated by the United States.[41] What they appear to share, with each other and with a century of Peruvian film "pioneers," is the somewhat utopian vision of a stable and independent infrastructure for Peruvian national cinema, as expressed by one of the main spokespeople for the decade, Perla Anaya:

> I continue to believe that these legal and economic problems can be overcome if we really work at it. All I ask is that those who really love our national cinema never tire of working in it and for it, however deficient or limited our actions might seem to be.[42]

In summary, Peru's filmmakers moved from having a clear if somewhat functional role within the inward-looking nationalist modernization agenda of General Velasco, to the promise of a broader cultural one under President Fujimori. The latter's neoliberal approach, leaving national filmmakers to compete against international industries under economic conditions that favor product from outside the country, appears in some ways to have more in common with those of earlier regimes led by Piérola and Leguía, who were seduced by the films, lifestyles, and investment opportunities of Europe and the United States. In the end, the promise of an overarching cultural policy remained unfulfilled, and just a few years after Fujimori's dramatic disappearance from the political scene it still appears to be too early to weigh up the possibility of renewed support from a regime whose leader has promised to prioritize the basic needs of the rural and poor majority.[43] In the meantime, Peru's filmmakers continue the search for finance and a role in an increasingly crisis-ridden country that in many respects is still finding the transition to modernity a painful one, imposed upon it from the outside like the Hollywood blockbusters that dominate its screens.

Endnotes

1. Stephen Kern, quoted in Ben Singer, *Melodrama and Modernity: Early Sensational Cinema and its Contexts* (New York: Columbia University Press, 2001), p. 19.
2. Quoted in Vivian Schelling, *Through the Kaleidoscope: The Experience of Modernity in Latin America* (London & New York: Verso, 2000), p. 149.
3. Ibid.
4. I am indebted to Ricardo Bedoya's *Cien años de cine en el Perú: una historia crítica* (Lima: Universidad de Lima, 1995) for providing much of the historical detail upon which parts of this introductory section are based.
5. See Peter Elmore, *Los muros invisibles: Lima y la modernidad en la novela del siglo XX* (Lima: Mosca Azul Editores, 1993), pp. 11–51.
6. Bedoya, *Cien años de cine en el Perú*, p. 43 (our translation).
7. Jorge Larrain, *Identity and Modernity in Latin America* (Cambridge, UK: Polity, 2000), p. 40.
8. See Carlos Iván Degregori et al., *The Peru Reader: History, Culture and Politics* (Durham, NC & London: Duke University Press, 1995), pp. 215–218.
9. Bedoya, *Cien años de cine en el Perú*, p. 305 (our translation).
10. Between 1993 and 1997, just four films were made and released in Peru: *Sin compasión* (No Mercy, 1994) and *Bajo la piel* (Under the Skin, 1996) by Francisco Lombardi, whose film projects at that time attracted useful coproduction finance, mainly from Spain; *Anda, corre, vuela* (Walk, Run, Fly, Augusto Tamayo, 1995), and *Asia, el culo del mundo* (Asia, the Pits of the Earth, Juan Carlos Torrico, 1996). No Peruvian films were released in 1997.
11. 1998: *Coraje* (Courage, Alberto Durant), *La carnada* (The Bait, Marianne Eyde) and *No se lo digas a nadie* (Don't Tell Anyone, Francisco Lombardi); 1999: *La yunta brava* (The Brave Union, Federico García), and *Pantaleón y las visitadoras* (Captain Pantoja and the Special Services, Francisco Lombardi); 2000: *Ciudad de M* (City of M, Felipe Degregori) and *A la media noche y media* (At Half past Midnight, Marite Ugaz and Mariana Rondón); 2001: *Tinta roja* (Red Ink, Francisco Lombardi), *El bien esquivo* (The Elusive Good, Augusto Tamayo), and *Bala perdida* (Stray Bullet, Aldo Salvini). Just five of those received partial support from the state. The 1994 cinema law stated that up to six feature film projects a year should be awarded funding, starting in 1996, thus up to 36 projects should have been supported by the end of 2001.
12. I am grateful to Anglia Polytechnic University (APU, Cambridge) for the award of a bursary that enabled me to carry out a research trip to Peru in 2001 and acquire the mate-

rial for this and other essays on Peruvian national cinema. I also owe a huge debt of gratitude to Norma Rivera and her staff at the Filmoteca de Lima, who very patiently helped me to find the material I needed. And, finally, thanks to those filmmakers and critics who generously gave their time to be interviewed for this project.

13. José Perla Anaya, *Censura y promoción en el cine* (Lima, Peru: Deyco Instituto Peruano de Derecho de las Comunicaciones, 1991) p. 115.

14. Christian F. Wiener, "Tan duro de vivir, tan duro de morir: el cine en el Perú de los 1990" in Rob Rix and Roberto Rodriguez-Saona (eds.), *Changing Reels: Latin American Cinema Against the Odds* (Leeds, UK: Trinity & All Saints College, 1997), pp. 17–31 (p. 22).

15. Financial support for production, marketing, distribution, and exhibition was not the sole contributor to the success of *Gregorio*, although it undoubtedly helped that the film was shown throughout the country, in the most remote areas, by a mobile cinema unit. Critical comment at the time praised the film's effective neorealist style and sensitive portrayal of social deprivation amongst street children in Lima. See the entry for this film in Ricardo Bedoya, *Un cine reencontrado: diccionario ilustrado de las películas peruanas* (Lima: Universidad de Lima, 1997), pp. 255–257.

16. These are just the main aspects of the 1972 cinema legislation. Exhaustive detail can be found in Perla Anaya, *Censura y promoción en el cine.*

17. See Jorge Schnitman, *Film Industries in Latin America: Dependency and Development* (Ablex, 1984).

18. See Ernest Gellner, *Nations and Nationalism* (Oxford: Blackwell, 1983).

19. Bedoya, *Cien años de cine en el Perú*, p. 188.

20. Wiener, "Tan duro de vivir, tan duro de morir," pp. 22–23.

21. Christian Wiener's essay examines in detail the political decisions that made the abolition of the cinema law inevitable. In summary, in December 1992, Fujimori and his ultraneoliberal chancellor, Carlos Boloña, decided to terminate the laws regarding tax exemption and privileges, which in effect made the old cinema law obsolete.

22. Wiener, "Tan duro de vivir, tan duro de morir," p. 24 (our translation).

23. José Perla Anaya, *Los tres primeros anos: memoria 1996–1998* (Lima: CONACINE, 1998), p. 74 (our translation).

24. In fact, the economic resources committed by the government were by far the greatest concern. As Perla Anaya summarizes in his 1998 report, CONACINE worked for seven months in 1996 with no funding; in 1997, they requested approximately $1.16 million (4 million nuevos soles) and received $290,000 (1 million nuevos soles); in 1998, they requested $1.305 million (4.5 million) and received $290,000 (1 million); in 1999, they requested the same amount and received nothing. Over 80 percent of the funding received was spent on competition awards, leaving little for the remaining responsibilities.

25. Perla Anaya, *Los tres primeros anos*, p. 19 (our translation).

26. Ibid., p. 20 (our translation).

27. Ibid. (our translation).

28. Ibid., p. 74.

29. Ibid., p. 66.

30. Armando Robles Godoy, *La República*, November 22, 1998 (our translation).

31. Andres Malatesta, *La República*, November 22, 1998 (our translation).

32. Interview with author by e-mail, August 9, 2001 (our translation).

33. Wiener, "Tan duro de vivir, tan duro de morir," p. 26.

34. For example, see Jorge Zavaleta Balarezo, "El Cine en el Perú: ¿la luz al final del túnel?" in Karl Kohut et al. (eds.), *Literatura peruana hoy: crisis y creación* (Frankfurt, Germany: University of Eichstatt, 1998).

35. For a full analysis of Lombardi's films see Ricardo Bedoya, *Entre fauces y colmillos: las películas de Francisco Lombardi* (Huesca: Festival de Cine de Huesca, 1997).

36. Zavaleta Balarezo, "El Cine en el Perú," p. 263.

37. Lombardi agreed to be interviewed by the author during her research trip to Peru in the summer of 2001. He spoke of having to suspend the operation of his production com-

pany Inca Films because of its links with the corrupt former Intelligence Minister, Vladimir Montesinos, via his colleague and head of the state television Channel 4, Crousillat. The Fujimori and Montesinos corruption scandals were closely linked to all the state television channels, in that the main broadcasters were allegedly bribed to support the President's regime.

38. Perla Anaya, *Los tres primeros anos*, pp. 94–96.

39. Ian Jarvie, "National Cinema: A Theoretical Assessment," in Mette Hjort and Scott Mackenzie (eds.), *Cinema and Nation* (London: Routledge, 2000), pp. 75–87.

40. Some are inevitably tempted to follow in the footsteps of Luis Llosa, who made several short films in Peru in the 1970s and then went to work with Roger Corman in the United States. His most (in)famous works to date include *Anaconda* (1997) and *The Specialist* (1994). He also has a television production company in Lima that specializes in the production of soap operas and employs much of the young filmmaking talent in the capital, including up-and-coming feature director Aldo Salvini, whose digitally filmed thriller set in Cusco, *La bala perdida*, starring two young and nationally well-known television actors, was released in late 2001.

41. Another new filmmaker, Álvaro Velarde, began to enjoy some success in the late 1990s. Having trained in New York, he went on to make three award-winning short films, *98 Thompson* (1994), *C. Lloyd, un cuento de crimen y castigo* (*A Tale of Crime and Punishment*, 1996) and *Roces* (*Social Graces*, 1999), and was due to release his first feature, *El destino no tiene favoritos* (Destiny has no Favorites), in 2002. He received some funding from CONACINE, but has had to look outside Peru for matched funding, postproduction facilities, and screening possibilities. By early 2003, this project had received support from the Rotterdam Film Festival's renowned Humbert Bals fund, and had been selected for a number of festival screenings, but the money had not been raised to transfer from video to film and the film had no release date scheduled in Peru.

42. Perla Anaya, *Los tres primeros anos*, p. 76 (our translation).

43. In the section on Peru in Peter Cowie's *Variety International Film Guide 2003* (London: Button, 2002), pp. 266–267, national critic and film professor Isaac León Frías explains that the "2002 Peruvian Film Congress stressed the need for a new legal framework to support production within the liberal economic model followed not only by the Peruvian government but by most Latin American regimes, and filmmakers have begun to put pressure on the new government of President Alejandro Toledo to do more for their industry." On these pages, León Frías mentions five other features that have been completed and are awaiting release, several of them made on the cheaper digital video format. He points out that while production continues, the films are often not released until two or three years after completion.

3

Crossing the Line in Mexico?: Luis Buñuel's *El ángel exterminador*

Robert J. Miles

Coterminous with but not circumscribed by the 20th century, the work and life of Luis Buñuel (born in Calanda, Spain, 1900) represent a complex interrelation between the artistic and ideological modes and movements of the last century and beyond — in both directions. Buñuel was raised by a bourgeois Aragonese family that had the requisite resources to see him educated by the Jesuits in Spain and also later, in the 1920s, at the progressive, Oxbridge-inspired Residencia de Estudiantes in Madrid. It was there that he was able to meet and fraternize with other unquestionably gifted contemporaries, including Federico García Lorca and Salvador Dalí, the latter becoming one of Buñuel's earliest collaborators on the epoch-transcending movie written in Spain, filmed in France, *Un Chien andalou* (*An Andalusian Dog*) of 1929.[1] It was their contributions to bourgeois bashing, an affront to the class that had raised and (certainly in Buñuel's case) unwittingly funded these artistic ventures, that were to prove filmic milestones in recent visual-cultural history. To the young Buñuel and Dalí, the surrealists, Arp, Breton, Ernst, Éluard, Tanguy, Unik, et al., were *the* art grouping in Europe, if not the world.[2] As much as their infamous short film was a calling card to the group, it was also Buñuel's step up to an international stage that would see him continue to weave a diverse range of medicoliterary and artistic influences from the psychoanalytic to the Sadean into his films, including a significant number he worked on in Mexico, with 18 films as director.[3]

The retrograde mindset and combined force of Spain's famously reactionary triumvirate made up of the military, the upper classes, and the church,[4] which functioned inexorably as a nursery for the young Buñuel's ever-budding will to subvert, were also the coalescent forces that had triumphed absolutely with the defeat in the Civil War (1936–1939) of the democratically elected Republic. No matter how tempting the opportunity to provoke, open dissent would at that point have been a matter of life or death, and Buñuel left Spain altogether. Realizing that under Francisco Franco there was no way of making the kinds of films that he wanted to make, Buñuel went where the work was. This was set in the context of the continued need for a voluntary exile based on both political and artistic-aesthetic dissonance with the regime in Spain. So he moved first to France and then to the United States to work at New York's Museum of Modern Art. He was subsequently hounded out of there owing to accusations of anti–Americanism and Communist involvement, largely originating from Dalí,[5] and then went on to Mexico in the 1940s where he took Mexican nationality in 1949.

Buñuel and Mexico

Given that Buñuel once professed, "I had so little interest in Latin America that I used to tell my friends that should I suddenly drop out of sight one day, I might be anywhere — except there," this was perhaps an odd choice of a place to settle.[6] Although David Thomson noted in 1995 that Buñuel's "Mexican films are the least well known, but they showed rapid development,"[7] the films completed there are commonly considered to be of an extremely mixed quality individually and as a group, perhaps echoing the director's initial ambivalence. In some cases the entire Mexican oeuvre has been disaggregated mercilessly, as the epigraph chosen from Virginia Higginbotham for Acevedo-Muñoz's 2003 book reminds us: "Many of [Buñuel's] films made in Mexico are inconsequential. Only five of the nineteen films of this period can be considered memorable."[8] The "most memorable and most durable" to Michael Wood are the last six. He adds, "but almost all have flickers of interest, flashes of Buñuel's cinematic signature."[9] They have also been divided up, as Peter Evans explains,

> into two categories: those like *Gran Casino, El Gran Calavera* [1949], *Susana, La hija del engaño* [1951], *Subida al cielo* [1951] *El bruto, Abismos de pasión,* and *La ilusión viaja en tranvía* [1953] belonging to a *cine de consumo* largely obeying the generic laws of the popular *ranchera*, musical, or melodramatic films of the commercial Mexican cinema; others like *Los olvidados, El Ensayo de un crimen, Nazarín,* breaking free of commercial constraints, reflecting the more personal interests and obsessions of the Surrealist auteur.[10]

In his aforementioned important study, Ernesto R. Acevedo-Muñoz aims to "'nationalize' Buñuel's 'lesser' Mexican Films,"[11] in contrast to the majority of the criticism of the films of the Mexican period, in a study which "departs from the usual perspectives that ground Buñuel's work solely in Surrealism,"[12] (which is Evans's approach on the whole). Acevedo-Muñoz seeks to rethink "auteurist and psychoanalytical approaches to Buñuel's work as critical standards of evaluation for such a transnational, highly individualistic director."[13] Taking Gwynne Edwards's otherwise valuable study as an example, Acevedo-Muñoz comments:

> Edwards flirts with some notions of nationality that are important in shaping the director's "unity of vision." But she [*sic*] subordinates Spanishness to Catholicism, putting the weight on the director's struggle between his *upbringing* [Spanish, Catholic, Bourgeois] and his *formation* [French surrealism].[14]

This said, it was definitely the case that to be a "good Spaniard" in 20th-century Spain also meant being a "good Catholic," which was more especially the case during the Vatican-approved years of Franco's regime. Also, to ignore Buñuel's insistence that some apparent symbols, motifs, and images (surreal as they may seem when decontextualized) are based purely on personal memories would be mistaken.

Buñuel was aware of the various nation-focused, community-reinforcing cultural ventures undertaken in Mexico before his arrival and for some years afterward. The most obvious link is with his famous cinematographer, Gabriel Figueroa, who worked with Buñuel up until the last two films made in Mexico. Figueroa was very much aware of and inspired by attempts to figure the national in postrevolutionary Mexican visual cultures. He worked with directors as different to Buñuel as Emilio Fernández, a director who "seized on the unfinished but highly suggestive work of Eisenstein's and Tissé's *¡Qué viva México!*, for a vision of a transcendent grandeur absent in his experience of Mexico in film," while Figueroa's "influential cinematography adapted Eisenstein's metaphor for the binarisms of Mexican culture: the traditional, syncretic sarape (or poncho)." Both went on to construct "a much-emulated concept of authenticity out of the slippery division between the rainbow gaiety and quaintness of the tourist object and the sombre-hued nobility of the original garment."[15] Buñuel's awareness did not equal complete sympathy, however. Generally, he reacted negatively toward *anything* that began to resemble a consensus or cultural status quo, tending always toward revolution, anarchy, and nihilism, no matter how demotic, telluric, or epic the representation.[16] This is also true of the ubiquitous and very influential neo–Realist movement in cinema. Buñuel complained that "with few exceptions..., neo–Realism has done nothing to highlight what is unique to cinema in its films: mystery and the fantastic."[17]

Acevedo-Muñoz has an important point regarding the way that more abstract questions of sources, belonging, and national identity have been too readily generalized away, or dissolved into appreciations of a director constantly reindexed as only a pre–Mexico master in (largely academic) criticism. In recent years, a little more consideration has been given to this once usually neglected period of film production in Buñuel's career, and more distinctively, attention has been given to drawing out the sociopolitical and historical references and significance of the films with attempts to figure and focus on the problematics of cultural specificity. The films are being considered a little more in a Mexican production context, the "Mexicanness" or "Spanishness" of the films is being assessed along with reflections on Buñuel as a peripatetic artist. Whilst some of the focus has changed, such "traditional" analyses continue to concentrate on the films that reflect the "more personal interests and obsessions of the Surrealist auteur."[18] Notwithstanding the more auteurist or fundamentally more idiosyncratic, European style films made in Mexico, most scholarly attention has gone to those which hark back to that now ironically more accessible and recognizable Buñuelian repertoire of recurrent Freudian (or "Freudianized") and antibourgeois motifs, symbols, and themes in the early works. This critical deficit is convincingly tackled by Acevedo-Muñoz who points up how:

> The tendency to overlook many of Buñuel's Mexican films made before *El ángel exterminador* [*The Exterminating Angel*, 1962], because they are inconsistent with psychoanalytical analyses of surrealist filmmaking, also occurs in classic auteurist criticism. Originating with works published in *Cahiers du Cinéma* in the 1950s, auteurist critics deemed most of Buñuel's Mexican work too "commercial" or creatively crippled precisely because it had emerged from the tightly structured, often generic national film industry.[19]

Acevedo-Muñoz admirably seeks to understand "films from 1946 to 1955 as 'Mexican' movies, insofar as they relate to the issues and concerns, and often even to the styles of the genres, of Mexican 'national' cinema."[20] The purpose of this chapter is to meet and assess the criticism in the middle, to weigh up some of what has been said, not about films from the period that Acevedo-Muñoz concentrates on, but to supplement and bring some of his awareness of the questions of identity and cultural ownership to a new interpretation of a putatively neosurrealist, "European style," but Mexico-made film, *El ángel exterminador*.

Acevedo-Muñoz sets about addressing the suppression of the native with his own analyses, which take into consideration the "production history, context, and content" of the films made before *El ángel exterminador*.[21] Despite Acevedo-Muñoz's objections, the discourse of national ownership and the perceived identity of Buñuel and his work in the contemporary Latin American imaginary collective, as perpetuated by the popular press, still serves to confuse the issue by sustained association of the director with, for example, the stars of Latin America and those heretofore critically favored "personal interest" films.

Amongst others, *La Prensa*, the web-based Nicaraguan daily newspaper (October 15, 2001),[22] and the Mexican newspaper *La Vanguardia* (Mexico City, January 22, 2002) announced the return of Silvia Pinal to the big screen. Pinal (born in Sonora, Mexico, 1931) was a member of the more "actorly" second wave of Mexican movie stars along with the likes of Marga López, Silvia Derbez, Pedro Infante, and others. The reports announce her starring role in the resonantly titled *Ya no los hacen como antes* (They Don't Make Them Like They Used To), directed by Juan Fernando Pérez Gavilán. The film was subsequently released in 2003. Curiously, to remind the reader of the significance of Pinal, the press concentrated on parts she played in films by Luis Buñuel in the 1960s. All this despite her appearances in at least 54 films with a range of directors as distinct in approach and caliber as Roberto Rodríguez, Joaquín Pardavé, Fernando Cortés, Emilio Fernández, and Rogelio A. González, before her work with Buñuel. There is no mention of her contributions to television production, her singing career, and (controversial) status as a theatrical proprietor, her appearances in musicals, her political activism, nor her famous progeny (her son is a musician, two daughters became successful actresses, and a third and a granddaughter are pop singers).

Pinal's more recent return to the screen and the press discourse constructed around her does not have anything like the same resonance as her return to Mexico from Spain (like Buñuel's in the same year), on a veritable tide of opprobrium and controversy with the release and garnering of prizes for *Viridiana* (Spain, 1961), to work once again with Buñuel and his producer — and her husband — Gustavo Alatriste. Certainly, some of Pinal's reputation must rest on her superb handling of complex roles in the pointedly sacrilegious, darkly humorous, and bitingly pessimistic *Viridiana* and the apparently absurdist follow-up in Mexico, *El ángel exterminador*. However, the press releases announcing her return perpetuated and reinforced not just the association of Pinal with Buñuel in two of his finest moments on either side of the world. With the conspicuous suppression of any mention of arguably less equivocally indigenous works that she

appeared in, they also implicitly perpetuate and reinforce Buñuel's association with Mexican cinema in the form of his later, personal and idiosyncratic, ostensibly back–to–Europe style films, rather than the more
Mexico-focused, or Mexico-derived "issues and concerns" variety, as
argued by Acevedo-Muñoz.[23] The press inevitably restated the critical
party line by referencing Buñuel's more "European" films, as these were
the kinds of films in which Pinal starred for him. But seen the other way
around, regardless of her status, she has been used by the press in this
instance as a way to shoehorn Buñuel back into the Latin American cinematic discourses of reminiscence, the film star system, and artistic success certainly on a national or continental level, if not of a particularly
patriotic or continentalist stripe. Pinal is being reassociated with a director whose so-called most respectable work is based in Europe, if not, certainly laced with Europe. Some of the irony of the use of Pinal's persona(e)
in this way should become apparent in the light of the debate surrounding the critical understanding and placement of El ángel exterminador.

El ángel exterminador

The film premiered in Mexico on May 8, 1962, and was also sent to
the Cannes Film Festival, where its reception was mixed.[24] This was probably because of the superlative hybridity of the critical succès d'estime and
the general public succès de scandale that was Viridiana at Cannes the year
before. Viridiana was Buñuel's unmistakable statement of intent and his
incisive and definitive rebuke to his detractors still in exile who suspected
some form of capitulation to Franco and Francoism with his agreement
to make another film during the dictatorship. It was a time when the likes
of Casals, Picasso, and many other Spanish figures of international standing claimed to be staying away from home as a matter of political principle. Thus, attention at the awards turned instead to Luchino Visconti's
The Leopard, which took the Palme d'Or, with Special Jury Prizes going
to Masaki Kobayashi's Seppuku/Harakiri and Vojtech Jasny's A Cat. Inter-
estingly, El ángel exterminador did win Best Non-European Film (Bedste
ikke-europæiske film) in 1963 at the Danish Bodilprisen cinema awards,
and the International Federation of Critics (FIPRESCI) awarded their own
prize to the film.[25]

The film starts as it ends, with the image of a church and a Te Deum
that acts as a background for the credits. The first sequence opens at night,
on a street sign indicating the location of the action for the entire narrative — excepting the closing sequences in a church. Following the initial

title of Buñuel and Alcoriza's screenplay, the camera is on the ironically named Calle de la Providencia (Providence Street), and it is to a fine mansion on this street that its owner Edmundo Nobile (Enrique Rambal) and his wife Lucía (Lucy Gallardo) return with 18 dinner guests after a night at the theater to see Gaetano Donizetti's *Lucia de Lammermoor* (1835, based on Sir Walter Scott's *The Bride of Lammermoor* 1819, revised 1830) starring one of the guests, Sylvia (Rosa Elena Durgel). Before the guests have even set foot in the house, the servants have been leaving hurriedly for one reason or another (or apparently for no reason at all) as if all of them experience a collective, but unarticulated premonition of some forthcoming disaster for the household.

The guests are all served eventually by the one loyal butler, Julio (Claudio Brook) who is the only servant to share the same fate as those who sat down to dinner.[26] After an absurdly platitudinous meal that sees the same people being introduced repeatedly, an identical toast being proposed twice, and a good deal of duplicitous gossiping in which, for example, the doctor (Augusto Benedico) turns to his patient, Leonora (Bertha Moss) and tells her that she is cured of cancer, only to almost immediately turn to another guest, Eduardo Gómez (Xavier Masse) to tell him that there is no hope for her at all, and that all her hair will soon fall out. Silvia Pinal's character, Leticia receives a sobriquet from Alicia (Jaqueline Andere), and she becomes known as "la Valkiria" (the Valkyrie). Alicia insists that Leticia's insistent preservation of her virginity is redolent of some kind of "perversión," a theory graphically enacted and perhaps vindicated when Leticia is seen hurling an object through a dining room window with apparent sexual frustration. The other guests comment that "someone broke a window, must have been a passing Jew" and so on, relentlessly. Here, Buñuel is doing one of the things he does best, which is to lambaste the middle and upper classes and satirize an entire worldview to which they cling and against which the director responded violently.

The spoof does not stop there. Inexplicably after dinner, and once Blanca (Patricia de Morelos) has finished playing a sonata by Scarlatti on the piano, they all simply fail to leave. As the hours pass and the guests circulate before the threshold that divides a drawing room from the main dining room, they begin to find each others' (but not their own) behavior odd. They still manage to find justification for each other in the name of politeness. Edmundo comments: "I'm pleased to note that the old spirit of improvisation is alive and well" as the guests prepare themselves to sleep in the room. Lucía begins to complain, but still making no effort to leave, is reminded in all seriousness as an explanation by Edmundo: "don't forget that Leandro [José Baviera] lives in the United States." As the guests plump cushions and pull their shawls and coats about them to settle down for the night, their hosts include themselves in this communal dilution of responsibility. Edmundo capitulates: "let's go to their level, to mitigate their bad behavior a little." In the morning they wake and share stories of dreams and delight in the novelty of not having spent the night in their own homes, with their own families and servants. Over breakfast the guests begin to accuse each other politely. A jumbled replay of the dinner dialogue from the night before also serves to "surrealize" the morning. A range of "reflexive" moments characterize their explanations: Alicia comments tautologically, "I find novel all those things that aren't routine" and Sylvia remarks, turning from the mirror where she is attempting to remedy her disheveled hair, "I didn't speak out of politeness."

Beginning to ask real questions about why none of them has left, they realize they are trapped for no apparent reason. Thus begins one of cinema's best representations of physical and psychological disintegration: these guests become hostages, or rather they are unwilling "guestages" of the Nobile household. They quarrel, fight over any remaining food and water (they are driven to hack away at the water pipes in the walls), they sweat, scream and starve, suffer delusions, punish each other, and behave obsessively, repeatedly shaving themselves, or brushing their hair. One guest breaks another's hair comb because she was becoming unbearable, Leticia slams the piano lid barely missing Blanca's hands as she monotonously fingers the keys, Leandro finds the little box of pills brought, lost, and urgently needed by another guest and throws them over the invisible border, two lambs and a small bear brought by Lucía as entertainment for the guests break free and run wild about the house.[27]

Ultimately one of the unfortunate invited, Russell, becomes ill and dies after the doctor fails to rouse him from a coma. They place the corpse in one end of a giant three-door cupboard and make efforts to block out the smell of its putrefaction. They use another part of the cupboard, which is full of tall urns, as a toilet, and the two young lovers, Beatriz and Eduardo hide and eventually expire behind a third door, thus making the toilet the site of all kinds of horrible endings. Days and nights seem to pass and all, including the spectator, lose track of the amount of time they have spent in the room. Eventually they make their way out in a state of hysteria, but only with the help of Silvia Pinal's character, Leticia, the once frustrated Valkyrie. Throughout, the camerawork of Gabriel Figueroa suggests intensive and sometimes hyperactive social interaction and then disintegration. Taking in the characters mostly in medium and medium-long shots, the camera glides elegantly from one set piece of chat and patter to the next, panning and tracking, as if just another guest at the party. With the onset of the guests' psychological breakdown there are more close-ups, and the earlier basic contrasts possible in a black and white film of this period give way to more studied, complex light and shadow effects. Durgnat comments eloquently that, "it looks more crowded, messy and inelegant than it is. It has the slovenly disorderliness of a tired capsizing mind."[28] In all, the film has a macabre, Gothic ambience accentuated by the precise and alluring choreography between those invited and the camera, which often also takes up more observational posts in the corners of the room, as the film progresses, monitoring the overall primal scene.

DIVERGING INTERPRETATIONS: THE SACRED AND THE PROFANE

Seemingly as inexplicable as what becomes of the protagonists, the original idea for the narrative and its unusual title (which seems to bear no clear relation to any one particular theme, image, symbol, or character in the film) has sometimes been erroneously attributed to a work purportedly completed by Buñuel's friend, José Bergamín.[29] There is no such completed work, although Bergamín, according to Buñuel, had been working on a play entitled *El ángel exterminador*, which Buñuel considered a crowd-tugging title in its own right, declaring that if he were to see such a title at a theater he would be compelled to attend. Later, Buñuel and his long-time cowriter, Luis Alcoriza (they had collaborated on at least 10 films together in Mexico) worked on a script they titled *Los náufragos de la calle Providencia* (The Castaways of Providence Street).[30] Buñuel decided that the title was altogether too "long and literary" and opted for a reversion to Bergamín's speculative dramatic title, with no quibble from the latter regarding rights.[31] Buñuel points up that the notion of an exterminating angel has biblical roots, while he also asserts "this was also the name used by a Spanish association, the Apostolics of 1828, and, I think, a group of Mormons too."[32]

Sánchez Vidal does implicitly refer to one of the most "colonial" critical strategies when he outlines what he calls the "'religious' interpretations" of the film:

> Given the many religious allusions in the film, explanations in this vein have been offered, considering that the basic scenario comes from the Passover, with the Jews locked in their homes like the castaways of Providence Street.... For Maurice Drouzy, it would take the "direct intervention of God the Father [Nobile the host], the sacrifice of Christ, and the linking of the Virgin and the Holy Spirit."[33]

Nevertheless, with equal certainty, though not of course *finality*, religious "readings" of the film are persuasive. The spectator witnesses the guests' utter degeneration, this mysterious captivity causing them to squabble and scheme. Their "ritual repetitions and liturgical lip service"[34] degenerate until their community becomes implosive and they call for the blood of a scapegoat elected among their number. Intriguingly, the requisite atoning sacrifice is implicitly acted out in more ways than one. One of the two lambs that have run free about the house is captured after it wanders into their new drawing room-prison and Leticia, having blindfolded the animal, hands Edmundo a knife to kill it, in what became one of the most emblematic sequences of the film. All the while the voice of Alicia is almost inaudible, chanting something off-screen. The next shot shows her acting out a ritual with the help of two others holding chicken legs. She tosses white feathers from her handbag (recalling the mysterious, ubiquitous, quasi-symbolic birds in *Los olvidados*, and then stops, saying that she cannot go on because they lack "innocent blood" and must "await the sacrifice of the last lamb."

Sure enough, it is "knife-bearing" Edmundo who makes such a "sacrifice" of Leticia's virginity. The lamb's blood shed, in a short speech full of double meanings Nobile declares to the throng, which has descended

Virgin on the edge: Nobile (Enrique Rambal) and Letícia's (Silvia Pinal) dramatic entrance in *El ángel exterminador* (Luis Buñuel, 1962).

into a wild brawl, that it is "hopeless to fight for something that is so easy to accomplish." He then turns, thanks and then kisses the hand of a disheveled but still dignified looking Leticia. It would seem that the erstwhile Valkyrie has surrendered herself to him. They have emerged from behind large curtains, which dramatically and suggestively swing apart, reminding us of Buñuel's no doubt mordant perception of the theatricality of the guests' enclosure, but also the performative ritualization of her implied loss of virginity. Leticia is suddenly and amazingly able to help the guests escape. The frustrations of earlier repetitions, manners, rituals, and dinner etiquette momentarily appear to be their salvation: Leticia realizes that one "last" reenactment/ repetition of their positions at the exact moment they all began to refuse to cross the imaginary barrier will be their release. Indeed, after smashing the window (another transparent barrier — her salvation perceived but still unreachable on the other side), and as she was the first to complain that she was hungry, the first to begin to use the cupboards as a toilet, she is naturally the first to cross the line, pausing, glancing up and around at the edges of the prison door that they made for themselves before she calls on the others to break on through with her. In a riot of collective fervor they escape.

The next sequences show the guests in church offering a Te Deum to give thanks to God for their release, as they promised they would earlier in the film. The priests make their way down the aisle at the end of the ceremony, but elect to allow the faithful to leave the church first. So, the captivity begins again. The guests and their intercessors are trapped in the place of worship as they all make excuses not to leave. In one way this is just thoroughly typical subversive Buñuel: entertaining, unrelenting, resolutely unrepentant, and profoundly blasphemous to the end. The last sequence shows a fresh cohort of surrogate sacrifices, in this instance an entire flock of sheep, which makes it through the town, now, inexplicably, in a state of uprising. They approach the church door as if to offer themselves to the newly entrapped. It would seem there is only one much more celebrated virgin who will be able to complete the formula and save them now.

Alternatively, at the Godless end of an imaginary scale between sacred and secular, in an article originally published in *Études Ciné-matographiques*,[35] Michel Estève slightly derails his own argument when he states that

> [C]onnections between *No Exit* [Sartre's *Huis clos*, 1944] and *The Exterminating Angel* are numerous and significant.... In Sartre's drawing room with the door bolted on the outside and the bell broken, help from without is

inconceivable. In Buñuel, the characters, as if held in by an invisible force, cannot leave in spite of the open doors, and the curious bystanders who wait outside cannot be of any service whatsoever.[36]

Bearing the existential interpretation in mind, and recalling the various possible roots of the title of the film, on one level it would be absolutely typical of the director, who famously thanked God he was still an atheist, to juxtapose the secular and the sacred to suggest something ultimately profane. *El ángel exterminador* is also like an adult version of *Lord of the Flies* (1954). The circumstances for the characters take a turn for the worst in the same vein as in William Golding's book, as Buñuel's boundless capacity for acidic humor ensures the guests' inexorable decline from equivalent bourgeois to a reequalization as thug infants: they all just collapse at different rates. Certainly, ever the amateur entomologist, Buñuel enjoyed spying on the interactions of his subjects given a clearly delimited scenario. But such interpretations as these are also typical of the kind of criticism that has focused on Buñuel's ambivalence, his unambiguous aestheticized religiosity, but vehement counterclericalism, the kind of writing of the nostalgic, Eurocentric, Buñuel as surrealist variety.

Some of the critical ambivalence relating to *El ángel exterminador* may stem from Buñuel's own mixed feelings about the filmmaking process and the finished product. Positively, with Alatriste as producer, he was once again permitted, with Pinal as renewed star (in the wake of *Viridiana*), to explore his own fantasies in Mexico, away from the uproar in Spain. He was somewhat gladly trapped for a moment in the place it would seem he was about to move away from more permanently.[37] Buñuel also commented negatively on the film, considering it poorly realized. Certainly, some of the acting in *El ángel exterminador* is simply very poor. Although hard to judge objectively, some dialogue delivered, particularly by the actors playing staff in the kitchen, is extremely stilted, as if read from cue cards. There is also some implausible hamming from hysterical guests. In the interview with Pérez Turrent and de la Colina, Buñuel claims that European audiences did not seem to notice this although he did and it pained him.[38] De la Colina also comments of the later film, "*The Discreet Charm of the Bourgeoisie* is a kind of *Exterminating Angel*, but better acted, with better costumes and sets, more subtle on the whole."[39]

Although it has been noted above that Buñuel was no fan of collective cultural initiatives of national self-definition, which were treated by the director as another bourgeois indulgence, perhaps hypocritically, the "national feel" of *El ángel exterminador* seemingly did become an issue. The entire location was unsatisfactory to Buñuel from the outset. Indeed he wished for a certain Europeanization of the film perhaps in order to impart some of the snob value required to truly relish the social disintegration of the guests. Some of his own roots and snobbishness would seem to be playing a part here, with the controversial implication being that the degradation of the European bourgeois would have been more "complete and poignant."[40] Buñuel bemoaned the fact that "Ideal, perhaps, would have been to have made it in England, in a place where a type of 'high society' really exists," whilst conversely accepting, as noted above, that "with Alatriste I had all the freedom in the world."[41] Buñuel was no doubt aware of some of the satirical effect (not to mention scandal) that had been achieved with *Les Règles du jeu* (*Rules of the Game*, Jean Renoir, 1939), and one can imagine the delight he would have taken in deflating a roomful of effervescent costume drama character types hired with the bigger budget (in addition to the lack of artistic and ideological/ religious restrictions, thanks to Alatriste) in something like Robert Altman's homage to Renoir, *Gosford Park* (2001), or a full-scale, stately home as in *Remains of the Day* (James Ivory, 1993), where all the characters, having shown themselves to be very worthy and solemn, are suddenly simply unable to leave the dining room.

Pérez Turrent and de la Colina comment on the difficulty of reimagining "such well-known actors as Loya, Beristaín, Del Campo, Patricia Morán, Jaqueline Andere from popular Mexican melodramas" as "haute bourgeoisie."[42] The critic, Michael Wood cuts a swath through the critical ambivalence that has stemmed in part from Buñuel's own disappointment, not so much at the final "Mexicanness" as at the apparent lack of "Europeanness" of the finished film. He argues:

> *El ángel exterminador* is a Mexican movie in the straightforward sense: shot by Gabriel Figueroa, in a Mexican studio, produced by Gustavo Alatriste; Mexican actors, Mexican technicians. The script is by Buñuel and Luis Alcoriza, another exiled Spaniard. But it is also one of the two films Buñuel said he would have liked to remake…. The target is the middle class, not particularly the Mexican middle class; the servants have the necessary intuitions, know they must leave, not because they are Mexicans, but because they are servants. Class not nation…. The irremediable specificity of film as a medium anchors this movie in Mexico, it cannot be anywhere else.[43]

But there is nothing "straightforward" about the finished film. It has been argued by another critic, Marsha Kinder, that there is, in fact, an implicit and, albeit inadvertent, negotiation of the matter of nation. This is not through the planned planting or accidental accretion of signifiers of "lo mexicano" ("the Mexican") or because of the forces employed in the making of the film, but through subject matter. The nation in history *through* class:

> Although many of Buñuel's Mexican films present stories and characters that could be easily transposed to Spain ... they tend to emphasize the legacy of that colonialist history through an emphasis on class—from the abandoned children of *Los olvidados*, whom Buñuel refuses to sentimentalize, to the trapped haute bourgeoisie in *Exterminating Angel*, the class he subjected to the severest irony and to which he himself belonged.[44]

Buñuel's primary target would seem to be the transnational class of the bourgeoisie as, he considered, best exemplified by the European of the variety. They were the upholders of—sometimes even imaginary—traditions for the sake of privilege and distinction from the masses thought of as contaminated and unworthy according to a value system that insisted on the link between ancestry and notions of purity with legitimacy.

Despite Buñuel's disappointment and what Wood says (above) regarding the unmistakable surfeit of "Mexicanness" in the film through knowledge of its production, Kinder manages to claim it back momentarily for her "reconstruction of national identity in Spain." She argues that "many of his best Mexican films suggest a strong parallel with at least one of the films he made in Spain," and that there is:

> [U]sually a pivotal inversion of class or gender, two registers that are frequently combined [or opposed] in his texts as agents of subversion. For example, despite their obvious differences, both *Exterminating Angel* and *Land without Bread* are ensemble films where characters are divided between insiders and outsiders.... In both cases a woman — the Virgin who performs a ritual of repetition or the poor old woman ringing the death bell — arouses some hope of liberating the insiders. Though the insiders at first seem to be the only ones who are trapped, the films eventually reveal that the outsiders [and by extension, we spectators] are caught in the same social structures on a larger scale. Yet the insiders in the Spanish film are poor, whereas the insiders in the Mexican film are rich — an ironic inversion of expectation when set against the colonial past.[45]

Kinder states that this idea of pairing is also the critical consensus with regard to *Viridiana* and *Nazarín*. The question of some mirroring or an inversion is undeniable, but again, it would seem to rest on the supposition that his "best Mexican films" are again those films that are "read" more easily in terms of their recurrent Europe-derived Buñueliana — the approach strongly contested by Acevedo-Muñoz, who also points up how Kinder tends to see "an extraordinary set of heroines who are characterized as 'agents of subversion of the patriarchal symbolic order'" in Buñuel's Mexico-based, if not really Mexico-inspired, works.[46] Moreover, at least seven critics consider the film a simple extension of sequences from *L'Âge d'or* (*The Golden Age*, 1930).[47]

What has been described thus far is the perpetual tension between critical responses to the film, Buñuel's condition as recently reminded of his roots, but also his vehement rejoinder to the regime in Spain. This is a tension that the film itself embodies with the guests' simple inability to leave, as well as the outsiders' (the authorities, a priest, some children and other onlookers) inability to cross the threshold and enter. So, first, to psychologize the director: as much as Buñuel is the objective observer/ *voyeur*, it would seem that he too was apt for captivity, was not immune to the problematics of belonging. This is certainly apparent when after contemplating the imaginary divide into the next space, Julio, the butler, explains to another why he is attempting to survive their confinement by eating small pieces of rolled up paper. He says that this was taught to him by the Jesuits (like Buñuel), whom he describes as "buena gente" ("good people"). The delight and particular incisiveness of the film are partly symptomatic of Buñuel's ambivalence regarding his own class: his apparent affection for them is the reason he can represent them so devastatingly; his hazardous proximity to them is the source of the embarrassing frisson of recognition his films often elicit. Following Kinder's comments, one can see how the butler might be figured as Buñuel's ironic mirror counterpart: Julio is trapped there through aspiration, whereas Buñuel is about to leave to return to his indisputable roots. Indeed, mirrors and self-observations are shown on various occasions throughout the film, reinforcing the suggestions of the double and weird inversions, which have normally been applied to Buñuel's output in Freudian terms, including such readings of some of the Mexican films. This can also be a starting point for a new analysis of *El ángel exterminador*.

Converging Interpretations: The Uncanny

Any critical-psychoanalytical "pick-n-mix" miscellany of fetishism, the Oedipus Complex, penis envy, the death drive, male and female desire couched (with some license) in further Freudian terminology, and much else besides, is of course redolent of the neosurreal, Eurocentric account of Buñuel. With this film in so many ways at the edge, such an interpretation can be adapted and updated when, for example, the likes of the double, those odd inversions and the mysterious are considered in the context of perceptions of belonging, and more specifically the question of national identity or experience of life in the margin for naturalized exiles and semi-consecrated "national" directors. Freud's essay on the uncanny has facilitated a valuable reading of *Los olvidados* by Peter Evans.[48] Freud's writing explores the subtle difference between what he termed *heimlich* and *unheimlich*, the closest translations in English being "homelike" or "comfortable," "uncanny" or "uncomfortable." The idea has been taken up by Bernardo Pérez Soler, who argues convincingly that the uncanny is likewise the "main source of inspiration" for *El ángel exterminador*.[49]

To recapitulate, and to compare treatments of *Los olvidados* and *El ángel exterminador* in this way, on the surface it would seem that many of Evans's findings could certainly be applied productively to *El ángel exterminador* too. First, however, the eye. Evans particularly follows Freud's lead in looking at the notion of blinding and our profound revulsion at assaults on the eye. The latter, Evans reminds us, is a recurrent feature in Buñuel's films, from *Un Chien andalou* to *Los olvidados*. In the former (and it has not lost its power) Buñuel's razor (he plays the assailant) slices the eye of a woman, foretelling, or rather, demanding a new interiorization for the filmgoer. The blinding was a prescription for a new way of seeing: the mind's eye. Similarly, in *Los olvidados*, the assault on the "eye" is an egg directly on the camera, a riposte to neo-realism and a development in that Buñuel directly reminds the spectator of the machinery behind the magic and deconstructs the medium to, as ever, subvert expectation and challenge spectatorial acquiescence. The idea of the assault directly on the eye is not apparent in *El ángel exterminador*.

Evans also draws on some of the finer detail, the accessories of Freud's essay, to make some very interesting points about *Los olvidados*. He notes the uncanny feelings associated with newly perceived or missing body parts: "[t]he references to severed hands there must at least be responsible for the recurrence of the motif in *Un Chien andalou* and *El ángel exterminador*,"[50] and animals, which might be applied to the bear and sheep, certainly to the chicken's feet sticking out of Alicia's handbag, and to the famous cliff-edge lavatory where a bird can be seen in flight below whoever is relieving themselves, which "has its bizarre Surrealistic place in the claustrophobic ambience" of Nobile's drawing room full of bourgeois autoincarcerated.[51] The reality-fantasy dialectic of the uncanny is figured in Evans as a reminder of Buñuel's key link to surrealism. Evans also argues that the impact of neorealism cannot be dismissed as easily as Buñuel might like with reference to *Los olvidados*. Whilst this is arguable of Buñuel's film about young and neglected toughs on the streets of Mexico (that some in Mexico considered just too beyond the pale, or rather, too close to reality for comfort) and regardless of Buñuel's attitude toward contemporary cinematic movements, *El ángel exterminador* is far less easy to associate with neorealism with its emphasis on the opulence and pomp of the upper middle classes as well as the extensive use of, for example, special effects associated with dream sequences like superimposition, the inexplicable repetitions, or the stylization of dialogue. But generally, Evans rightly reminds us that "his [Buñuel's] commitment to fantasy and mystery does not imply repudiation of the preoccupations of ordinary daily life, affirming Breton's view that Surrealism is a *sous-* as well as a *sur-* realism, in which reality itself is the focus," recalling Italo Calvino's famous comments in a television interview.[52] He remarked: "Fantasy is like jam, you have to spread it on a thick slice of bread."[53]

Even if, for example, *Los olvidados* opens with a voice-over sardonically naming the great cities of the world as if to recommend them from the back of a perfume bottle, "London, Paris, New York," and, as has been shown in Wood,[54] *El ángel exterminador* has been considered simply Mexican in terms of production, neither Evans nor Pérez Soler really pursue their understanding of the uncanny into its significance in the discourse of national or continental identity in these Mexico-made films, although the subtext of both writers is replete with reference to questions of belonging. The question has also been taken up by Acevedo-Muñoz who states, "*Los olvidados* is not much concerned with understanding the abstract psychoanalytic construction of Mexican national identity,"[55] but with reference to Octavio Paz's work of psychohistory, *El laberinto de la soledad* (*The Labyrinth of Solitude*, 1950), he concedes in terms which are also consistent with *El ángel exterminador*: "[t]he characters that populate *Los olvidados* are, like Paz's Mexican, traumatized and trapped in their own 'drama of identification.'"[56]

In terms of "identity" in the most general terms, the debate remains one not of nation but of class and its representation in relation to these films. Yet it is in a quite different way that *El ángel exterminador* lends itself rather well to such a debate, with the uncanny aspects of the film representing a Freud-based and concessionary starting place for a different understanding of the film as generally in line with much treated notions of life at the margins, the experience of the interstitial, and the construction of otherness in concurrent Latin American literary and artistic developments. Freud refers to the uncanny as that near-unnamable sense of disjunction from or interference with or inflection of, but always relation to that which is "long familiar."[57] The uncanny is an experience that takes:

> [T]he form of something familiar unexpectedly arising in a strange and unfamiliar context, or of something strange and unfamiliar unexpectedly arising in a familiar context. It can consist in a sense of homeliness uprooted, the

revelation of something unhomely at the heart of hearth and home…. But it is not "out there" in any simple sense: as a crisis of the proper and natural, it disturbs any straightforward sense of what is inside and what is outside. The uncanny has to do with the strangeness of framing and borders, an experience of liminality.[58]

The uncanny in this sense is part of the larger discourse of the perception of the borders, limits, divisions, and all forms of experience of the "other side." Arguably, El ángel exterminador—with its fantastically inexplicable central event—represents the tail-end of a curious modern hybrid: taking the tried and tested elements of Buñuel's Freudian-inspired surrealist films to Latin America to blend them with cultural developments, particularly new literary initiatives. Víctor Fuentes illustrates how Surrealism meets (another Euro-American derived category) "magical realism" in El ángel exterminador, and certainly Buñuel's paralleling of themes and techniques from the contemporaneous "boom" period of literature in Latin America is, to say the least, uncanny.[59] A range of—notably non–Mexican—writers seems to have been a strong influence. Certain tropes recurred suggestively in such works whose authors were concerned with the discourses of postindependence and postrevolutionary continental and national cultural legitimacies: the mirror, the double, and the labyrinth were the obsession of the Argentine writer Jorge Luis Borges, who sought in his early poetry to eulogize Buenos Aires. Also, there was the reality-fantasy dialectic in the multilayered narratives of Julio Cortázar, who detailed in deeply uncomforting, uncanny narratives his sense of a ubiquitous, but ephemeral "otro lado" ("other side") in many of his short stories, such as "Casa tomada" ("The Taken House," 1951) or later, the structurally experimental novel Rayuela (Hopscotch, 1963). El ángel exterminador could represent an early proposition of a development in Mexican filmmaking for Buñuel toward some new "magical surrealism," or, more likely, it should be considered that the surrealism that Buñuel was so much a part of as a younger man had been fed into Latin American-produced plastic arts, literature, and film decades before (e.g., note the shifting status of Mexican painter Frida Kahlo in this way), and what Buñuel encountered in magical realism was another shade of himself. The indigenous nature of either surrealism or magical realism as artistic modes and movements would be extremely contentious. One can be left with nothing but a sense of the radical indeterminacy, or at best, ambiguous hybrid, when considering El ángel exterminador in this way, especially given a whole other range of sources in Buñuel: Evans, for example, lists: "Hollywood forms of expression…, Poe, Lewis, Maturin, the Brontës…, Quevedo, Goya, Rulfo, Cortázar."[60]

THE IMPASSE AND IDENTITY

The simply inexplicable nature of the guests' (and it would seem the critics') entrapment in an otherwise unthreatening and not particularly out of the ordinary dining situation has been raised by Pérez Turrent and de la Colina in an interview:

> The motif of enclosure and the circular is already apparent in your other films: the terrifying room of *Un Chien andalou*, the suffocating drawing room of *The Golden Age*, the "jungle living room" of *La mort dans ce jardin*, even the island in *Robinson*, the circular night ride of *A Tram-Ride of Dreams*. Also, the theme of impotence: the bandits of *The Golden Age* collapse on the road without reaching the beach, the bourgeois of *The Exterminating Angel* cannot leave the room; and those of *The Discreet Charm* walk along a road without getting anywhere, unable to find a place to dine.[61]

Buñuel's reply to this is that it was a well-observed list by the interviewer, but he insists that *El ángel exterminador* is different in that there are always physical or obvious psychological impediments to leaving in the other films: "*Robinson* [*Las Aventuras de Robinson Crusoe* (*The Adventures of Robinson Crusoe*, 1954)*] being an example of the case in point: he cannot leave the island, because he has no way of doing so."[62] In fact, Buñuel consistently responded to critics of *El ángel exterminador*, stressing that it was perfectly fine that it did not make sense at all.

Still, this purported meaninglessness is meaningful. Víctor Fuentes considers *El ángel exterminador* "the quintessence of his [Buñuel's] three currents (surrealist, realist, and theological) and a testament of his conception of life and the world."[63] Arguably, it is also indirectly philosophical. Although, after psychologizing Buñuel and considering this film his moment of uncanny hesitation in a biographical vein, it might be worth remembering that philosophy was Buñuel's major subject at the Residencia de Estudiantes in the 1920s. Víctor Fuentes remarks how this concept of mystery is revived in the film in modern millenarian form, when the ultimate edge, apocalypse, is approached:

> The bourgeois drawing room [in *El ángel exterminador*] has many of the "mysteries" or "moralities" of medieval theater, except here one does not celebrate the mystery of a controlling divinity, but the mystery of mystery itself.[64]

Buñuel's own "reassurance" regarding the film to his Paris audience became notorious:

> If the film which you are about to see seems to you enigmatic or incongruous, that is how life is also. It is repetitive like life, and, like life again, sub-

ject to many interpretations. The author declares that it was not his intention to play with symbols, at least not consciously. Perhaps the best explanation for *The Exterminating Angel* is that, rationally, there is none.[65]

The concern with border crossing and identification with insiders or outsiders is central to, indeed is the entire pretext for the narrative development of the film. This dynamic becomes the subtextual structuring mystery and metaphorics of the film (with "text" taken here to mean any planned or unplanned arrangement of meaning). The concept of inclusion versus exclusion and the figuration of an edge and the possible beyond, real or imagined, are ubiquitous in the film. The film betokens a metacritical function: it implicitly takes in and is structured by the dynamics of belonging by performing them. Something along these lines was noted in Buñuel's work in another essay by Octavio Paz in which the latter stresses the similarities between the artistic-political work of the Marquis de Sade and Buñuel articulated in the performance of godlessness and the figuration of an atheist world. Paz notes that, like Buñuel, "Sade was not concerned with showing that God does not exist: he took it for granted."[66] Paz does not reference *El ángel exterminador*, but it would have been ideal for his topic when one considers that "the film can be seen as a parable about meaning: not about the meaninglessness of the world, or of social life, but of our rage for meaning in those areas."[67] This recalls the initial existential take on the film, but there is still the simple problematic fact of not being able to leave, which could be explained away as group hysteria, but why did the servants leave when there was no interaction between servants and guests before the meal? Why can the people on the outside not get in? Punning on his French, Jacques Derrida expands:

> The crossing of borders always announces itself according to the movement of a certain step [*pas*] — and of the step that crosses a line. An indivisible line. And one always assumes the institution of such an indivisibility. Customs, police, visa or passport, passenger identification — all that is established upon this institution of the indivisible, the institution therefore of the step that is related to it, whether the step crosses it or not ... the crossing of the line becomes a *problem*. There is a problem as soon as the edge-line is threatened. And it is threatened from its first tracing.[68]

One can argue that *El ángel exterminador* goes beyond foregrounding the uncanny more cannily and can be studied beyond psychoanalytical categories to represent the entire identity question via a performance of the ultimate puzzle, the pathless path: an *aporia*. Derrida uses some interesting mnemonics to convey the complex concept of the aporia. The "step"

Lapping it up: The beggars (uncredited actors) invade in *Viridiana* (Luis Buñuel, 1961).

to Derrida (*pas*) is also taken to be the negation of the movement too: the "not" also signified by *pas* (curiously enough, and ignored by Derrida although he looks at other languages, a "step" in Spanish is *paso*, also meaning "I pass," or "I go through"). Of course, Derrida concerns himself with and concentrates on difference in language and its precedence to and construction of a permanently equivocal reality, the tension of which is only heightened in those uncanny moments of perceptions of the edge. Culler reminds us how, in the Derridian deconstructive worldview:

> [S]ignifying events depend on differences, but these differences are themselves the products of events. When one focuses on events one is led to affirm the priority of differences, but when one focuses on differences one sees their dependence on prior events. One can shift back and forth between these two perspectives which never give rise to synthesis. Each perspective shows the error of the other in an irresolvable dialectic.[69]

Viridiana

In a postscript to his prologue for the published script of *Viridiana*, Georges Sadoul refers to "*El ángel exterminador*, a Mexican film, left out of the running for the Palme D'or," but also remarks how "this new film, also more Spanish than anything, continues with the aim of *Viridiana* in a more convincing and buñuelian tone."[70] Whilst *El ángel exterminador* is not necessarily more "essentially" Spanish than Mexican, or vice versa, to treat *Viridiana* in relation to it is revealing. The questions of identity and belonging are more salient in intracinematic terms when the films are considered with each other as an "uncanny" pair, with particular attention paid to the crisscrossing on-screen cipher that links them: Silvia Pinal. Although it has been noted that Julio, the butler, appears as Buñuel's possible on-screen cipher, as his double, one cannot overlook the association between what Pinal signifies to the director. Whilst Kinder pairs films which mark Buñuel's departure from Europe with those that mark the beginning of the end of the Mexican period and his return to Europe, she ignores the reflection of *Viridiana* in *El ángel exterminador*. One major inversion is the troupe of motley beggars which breaks into the house in *Viridiana*. They play at being wealthy and well-to-do, parodying their benefactors and end up being forcibly ejected, while the real wealthy and well-to-do of *El ángel exterminador* mock the poor and end up trapped. There is further doubling in both films, the most significant being structured through Pinal's characters. For example, in *Viridiana*, her experience is framed by two failed rapes and two aborted "marriages," one to God and another to her estranged uncle, Don Jaime. In *El ángel exterminador* the notion of opening up at the finale is fostered in the mind of the film's spectator when presaged by earlier subtle moments like Leticia's careful, almost studied folding up of a napkin in the seconds before she breaks the window in the early stages of the film. She has new significance appearing within each film, but also operating *between* each film. As the obvious, on-screen, common denominator, Pinal has a subversive, repeat, dynamic narrative function, shifting back and forth, also linking the films and eliciting more associational significance for each when *Viridiana* and *El ángel exterminador* are paired. Both films articulate the classic stereotypically Hispanic virgin-whore dichotomy. In *Viridiana* she progresses from self-control, piety, and helping others, to apostasy, resignation, and self-interest. In *El ángel exterminador* she is out of control early on, a vandal, she puts her needs first, but once she has given herself to Nobile she is able to help the others to escape. In *Viridiana* she finally capitulates to Don Jorge after a second attempted rape (with the spectator and Viridiana herself still unsure whether she was ever really raped earlier in the film by her uncle, Don Jaime, played by Fernando Rey). After some days of general antagonism and ferociousness toward the bourgeois guests in *El ángel exterminador*, she seems to have given herself freely to one (Nobile) and, in a way, all of them. In both films the way she is referred to or addressed directly is a contradiction in terms: *Viridiana*, whether a real saint from Buñuel's childhood or not (it is yet to be ascertained) still seems a compound word of the Spanish *viril* (virile) and Diana (the chaste goddess of the hunt). In *El ángel exterminador* Leticia is similarly described as virgin and Valkyrie, repressed, yet unmistakably fiercely sexual. In *Viridiana*, originally she offers her services freely, but the beggars invade, intrude upon her hospitality, and she must resist them. In *El ángel exterminador* Nobile and others consider that she is begging for it.

Of course, there is every reason to suppose simply that the continuation with Pinal from Spain to Mexico has much to do with Buñuel's con-

The Valkyrie-virgin at play: Silvia Pinal in *El ángel exterminador* (Luis Buñuel, 1962).

tinued collaboration with Alatriste, and her various personae, nothing more than the result of Buñuel's self-indulgence: the witnessing of Pinal embodying the arch Hitchcockian icy blonde in danger, as would be the case with later variations on the image with Catherine Deneuve in *Belle de jour* (1966) and *Tristana* (1970). Politically correct or not, Pinal functions as a cipher of the ever-interstitial. She must undergo marked transformation, which she was to continue to do, going all the way from sexless nun to high-octane, shape-shifting Satan in the last Mexico-made film, *Simón del desierto*. Pinal's character in both *Viridiana* and *El ángel exterminador* must give up something of her identity, spirit or flesh, to save her and possibly others. Raymond Durgnat pointed this out some time ago:

> A step [though only a step] in the direction of liberation is taken when Letitia [Silvia Pinal], the Valkyrie, allows herself to be deflowered by Nobile.... Letitia is an intransigent; her virginity [with attendant perversions] is, like

Buñuel's little angel: Silvia Pinal as Satan in *Simón del desierto* (Luis Buñuel, 1965).

the saintliness of another Valkyrie, Viridiana.... Maybe Nobile and Letitia should have stepped out into their freedom, leaving the dead to slaughter the dead. But at this last moment the "collective" enwraps them.[71]

The return to Mexico with Pinal as vehicle (in many senses, if not all of them particularly politically correct) would have proved a fascinating, but truly uncanny multilocational experience of "the same, but different": leaving the now familiar exile's Mexico to return to an old, now unfamiliar home, and then to return to the new home, Mexico, from a refamiliarized exile's Spain. In Spain, Mexican Pinal will play a European woman and on return to Mexico, she will play a Mexican in a cast of actors Buñuel wished were more European. Pinal is a reminder, but also a way through the "uncanny" experience of perceiving or attempting to cross the line, or to attempt some synthesis of differences into one meaningful but impossible totality or essence, to be at home and away, to be in two places at once or perhaps never really in either.

Concluding Remarks

Acevedo-Muñoz concedes from the outset that "Buñuel's surrealist formation certainly justifies his creative and ideological independence from any concept of 'national cinema.'"[72] As has been shown, his relationship with the idea of national cinemas is complex, but I would argue that *El ángel exterminador* represents the look back over this issue, the film having an added resonance of the interstitial given Buñuel's return to Mexico, and a look forward. It is particularly interesting, but not entirely surprising that *El ángel exterminador* has become something of a boundary marker for Acevedo-Muñoz, who considers the film "the logical conclusion, the closure, of that period of Buñuel's career," and how:

> [W]hether Buñuel desired it or not, they [he includes *Simón del desierto* also starring Pinal] suggested, if not initiated, the wave of independent experimental films of the Mexican "new cinema" which is historically placed precisely in the period 1964–1965. Furthermore, the rise of auteur criticism in the 1960s and of the auteurist journal *Nuevo Cine* [1961–1962], which picked Buñuel as a symbolic, inspirational figure, confirm the bridging function of Buñuel's films between two distinct eras of Mexican cinema.[73]

Pinal is a bridge between Europe and Latin America, and she is the free variable that blurs the subtle distinction between the director's famous status as multilocated exile and the creation of a new Buñuelian heterocosm ahead of debates regarding transnationalisation, transculturation, and eventual denationalization — reflected in an even more recent post-modern, perhaps utopian, politics of representation, where the indige-nous nature of the film has become secondary or irrelevant:

> The film historian Emilio García Riera writing about ["the situation of Mex-ican cinema"] in 1992, suggested that the term itself was a misnomer, indi-cating the notion of a national industry nurtured in the 1930s and 1940s that was no longer tenable.[74]

El ángel exterminador lacks anything like previous methods of decon-structing the medium (the assaulted eye particularly), has its fair share of dream sequences and surreal paraphernalia, but it functions, like the char-acters do, around a simple, absurd and unfathomable premise: the imag-ined border. In one way the emphasis on class is a superficial diversion, in another way *El ángel exterminador* can be taken as an attack on the bour-geoisie as a particularly exacerbated case of belief in a putative linearity, an imaginary order to history with some originary or transcendental point expressed through rituals and repetitions.

   El ángel exterminador is a synchronic slice across the diachronicity of the bourgeois mindset: it demonstrates an opening into *modes* of legiti-macy and authenticity, and suggests, albeit cruelly, how some communi-ties are delimited and die or develop according to the borders they envision for themselves in relation to an imagined unique center or source. The film is structured around binaries within a binary with *Viridiana*: com-plementary and clashing pairings and unresolved oppositions; upper and lower classes, male and female, inside and outside, plenty and depriva-tion. Moreover, Pinal is the free variable who also serves to offset the Mex-ican melodrama associations of the other actors. In this way, the claiming of Pinal back through Buñuel in the press reports of her new film, as noted above, suggests that her personae remain useful not so much as the indige-nous film player and the reminder of a native, centered, cinematic hey-day and how "they don't make them like they used to," but as the postmodern, transnational changeling. Derrida continues:

> In one case, the nonpassage resembles an impermeability; it would stem from the opaque existence of an uncrossable border: a door that does not open, or that only opens according to an unlocatable condition, according to the inac-cessible secret of some shibboleth.... In another case, the nonpassage, the impasse or aporia, stems from the fact that there is no limit. There is not yet or there is no longer a border to cross, no opposition between two sides: the limit is too porous, permeable and indeterminate. There is no longer a home [*chez-soi*] and a not-home [*chez l'autre*].[75]

Much of what has been discussed regarding ambiguity and the multilocational is arguably intrinsic to cinema. Because the medium is recent in development, it is not necessarily possible to trace its origins to a fixed point. Cinema is multirooted and continues to be a collaborative medium per se. As Paolo Cherchi Usai makes clear in his introduction "The Early Years" in *The Oxford History of World Cinema*, despite the apparent suddenness and speed of cinema's development, the beginning of cinema was not characterized by "a 'big bang'" but by a multioriginary evolution:[76]

> No single event — whether Edison's patented invention of the Kinetoscope in 1891 or the Lumière brothers' first projection of films to a paying audience in 1895 — can be held to separate a nebulous pre-cinema from a cinema proper. Rather there is a continuum which begins with early experiments and devices aimed at presenting images in sequence.[77]

Born with the century of cinema, any universalization of Buñuel's *El ángel exterminador* (borders, margins, belonging) can easily be taken as another Buñuelian personalization (by referring the film back to the question of identity and subjectivity mediated again by postsurrealist psychoanalytic categories and terminology). Likewise, the personalization of the film, for example, his returning to Mexico after Spain, can be taken as another basis for an analysis of the film in terms of (national) identity. Kinder notes, "Buñuel's career of exile dialogizes the auteurist and national contexts, revealing that neither perspective is sufficient by itself."[78] I agree with Kinder, but arrive by a different route. Arguably, Pinal (not forgetting she was married to Alatriste) embodies the problematization of any notion of a creative organizing presence or even auteur in this later phase of Buñuel's career. Pinal represents a way out, but also the possibility of impossibility. The guests have to work out their way back to escape — they trace a circle, and reenact the earlier events — although the repetition is their *temporary* salvation. What they really trace is the spiral. *Avant la lettre*, postmodern Borges pointed this dynamic out in his "Pierre Menard: autor del *Quijote*" in *Ficciones* (*Fictions*, 1944). No matter how one attempts to repeat it, it is inevitably different — at best, the experience can only be uncannily similar, never the same. To trace Buñuel's filmmaking around the globe is seemingly to chronicle an uncannily serendipitous career that saw him move from one "center" to another:

> Paris as an international center of modernism in the late 1920s, when surrealism was a major movement; Hollywood as the center of hegemonic practice in 1930; ... Paris in 1936 and then New York in 1938; ... Mexico as a

political and economic refuge; ... and France as the center of the European art film in the 1960s and early 1970s.[79]

Relating less to the question of region and more to the metaphorics of the margin, *El ángel exterminador* is Buñuel's first truly postmodern film. The film subsumes surrealism, magical realism, and treats class, gender, and sexuality as media for a never-ending discussion with itself. The spectator of *El ángel exterminador* is never really sure if the guests will escape (especially given the reincarceration at the end), and never sure if Pinal has really sacrificed her innocence. The ambiguity is the (ever-shifting) point of the film. Arguably the idea was taken to another level in Buñuel's last film, *Cet obscure objet du désir* (*That Obscure Object of Desire*, 1977). This film revives the theme of male predator and apparently innocent female prey; except that in this instance the female protagonist is inexplicably interchangeable, played by both (French) Carole Bouquet and (Spanish) Ángela Molina. The film functions as if to disrupt even the new binary of *Viridiana* and *El ángel exterminador* where one actress (Pinal) plays her own internally reversing roles in two different films. Uncannily, among Zygmunt Bauman's list of "examples of 'undecidables' discussed by Derrida," he notes:

> The *hymen*: a Greek word again, standing for both membrane and marriage, which for this reason signifies at the same time virginity — the uncompromised and uncompromising difference between the "inside" and the "outside" — and its violation by the fusion of the self and the other. In the result *hymen* is "neither confusion nor distinction, neither identity, nor difference, neither consummation nor virginity, neither the veil nor the unveiling, the inside nor the outside, etc."[80]

Like the protagonists, the film sits at the edge. The guests perform the aporia, which is a sort of "perforia," if one allows for a pun on the notion of perforation in relation to Pinal's ambiguous sexual status. The film is looking backwards and forwards, bound up with the problem of roots and the possibility of return, but disavowing them it acts out *and* critiques the interstitial and irresolvable. *El ángel exterminador* embodies an awareness of postmodern, transnational centerlessness, perpetual exilic indeterminacy, the plurality of identity, and that exotic contingency that was always innocently *over there*, but is now forever here — in the global nowhere?

Endnotes

1. John Baxter, *Buñuel* (London: Fourth Estate, 1994), pp. 77–84; Luis Buñuel, *My Last Breath* (London: Vintage, 1984), pp. 103–106; Ian Gibson, *The Shameful Life of Salvador Dalí* (London: Faber & Faber, 1997), pp. 191–212.

2. Buñuel, *My Last Breath*, p. 105; Gibson, *The Shameful Life of Salvador Dalí*, pp. 204–205.

3. Gibson, Ibid., pp.195, 235.

Amongst other Franco-Mexican and Franco-Italian projects: *Gran casino* (1947); *El gran calavera* (*The Great Carouser*, 1949); *Los olvidados* (*The Young and the Damned*, 1950); *Susana* (1951); *La hija del engaño* (*Daughter of Deceit*, 1951); *Una mujer sin amor* (*A Loveless Woman*, 1951); *Subida al cielo* (*Stairway to Heaven*, 1951); *El bruto* (*The Brute*, 1952); *El* (*He*, 1952); *La ilusión viaja en tranvía* (*A Tram-Ride of Dreams*, 1953); *Cumbres borrascosas* (*Wuthering Heights*, 1953); *Robinson Crusoe* (U.S. coproduction, 1954); *El río y la muerte* (*The River and Death*, 1954); *Ensayo de un crimen / La vida criminal de Archibaldo de la Cruz* (*The Criminal Life of Archibaldo de la Cruz*, 1955); *Nazarín* (*Nazarin*, 1958); *The Young One* (U.S. coproduction, 1960); *El ángel exterminador* (*The Exterminating Angel*, 1962); *Simón del desierto* (*Simon of the Desert*, 1965).

4. These three institutions would be most obviously lampooned in *Le Charme discret de la bourgeoisie* (*The Discreet Charm of the Bourgeoisie*, 1972) when an upper-middle-class coterie, joined by a bishop suffers repeatedly aborted attempts to finish dinner. One of the many distractions is a group of inept and fantasizing soldiers who spontaneously arrive, are asked to join them, and then leave suddenly to continue their "maneuvers" apparently right outside the house.

5. Gibson, *The Shameful Life of Salvador Dalí*, p. 419; Tomás Pérez Turrent and José de la Colina, *Buñuel por Buñuel* (Madrid: Lavel, 1993), p. 43; Buñuel, *My Last Breath*, p. 194.

6. Ibid., p. 197.

7. David Thomson, "The Razor's Edge," *The Independent on Sunday*, January 15, 1995, pp. 18–20 (p. 20).

8. Ernesto R. Acevedo-Muñoz, *Buñuel and Mexico: The Crisis of National Cinema* (Berkeley: University of California Press, 2003), p. 1. This quotation originally appears in Virginia Higginbotham's book, *Luis Buñuel* (New York: Twayne, 1979), p. 63.

9. Michael Wood, "Buñuel in Mexico," in John King, Ana López, and Manuel Alvarado (eds.), *Mediating Two Worlds: Cinematic Encounters in the Americas* (London: BFI., 1993), pp. 40–52 (p. 42).

10. Peter W. Evans, *The Films of Luis Buñuel: Subjectivity and Desire* (New York, Oxford University Press, 1995), p. 36.

11. Acevedo-Muñoz, *Buñuel and Mexico*, p. 1.

12. Ibid.

13. Ibid.

14. Ibid, p. 3.

15. Erica Segre, "Visualizing Mexico: The Interplay of Mexican Graphic Arts and Film in the 1930s and 1940s," *Hispanic Research Journal*, (February 2000), pp. 87–95 (p. 91, 93–94).

16. In 1991, Chicago-born photographer Mariana Yampolsky, whose works represent the epitome of Mexican postrevolutionary pictorialism — she was the first female member of the Taller de Gráfica Popular (Workshop for Popular Graphic Arts)— produced a powerful image of the back of a broken, one-armed angel against a vast Eisensteinian sky titled, "El ángel exterminador" as if to correct the lack of Mexican particularity in Buñuel's film, in a fascinating reclamation; q.v. Mariana Yampolsky, *The Edge of Time: Photographs of Mexico* (Austin: University of Texas Press, 1998), foreword by Elena Poniatowska, introduction by Sandra Berler.

17. Luis Buñuel, "El cine instrumento de poesía," *Universidad de México*, Vol. 13, No. 1, 1958, pp. 14–15. (p. 15) (our translation).

18. Evans, *The Films of Luis Buñuel*, p. 36.

For example, at an unusual exhibition entitled "Mexperimental Cinema," which ran from June 23 to July 20, 1999 at the Guggenheim Museum in New York and from May 26 to June 4, 2000 at the sister museum in Bilbao, several of Buñuel's films including, *Simón del desierto* and *Ensayo de un crimen/La vida criminal de Archibaldo de la Cruz* were shown in the context of the thematic and aesthetic relationships between the imagery of postrevolutionary experimental cinema developed in Mexico and the international cinematic avant-garde, as well as photography, ethnography, painting, and theater. At *Buñuel 2000: Centenary Conference*, September 14 to 16, 2000 at the University of London, a range of papers was presented including: "Buñuel, un cine del exilio redimido" (Buñuel, a Cinema of Redeemed Exile), by Víctor Fuentes; "Buñuels Miracles: The Case of *Simón del desierto*," by Xon de Ros; "Exterminating Visions: the Collaboration of Luis Buñuel and Gabriel Figueroa," by Ceri Higgins; "Buñuel's Mexican Period: Space and the Construction of Myths," by Pietsie Feenstra; "Text and Context: Buñuel, Paz and Mexico," by Ernesto Acevedo-Muñoz; "The Mexican Dimension of Buñuel's Work: Technique in *Los olvidados*," by Stephen Hart, and "Subversive Travel: The Transnational Buñuel in Mexico," by Marvin D'Lugo. Also, in a paper titled "Buñuel's Outsiders," presented at the conference, *World Cinemas: Identity, Culture, Politics* at the University of Leeds, June 25 to 27, 2002, Peter W. Evans continued to investigate the Freudian aspect of Buñuel's work in Mexico, but his essay began to take in issues of displacement, exclusion, and race. More recently, Sebastiaan Faber has taken a closer look at *Los olvidados* and exiled European artists' fascination with but also preconceptions of Mexico in the 1940s and 1950s. See Sebastiaan Faber, "Between Cernuda's Paradise and Buñuel's Hell: Mexico Through Spanish Exiles' Eyes," *Bulletin of Spanish Studies*, 53: 2, (2003), pp. 219–239.

19. Acevedo-Muñoz, *Buñuel and Mexico*, p. 4.

20. Ibid., p. 5.

21. Ibid., p. 4.

22. http://www-ni.laprensa.com.ni/archivo/2001/octubre/15/revista/revista-20011015-02.html

23. Acevedo-Muñoz, *Buñuel and Mexico*, p. 5.

24. Edwards, *The Discreet Art of Luis Buñuel*, p. 171.

With typically Buñuelian expedition, *El ángel exterminador* was filmed between January 29 and March 9, 1962 in the studios of Churubusco, Mexico City.

25. Georges Sadoul, Prologue to *Viridiana* (screenplay), by Luis Buñuel (Mexico City: Cine Club Era, 1963), p. 37; Edwards, *The Discreet Art of Luis Buñuel*, p. 171.

26. Buñuel insists "[u]n mayordomo es burgués de corazón" ("a butler is bourgeois at heart"). Pérez Turrent and de la Colina, *Buñuel por Buñuel*, p. 127.

27. See Juan Buñuel on his father's experiences for one possible source of some of the film's imagery in Joan Mellen, (ed.), *The World of Luis Buñuel: Essays in Criticism* (New York: Oxford University Press, 1978), pp. 254–256.

28. Raymond Durgnat, *Luis Buñuel* (Berkeley and London: University of California Press, 1977), p. 129.

29. For example, q.v. Edwards, *The Discreet Art of Luis Buñuel*, p. 171.

30. Francisco Sánchez offers an explanation for the root of the confusion:

"In issue number 6 (March 1962) of *Nuevo Cine* magazine, because of some misunderstanding it states that the film was based on a theatrical work by José Bergamín entitled *Los náufragos de la calle de la Providencia*. This error has subsequently shown up in numerous filmographies. The truth is that such a theatrical work does not even exist. What certainly does exist, in Mexico City, just a few blocks from where Buñuel was living, is Calle Providencia." Francisco Sánchez, *Luis Buñuel* (Mexico City: Cineteca Nacional, 2000), p. 109 (our translation).

31. Pérez Turrent and de la Colina, *Buñuel por Buñuel*, p. 125; Edwards, *The Discreet Art of Luis Buñuel*, p. 171.

32. Pérez Turrent and de la Colina, *Buñuel por Buñuel*, p. 126.

See, for example, II *Samuel*, 24.16; *Kings* II, 19.35; and 19:35; *Exodus*, 12.23; *Psalm; Chronicles* 21:15; 78.49; *Numbers* 17:11–15; *Revelation* 9:11. Note also: a distinction between the angel of death who comes to an individual at the time appointed for him to die and the Destroyer who massacres entire populations with premature violent deaths. Later traditions, however, fuse the two conceptions. Thus "Destroying Angel," in Karel van der Toorn, Bob Becking, and Pieter W. van der Horst (eds.), *Dictionary of Deities and Demons in the Bible (D.D.D.)* (Leiden and New York and Cologne: E. J. Brill, 1995), p. 462.

33. Agustín Sánchez Vidal, *Luis Buñuel* (Madrid: Cátedra, 1991), pp. 237–238 (our translation).

34. Ibid., p. 237 (our translation).

35. Michel Estève, "L'Ange exterminateur," *Études Cinématographiques* (Spring 1963), pp. 22–23.

36. Quoted in Mellen (ed.), *The World of Luis Buñuel*, pp. 245–246.

To be fair to Estève, he concedes, "[t]he undeniable presence of these three themes, however [the theme of the absurd, the failure of communication, and the conception of the other as executioner] is not enough to make us define *The Exterminating Angel* as a totally existential work." Ibid., p. 249.

37. He would not move away more permanently until he had traveled back and forth some more, completing *Le Journal d'une femme de chambre* (*Diary of a Chambermaid*, 1964) in France, then back to Mexico with *Simón del desierto* and then back to Europe, where he remained pretty much, with *Belle de jour* (1967), *La Voie lactée* (*The Milky Way*, 1969), and others until his death, again back in Mexico in 1983.

38. Pérez Turrent and de la Colina, *Buñuel por Buñuel*, p. 128.

39. Ibid. (our translation).

One intention/theme that was continued from *Viridiana* through *El ángel exterminador* into *The Discreet Charm of the Bourgeoisie* was a vehement, if oblique, anti–Francoism, which implicated various figures who had vowed to remain opposed to the regime in Spain. The cello being bashed to pieces to make firewood to cook with in *El ángel exterminador* is recalled in *The Discreet Charm of the Bourgeoisie*: Florence (Bulle Ogier) expresses her irrational, but unquestioned horror at the cellist in a café, suggesting Buñuel's disgust at Pablo Casals taking part in a concert of chamber music at the White House on November 13, 1961, at the invitation of President John F. Kennedy, whose administration recognized the Franco regime.

40. Wood, "Buñuel in Mexico," p. 50.

41. Pérez Turrent and de la Colina, *Buñuel por Buñuel*, p. 125 (our translation).

42. Ibid., p. 128 (our translation).

43. Wood, "Buñuel in Mexico," p. 50.

44. Marsha Kinder, *Blood Cinema: The Reconstruction of National Identity in Spain* (London: University of California Press, 1993), p. 301.

45. Ibid.

46. Acevedo-Muñoz, *Buñuel and Mexico*, p. 41.

47. Ado Kyrou, "The Exterminating Angel," in *The Exterminating Angel, Nazarín and Los olvidados* (London: Lorrimer, 1972), pp. 6, 8, 10, 13; Durgnat, *Luis Buñuel*, p. 126; Edwards, *The Discreet Art of Luis Buñuel*, p. 172; Sánchez Vidal, *Luis Buñuel*, p. 236; Pérez Turrent and de la Colina, *Buñuel por Buñuel*, p. 126; Víctor Fuentes, *Los mundos de Buñuel* (Madrid: Akal, 2000), p. 106.

48. Evans, *The Films of Luis Buñuel*, pp. 72–90.

49. Bernardo Pérez Soler, "*Heimlichkeit* Destroyed: Freud's 'The "Uncanny"' and *The Exterminating Angel*," paper presented at *Buñuel 2000: Centenary Conference* at the University of London, September 14 to 16, 2000.

50. Evans, *The Films of Luis Buñuel*, p. 81.

51. Ibid., p. 83.

52. Ibid., p. 79.

53. Gore Vidal for Emory University: http://www.emory.edu/EDUCATION/mfp/eulogy.html

54. Wood, "Buñuel in Mexico."

55. Acevedo-Muñoz, p. 65.

56. Ibid., p. 66.

57. Sigmund Freud, "The Uncanny," in *Art and Literature*, Penguin Freud Library, Vol. 14 (London: Penguin, 1990), pp. 339–376 (first published 1919), (p. 340).

58. Nicholas Royle, *The Uncanny* (Manchester: Manchester University Press, 2003), pp. 1–2.

59. Fuentes, *Los mundos de Buñuel*, p. 107.

60. Evans, *The Films of Luis Buñuel*, p. 76.

61. Pérez Turrent and de la Colina, *Buñuel por Buñuel*, p. 126 (our translation).

62. Ibid. (our translation).

63. Fuentes, *Los mundos de Buñuel*, p. 106 (our translation).

64. Ibid., p. 107 (our translation).

65. Kyrou, "The Exterminating Angel," p. 5.

66. Octavio Paz, "El cine filosófico de Buñuel," in *Los signos en rotación y otros ensayos* (Madrid: Alianza, 1971), pp. 175–180 (our translation). This topic was taken up by Vicente Cervera Salinas, in his paper "Octavio Paz y el cine filosófico de Buñuel," presented at *Buñuel 2000: Centenary Conference*, held at the University of London from September 14 to 16, 2000.

67. Wood, "Buñuel in Mexico," p. 50.

68. Jacques Derrida, *Aporias* (Stanford, CA: Stanford University Press, 1993), trans. by Thomas Dutoit, p. 11.

69. Jonathan Culler, "Jacques Derrida," in John Sturrock (ed.), *Structuralism and Since* (Oxford: Oxford University Press, 1979), pp. 164–165.

70. Buñuel, *Viridiana* (screenplay), p. 37.

71. Durgnat, *Luis Buñuel*, p. 129.

72. Acevedo-Muñoz, *Buñuel and Mexico*, p. 1.

73. Ibid., p. 7, p. 13.
In the introduction to an interview with Alejandro González Iñárritu, the director of *Amores perros* (*Love's a Bitch*, 2000), Bernardo Pérez Soler shows the continued influence of Buñuel when he refers to certain sequences of the film as an "account of a relationship falling apart — and a painstaking exploration of the hold domestic spaces have over us — shot through with a line of dark absurdist humor that brings to mind Buñuel's treatise on bourgeois entrapment in *The Exterminating Angel*, a late entry in the Spanish director's Mexican period." Bernardo Pérez Soler, "Pup Fiction: *Amores Perros/ Love's a Bitch*," *Sight and Sound*, BFI, (May 2001), pp. 28–30.

74. Erica Segre, "'La *desnacionalización* de la pantalla': Mexican Cinema in the 1990s," in Rob Rix and Roberto Rodríguez-Saona (eds.), *Changing Reels: Latin American Cinema Against the Odds* (Leeds: Trinity and All Saints, 1997), pp. 33–59 (pp. 41–42).

75. Derrida, *Aporias*, pp. 20–21.

76. Geoffrey Nowell-Smith (ed.), *The Oxford History of World Cinema* (Oxford: Clarendon Press, 1995), p.6.

77. Ibid.

78. Kinder, *Blood Cinema*, p. 291.

79. Ibid., p. 287.

80. Zygmunt Bauman, *Modernity and Ambivalence* (London: Polity Press, 1991), pp. 55–56. Bauman quotes from Jacques Derrida, *Positions*, trans. Alan Bass (University of Chicago Press, 1981), pp. 42–43.

PART II

Gender and Sexuality

4

Nelson and Nelson: Mirror Images and Social Drama in *Boca de Ouro*

Ismail Xavier

Boca de Ouro (Gold Mouth), the play, was written in 1958, when Nelson Rodrigues was at the height of his creative power and was one of the most controversial playwrights in Brazil. Petit bourgeois spectators rejected him, for moral reasons, and he came into conflict with the official censors. Although he had been a successful author since the 1940s, only one of his works had been translated into film before the production *of Boca de Ouro,* directed by Nelson Pereira dos Santos, in 1962. This was an adaptation of one of his novels, *Meu destino é pecar* (Bound for Sin), directed by Manoel Pelufo for the Maristela studios in São Paulo in 1952. Film producers were cautious and did not want to challenge the censors, and the major Brazilian film production company of the 1950s, Vera Cruz, had its own playwright to sign the screenplays, Abílio Pereira de Almeida, who also wrote plays dealing with family dramas and moral issues characteristic of Brazilian patriarchal society. Nelson Rodrigues had to wait until the 1960s to see his plays and other texts adapted for the screen. To date 20 adaptations of his work have appeared on screen.

The late 1950s and the early 1960s saw the emergence throughout the world of a new way of treating sexuality on screen and a new acceptance of "adult themes" in film. The "Brigitte Bardot phenomenon" and the liberating role played by the "New Cinemas" in different countries, Brazil included, produced a significant change in the visual presentation of sexuality. It was no coincidence that *Boca de Ouro* and Rui Guerra's *Os Cafajestes* (*The Hustlers*) were released in the same year, both featuring what was then considered to be the scandalous exposure of women's bodies.

Since then, the status of sexuality in adaptations of Rodrigues's work has become an obligatory theme for debate, renewing the traditional tension between sex as a moral subject and sex as an attraction to be exploited in the marketplace. For his part, Nelson Pereira dos Santos was discreet, avoiding arbitrary excesses but remaining firm in his refusal to cut bolder scenes that could create problems with the official censors. (The clearest example of the latter is the scene in which the leading character, Boca de Ouro, hosts a contest in his house to find the woman with the most beautiful breasts from among a group of female visitors).

Nelson Pereira dos Santos was invited to direct *Boca de ouro* by Jece Valadão, the producer and leading actor of the film, a well-known star who also played the lead role in Guerra's *Os Cafajestes,* and who had worked on dos Santos's so-called neorealist films of the 1950s. Valadão had ample experience of playing tough characters from the poorer quarters of Rio de Janeiro, as he did in dos Santos's *Rio, 40 Graus* (Rio, 40 Degrees) of 1954, in which he played a typical *malandro* or hustler from the shantytown. Egotistic, smart, sometimes violent, the *malandro* always looks after his own interests. He can be poor and involved in small-scale acts of dishonesty or petty crime, or rich, like the gangster character Boca de Ouro, the self-made *bicheiro.*[1] A well-known figure in the social landscape of the city, the bicheiro has popular appeal, and Boca de Ouro, given his humble origins, exhibits a coarse personal style that integrates him well into the culture of Rio's outlying areas, forming part of a social milieu that, in the 1950s, could be seen as typical of a neo-realist film. The playwright was aware of this possible association but wanted to give other connotations, of a psychological kind, to the leading character. To avoid the identification with a realism he disliked, he introduces, in the play, a joke to mock the neorealist film school that was so seminal in film history. At a certain point in the story, a rich woman comes to see Boca de Ouro. She already knows him, and she has brought with her two friends who belong to a charitable institution, who want to ask him for money. She behaves quite frivolously, as if she were carrying out some kind of empirical research in the poor outlying districts, encountering the key figures of such an area and in the hope of being affected by the libido that supposedly circulates in the poor sections of town. Looking at him, with a mixture fascination and ironic distance, she says to her two curious friends: "He's rather neorealist, isn't he?"

On the one hand, Nelson Rodrigues recognizes the presence in his work of a character shaped by the same real world that was the inspiration for *Rio, 40 Graus* and *Rio, Zona Norte* (Rio, North Zone, 1957), two films made by Nelson Pereira dos Santos. On the other hand, he equates neorealism with those "artifacts" taken from real life and placed on display for the distanced curiosity of rich people. Nelson Pereira dos Santos, the Brazilian filmmaker most identified with the Italian school at that time, accepted the challenge and indeed turned his adaptation of *Boca de Ouro* into a kind of neorealist film, as much as possible, bringing to the creation of its protagonist all the experience he had acquired in his other films dealing with the poor of the "North Zone" of Rio. He kept the rich woman's line exactly as it appeared in the play, and turned the film version of *Boca de Ouro* into a new chapter in his continuous dialogue with neorealism and Brazil's social problems, shifting the balance between the moral and the political side of the text.

Considering the ideological perspectives of the early 1960s, there were clear tensions between the Cinema Novo filmmakers and Nelson Rodrigues's plays. Boca de Ouro's life is seen by Rodrigues as a moral parable that concerns the tragic effects of unrestrained human ambition. Rodrigues has a keen perception of crude reality, developed during his work as a newspaper reporter, but sometimes his plays acquire a conservative moral tone that inscribes powerful scenes and vital characters within an overall design meant to condemn concrete people, whoever they are. Human misbehavior is taken as an expression of a person's specific nature, and is measured against a radical moral scale that offers no choice: once absolute purity is made impossible, society can only produce unhappiness. The playwright displays a moral sense that derives from a Christian tradition aware of its own crisis (there are clear affinities between Rodrigues and Dostoyevski in their mistrust of modernity).

· Focused on family dramas— normally with a tragicomic flavor — Rodrigues's plays are concerned with the crisis of Brazilian patriarchal society and moral decadence. Resisting modernization, he constantly attacks mass communication and its central role in the construction of a new subjectivity shaped by a consumer society. This is, for him, a new stage in a slide toward moral corruption, embedded in a human nature that always reveals a vicious motivation at the root of any gesture. Although his plays were seen as too pessimistic and strict in their understanding of social problems, Cinema Novo's filmmakers, in different instances, tried to explore the points of conjunction in which the playwright's critique of society could be reworked to express a more historical view of human experience. For Nelson Pereira dos Santos, one challenge was to displace Rodrigues' negative view of the poor. The play depicts a corrupt world populated by weak men (husbands or fathers) who try to think and act as if they were great but can only show the gap between their pretense and their performance, their lack of competence, and their contradictions. In

Boca de Ouro, the moral debate develops around the powerful man who places himself at the center of a complex social game involving three kinds of experience: first, the illusions of poor people in search of the easy money generated by the illegal private lottery that he runs; second, the different legends that surround his charismatic figure; and third, the interests of the sensationalist press that exploits him as a media star. He is the gangster who builds his social image as a charitable benefactor by attracting poor people. Surrounded by a variety of legendary stories, he triggers people's imagination, becoming a source of both material gratification (the promise of money) and spiritual fulfillment (the fiction that satisfies a longing for myth typical of a population otherwise condemned to a dull everyday life).

Given this set of relationships, Nelson Pereira dos Santos creates an adaptation of the play that gives more emphasis to the historical and the social than to the mythic dimension of people's experience. To pursue his aim, the filmmaker maintains a tone of good-humored observation with regard to the milieu in question, and introduces new characters in a variety of urban spaces. His aim is a social chronicle that can move away from a sense of theatrical closeness and express a different sense of the popular, counterbalancing an imputed image of ignorance and bad taste with the representation of simple people as a source of value and hope. He searches for identification and complicity, casting poor characters in a sympathetic light, in a representation marked by an absence of moral judgment and less dependent on the traditional stereotype of Brazilians as weak fatalists who are obsessed with easy money, and who reject any work ethic.

Although the character of Boca de Ouro finds his major reference in everyday life in Rio de Janeiro, his composition owes something to the American gangster film, especially with regard to the moral parable designed to condemn vanity and an unrestrained quest for power. On a symbolic level, he represents a figure of resentment, shaped by his own sense of his "shameful" origins that gives impulse to his project of revenge against society. Working as a great compensatory plan, the major project that synthesizes Boca de Ouro's revenge is the construction of a coffin made of gold, a symbol of glory in death that amplifies what is already signified in his gold teeth. In his clichéd treatment of the question of humble origins and triumph in death, Rodrigues is again playing on that common sense derived from psychoanalytic knowledge and stereotypes, exploring Boca de Ouro's strong fixation on his mother. She is a dead woman whom he has not effectively known. The legend says that she gave birth to him in the restroom of a *gafieira* (a down-market dance hall), abandoning him in a sink. This story comes to the fore in more than one dramatic instance, usually to trigger the character's more violent reactions toward unfortunate offenders.

Together with Boca de Ouro's personal mythology, a conventional family drama emerges at the center of the play, entering the scene through the key role played by Dona Guigui, the bicheiro's former lover, in the unveiling of the plot. She is the character who narrates the past episodes of Boca de Ouro's life that provide most of the material for the three acts of the play. First, there is the paradigm of the search: the news of Boca de Ouro's death arrives at a newspaper office, and a reporter, Caveirinha, is sent to interview the gangster's ex-lover to discover any private secrets that could give him some advantage over his competitors. As in *Citizen Kane,* where the journalist goes to see Susan Alexander but obtains very little information from her, we follow Caveirinha's attempt to find a good story while Dona Guigui, proud of this public attention, takes the opportunity to come to terms with her own past. She once abandoned her family, composed of her weak husband Agenor and their children, to be part of the bicheiro's intimate world. Now she has returned to her legal marriage, but Boca de Ouro's presence in her life is far from over. When invited to say something about him she has a cathartic experience (with the journalist acting as a prototherapist).

As the source of the intradiegetic narration that dominates the play, Dona Guigui and her state of mind become major dramatic issues, together with her husband's present reactions to her words. Rodrigues uses Guigui's family to introduce the question of the "small man" and his private ethics, depicting a petty world of impotence that contrasts with Boca de Ouro's powerful figure, a kind of father (or husband) substitute. Dos Santos takes the couple as a pretext for a more panoramic view of society. His efforts to create a kind of chronicle of social life in the suburbs make him avoid heavy symbolism or dramatic resonance based on games of light and shadow. He distances himself from an expressionist reading of the play, a reading that could find its way through the opposition between the "small man" and the grotesque figure of evil. A dramatic display of human experience, the play *Boca de Ouro* is organized around a whole set of imaginary constructions that come from Guigui and other people that surround the protagonist. But Rodrigues himself, despite the gothic scenario, makes jokes about this side of his drama, balancing, for example, the pathetic ending with a comic speech made by a radio broadcaster who calls Boca de Ouro the "Dracula from Madureira," among other eloquent epithets.[2] Dos Santos understands quite well the role of comedy in the play, which is designed to provide local color for the drama. Therefore, avoiding an overly serious exploration of the grotesque implied in the golden teeth idea, he reinforces the naturalist side of the story, making Boca de Ouro a social type, eccentric but quite acceptable, inscribed in melodramatic codes but representative of a social reality. The film moves away from the archetypal and privileges a more down-to-earth psychological side of motivations. We have a story that unfolds in daylight hours, which features humor and indeed an expected neorealist flavor.

There is a tragic effect in the irony of Boca de Ouro's defeat: he is not buried in the golden coffin, and after he is killed, all his gold teeth are extracted, in a violent act that gives his corpse an even more grotesque appearance. At the same time, there is a comic effect in the festival of kitsch implied both in Boca's own style and in the distance between pretension and performance that marks all the "small men" around him. This mixture in tone and genre that results in tragicomedy is also explored in the film, but dos Santos tries to soften the image of the people, represented by the couple, Agenor and Guigui. Their precarious way of dealing with their lives does not result from fate or a fixed moral character. The film wants to suggest that people's mentality can change according to circumstance, and for the better, not only for the worse. In his adaptation, dos Santos expresses the central concerns of leftist art produced in Brazil in the early 1960s as outlined below.

Real Facts, Unreliable Narrators, Mental Projections: Dos Santos's Choices

The film opens with a prologue that gives a brief account of Boca de Ouro's career, from the young man of action who did the dirty jobs for the "firm," to the man at the top of the illegal lottery. The key moments of his ascent are presented as clips, a sequence of short scenes that run while we read the film credits. This kind of objective presentation of a bicheiro's life (in fact, the series of facts that precede his decision to become Boca de Ouro by implanting the gold teeth) introduces a major difference between the film and the play. Dos Santos gives us the standard trajectory of an outlaw, not far from the model taken from the Hollywood gangster film. We see him performing different kinds of violent acts, such as killing a man while a child looks on, seducing his boss's wife in order to gain some advantage in the "firm," and finally, stabbing his own boss in a bold move which, it is suggested, is his last step toward becoming the leader of the gang. The prologue gives us a first portrait that allows for a preliminary judgment supported by images presented as "the truth" in the diegetic world. There is no reason to question the invisible narrator, and the audience takes what it sees as fact, something that rarely happened in the past, gaining some objective knowledge about Boca de Ouro, namely that he is tough, he can be charming, and he kills people. Later, when we listen to Guigui's narration, this identity already shaped in the audience's minds will play a role in their perception of things. Facts about Boca de Ouro that a reader of the play can suspect or ignore become established truths in the film, neutralizing some of the effects that come from the ambiguities created by Guigui's narrations. The prologue anchors Boca de Ouro's image in the real world before we have to look at him as a projection of Guigui's mind.

After this opening credit sequence, the film follows the order already established in the text, taking us first to the major symbolic gesture that opens the play and introduces the protagonist, namely the scene in which Boca de Ouro obliges his dentist to extract all his teeth and implant the golden teeth that will become his personal mark of distinction. This is the only instance in which Rodrigues' play provides a nonmediated view of the protagonist. The next scene presents him as a dead man, the topic of a conversation between journalists who are preparing their strategies to exploit the news. Dead, Boca de Ouro will only return to the audience's view through Dona Guigui's memory. A particular set of projections composes his image on stage, filtered by her mind. Dona Guigui's behavior, heavily inflected by her emotions, complicates this mediated process: her account of the past produces three distinct and contradictory versions (one for each act of the play). When she receives the journalist who comes to demand a "good unknown story," she is not aware of Boca de Ouro's death, and Caveirinha deliberately does not tell her about it. Out of vanity, she starts showing off (the photographer is there too) as if she were the important figure in the story. Resenting her past with the bicheiro, she hesitates, but ends up being happy with the idea of the interview, which offers a chance for revenge. She recounts what she supposedly witnessed on a particular day in Boca de Ouro's house, a peculiar episode narrated three times, in different ways, according to her changing mood.

Since it lies at the center of the play, Guigui's account of the past raises the question of the "unreliable narrator," creating a seductive game for those who like to solve puzzles and pay attention to detail in order to dissipate ambiguities. There is something in the play that reminds the reader of Kurosawa's *Rashomon*, with its distinct versions of the same story told by different people in the solemn trial sequence. The difference here is that the same person repeats the story three times, recounting everything in her own house, with more than a touch of exhibitionism, and being transparent in the exposure of her motivations for acting that way. In each of

Guigui's versions, the facts and Boca de Ouro's style and behavior change. There are blatant differences in the plot that clearly result from Guigui's words (that is to say, the play's text). But there is something that is more decisive to our reading; the film's visual text introduces significant new elements, which stem from the camera style and specific connections produced by the repetition of the same frame in different circumstances. These formal aspects of the film cannot simply be interpreted as a result of Dona Guigui's unstable view of the past. There is something in the cinematic constructions that comes from the intervention of another narrative agency, invisible and external to the diegetic world. It is the combination of Guigui's emotional speech and the specific forms taken by the more calculated visual discourse that creates the main reference for the interpretation of the film. In other words, the play provides the material for the three versions as proposed by Guigui's accounts, but the final result of this game comes from the choices made by the filmmaker, the formal procedures and the cinematic creation that derive from dos Santos's realist stance. In the play the journalist arrives at Guigui's home during the evening, and the entire conversation is marked by a nocturnal atmosphere that enhances mental projections, and could be enacted with something closer to an expressionist tone. In the film, he arrives at her house in the morning, and the conversation is punctuated by the presence of other people, namely her children, a visitor, and the neighbors, whom Guigui meets when she runs from her house to the grocer's store to pick up a telephone and tell the newspaper to change her testimony. In her second account of the past she presents a more favorable view of the bicheiro and has to face her husband's protests. They quarrel, the journalist intervenes, and is instrumental in their reconciliation in a comic scene intended to demonstrate how people's weaknesses and incoherence can be manipulated by the media. The journalist takes them both with him to the municipal morgue to see Boca de Ouro's corpse. In the car, Guigui starts the third version of the story, out of her desire to consolidate her peace with Agenor. In the play, there are none of these spatial displacements. The reader/spectator remains in the house, from Act I to Act III, and the journalist leaves the couple alone when he goes to the morgue. The film brings the streets into the audience's view, and makes Guigui interact with other people, giving her words and action a sense of being more connected with her neighbors' everyday lives. Her face and gestures are all bound up with a clear-cut transparency, and her different versions of the story express her psychological naiveté. They clearly result from her overtly emotional reactions that are caused by the reporter's manipulation.

The Three Versions in Rodrigues's Play

Why did Nelson Rodrigues place a single character, particularly a woman, at the center of the narration? Broadly speaking, the following is a translation of a central idea of the play: the myth-making process implies multiple versions, from the media discourse to the variety of stories made up by different people. Boca de Ouro's identity must be an effect produced by the discourse of others. More specifically, Rodrigues chooses a female character because, aside from the rise and fall of the gangster, he wants to raise questions of desire and moral codes, and to discuss family affairs and the behavior of women like Dona Guigui. She is the center of a suburban family drama that requires more detailed observation to clarify how the pivotal social role played by a character like Boca de Ouro carries many implications and solicits serious moral debate. It is this concern that explains the kind of story chosen by Guigui when she meets the journalist's demands. Among the many "secrets" available, she selects the misadventure of a couple, Celeste and Leleco, in their confrontation with the protagonist.

One day the unemployed, relatively poor Leleco went to see Boca de Ouro and, after a complicated conversation involving his wife, was killed by the bicheiro (in the first two versions), or perhaps both him and his wife were killed in Boca's house (in the third version). The disappearance of the corpses, organized by the members of the gang, meant that the double murder remained unsolved. Guigui frames her story as a revelation but, as the film progresses, we understand that it is her, the narrator, that matters, not the story. First, this is suggested by the symptomatic similarity that exists between the two couples: Agenor-Guigui and Leleco-Celeste. Both present the figure of the "small man" as the head of the family, a kind of anti–Boca, and the unsatisfied woman who is attracted by the charming and rich bicheiro. Like Guigui, the wife who features in her story once had an affair with Boca de Ouro. The episode recalled in the flashbacks shows the complications that resulted from this affair, functioning above anything else as mental projections through which Guigui deals with her own past. Each of the three versions, besides being inflected by her mood in the present, corresponds to an imaginary resolution of her own affair with Boca de Ouro. In other words, they correspond to past events as they could have been but were not, when she started her affair with the bicheiro. This is the basic mirror relationship that structures the play and provides the key to this interpretation of the film.

When Guigui was seduced by Boca de Ouro and went to live with him, her husband, although humiliated, was obliged to accept things as they were, waiting for her return and for a reconciliation that did not prove entirely satisfactory for him (nor for Guigui), as their present reactions to the story demonstrate. Boca de Ouro is the source of a clear tension that affects both Guigui and Agenor, giving the journalist's visit that cathartic function referred to earlier. Rising to the provocation, the wife tells us three possible versions of how things could have occurred between her, represented by Celeste, and Boca de Ouro, and she recounts three unfortunate endings, marked by death. Each version suggests a different, although always tragic, denouement for the romantic episode that, in real life, ended with her return to a conventional family life.

In Act I of the play, Guigui's resentment caused by Boca de Ouro's rejection of her leads to a depiction of the protagonist as a villain. In Act II, we encounter a woman who, having learned that her ex-lover is dead, recalls the past, inspired by her remorse and by the desire to redeem the bicheiro. In Act III, we face a woman who, reconciled with her husband, weaves the last version of the story, and according to this new disposition, sends Boca de Ouro back to hell. The first version gives total emphasis to Boca de Ouro's sexual desire, and the way he took advantage of Celeste's innocence and Leleco's stupidity. Celeste's mother dies, the unemployed Leleco does not have enough money for the funeral and, playing the smart guy, tries to obtain money from the bicheiro. Boca suspects the naive plot set by Leleco and persuades him to bring his wife along with him, agreeing to hand over the money only after "talking" to her. Excited by the prospect of easy money, Leleco pretends not to understand what is implied in the offer, and calls his wife. Once in Boca's house she resists the gangster's advances and asks for protection from her husband. Under pressure, Leleco ends up "delivering" his wife to the bicheiro, but despite being seemingly heartbroken by this act, he only reacts when Boca refuses to give him the money. Furious (only because of the money), he cannot help reminding the bicheiro of his shameful birth in the dance hall, and Boca then loses his self-control and kills him. The melodramatic moral annihilation of Leleco is completed even before his physical death. The confrontation between the "small man" and the powerful figure, conducted in a dishonorable way, ultimately exposes Leleco's baseness, and his radical failure would perhaps never have happened if his perception of his own limitations had been better.

In the second version, Boca is the innocent party and both Celeste and Leleco are the corrupt figures from the start. The day his mother-in-law dies, Leleco discovers that his wife has a lover. The question of money is at the heart of events again, but this time the husband is also motivated by a desire for revenge. Jealous, he wants to humiliate his wife and forces her to seduce the bicheiro and take his money, as if implying "once a prostitute, always a prostitute." For her part, Celeste sees this seduction plot as a chance to leave her husband and stay with Boca de Ouro for a while (like Guigui, who was at that point living with the bicheiro). Once in Boca's home, she begins the planned seduction routine but the arrival of other people obliges her to wait for a while. Three rich women come to see Boca de Ouro, in awe of the media star and his kitsch macho style. The next scene features the beauty contest, already mentioned, in which the bicheiro compares the breasts of the four women present, and concludes that Celeste is the winner. She deserves the necklace that he had offered as a prize to encourage them to accept the embarrassing competition. The rich women leave the house and Leleco arrives. Looking at the necklace, he sees it as a sign that the seduction plot has already been carried out. He plays his role in the comedy and pretends to forgive her, supposing she is on his side. Celeste rejects his call to go home, since she has her own plans. Boca de Ouro intervenes to protect her, telling Leleco to leave the house. He is firm but polite. Violence will be perpetrated by Celeste in an impersonation of the femme fatale; she kills her husband with a knife, keeping Boca de Ouro out of the self-destructive conjugal war. The bicheiro's clean hands contrast with the lesson on family decadence given by Celeste and Leleco.

In the third version, there is no innocence. When Guigui's narration begins, Celeste is already having her affair with Boca de Ouro. Leleco discovers everything in a devastating scene that opens the story. He is on a bus that stops just beside Boca de Ouro's car. Recognizing Celeste, Leleco suffers while all the people around him joyously comment on the love scene performed by the two passengers in the vehicle. At home he demands that she identify her lover. Promising revenge, Leleco hears Boca de Ouro's name, which brings a bitter smile to his face. His hesitation about taking measures against such a powerful figure leads him to hatch a new plan involving extortion. Violence can wait. He warns Celeste that her life depends on the result of the lottery game run by Boca de Ouro. He has made his bet; if he wins she is on safe ground, but if he loses he promises to kill her. She goes to see the bicheiro and tells him about Leleco's planned revenge. When the husband arrives in Boca de Ouro's house, ironic and self-assured as never before, he threatens Boca de Ouro with a gun and demands "his" money although he has lost in the lottery game. Aggressive, he demands a violent reaction, and when he is hit on the head, he falls down. When he is lying on the ground still alive, the bicheiro comes up with a plan, and invites Celeste to help him consummate the murder. Celeste accepts the idea and seals her partnership with Boca de Ouro. But the circumstances do not give her much time to enjoy this new status. Again the rich woman, Maria Luiza, enters the scene to stop Celeste. Now she comes to the house alone and seems to be much more acquainted with the *bicheiro*. She already has a love story in mind. Eager to play her part in Boca's world, she confronts Celeste and ends up usurping the position of the girl from the poor suburbs sooner than the audience could imagine. In a complicated scene marked by melodrama, when the two women recognize each other (they had been classmates in a boarding school), the three characters develop a kind of psychodrama in which Celeste reveals to Maria Luiza the crime she and Boca de Ouro committed that same afternoon. She takes Maria Luiza to see Leleco's corpse. The truth uncovered, the bicheiro threatens Maria Luiza, since she knows too much, but ends up killing the "dangerous" Celeste, as he calls her. In this final version, there is no difference between good and evil, and all the characters are equal in their displays of self-interest, including the apparently timid and naive Maria Luiza. Later in the play the reader/audience will learn that Boca de Ouro made a mistake, killing the wrong femme fatale, because, as his lover, Maria Luiza will show her perverse side, already suggested in Guigui's narration, killing Boca de Ouro and stealing all his gold teeth. (The news will be relayed to Caveirinha in the last scene by a radio announcer.)

It is impossible to decide which version is closest to the truth. The third one is more plausible, for its degree of compatibility with the rest of the story, especially the details concerning Maria Luiza, the woman who will go on to kill Boca de Ouro. Despite this particular sign, the play itself mocks our anxiety to solve the problem. A clear example of this is the scene in which the journalist argues with the photographer about the number of unidentified corpses found in the bushes, supposedly at the time of this episode recalled by Guigui. Strictly speaking, there is no sense in talking about verisimilitude in Rodrigues's plays, a fact that dos Santos's realist reading of *Boca de Ouro* could not radically change. It is impossible to say anything certain about this matter, because there is no teleology of a factual truth implied in the order in which the three versions appear.

What we have here is indeed a teleology of drama, in other words, the concern for an order that can best explain what each character means to the others in their confrontation as social types. The play, and subsequently the film, exhibits an order that best characterizes, without concern for chronology, Boca de Ouro's experience, from the implantation of the gold teeth to his death. At the same time, the order in which the three versions occur suggests a progressive pattern, not in the facts narrated, but in the way Guigui deals with the different characters, namely Boca de Ouro, Celeste, Leleco, and Maria Luiza. The changes introduced with each new version obey a certain rule that can be referred to as Guigui's mental projections. The three flashbacks create mirror relationships that make evident how Guigui, in her symbolic revisiting of her past, projects herself onto Celeste's body.

In the first version, Celeste embodies a figure of innocence who became involved in the affair with Boca de Ouro as a result of an incident for which the people to blame were Boca de Ouro (the villain) and Leleco. Her husband's weakness and cowardice are punished with death (Agenor's symbolic death). In the second version, she makes progress in recognizing her own responsibility in the whole affair. Embodied in Celeste, she loses her innocence. For his part, Leleco, as Agenor's representative, is even worse than before. Now the people to blame for the whole affair are the husband and wife, not Boca de Ouro. Guigui starts to acknowledge the affair as something that resulted from her free will. Guilty feelings can surface: in her account she makes Celeste kill Leleco. In other words, she sees herself killing Agenor symbolically. In the final version, all the characters involved are perverse. Celeste does not wait for any complicated plot set by Leleco to start her affair with the bicheiro. Guigui seems to accept her responsibility for the affair in the past and creates a horrible figure to mirror herself, a specular image made to be killed (Boca de Ouro kills Celeste). The husband suffers his symbolic death again, both because he is the bad husband and, in practical terms, the victim of betrayal. With this last turn of memory Guigui finally comes to terms with her past, emotionally "killing" that experience and that part of her own self still linked to it.

Taking what is proposed by the play, one can read the present as the occasion for the elimination of the remnants of that past experience involving Boca de Ouro, Agenor, and Guigui. But the text does not give much emphasis to the couple at the end, instead paying more attention to the journalist's investigation, because Boca de Ouro is what really matters to him. When Guigui finishes her story, the journalist is satisfied and, because she has already given him everything he wanted, he quickly leaves the house and goes to see Boca de Ouro's corpse in the municipal morgue. In the play, we follow him there while Guigui and Agenor are forgotten, left at home to decide their own affairs out of our view. The idea that Guigui and Agenor might have freed themselves from Boca de Ouro's ghostlike figure remains open to question.

Nelson Pereira dos Santos's Formal Strategy

The film, although apparently simple in its formal composition, in fact presents very careful camera setups that suggest dos Santos's interpretation of the role played by the flashbacks in Guigui's life. Given his realist framework, he provides a different ending for the story in order to reinforce his view of her psychological process as an experience of liberation. Clear evidence of this is the way in which Maria Luiza's image is presented in the film, from the first to the third version of the past.

In the first version, we see Boca de Ouro arriving at his house and meeting some people who are waiting for him. They hope to be received by the bicheiro in order to present their demands. When the camera pans in the front yard of the house, Maria Luiza is seen mixed up with the people who stand there and look at the big boss when he goes into the house. Then she is forgotten, and the entire scene in the house only involves Boca, Leleco, and Celeste. Guigui appears when Boca enters the house. She says hello, talks to him before he receives his guests, and then she disappears. (She is supposed to be in the house all the time during the three versions.) In the second version, Maria Luiza comes into the foreground for a brief period. She enters the house, followed by her two friends, interacts with Boca de Ouro, and only leaves the house when Boca de Ouro decides to give the necklace to Celeste. In the third version, Boca de Ouro's arrival at his house is repeated for the last time. Now Maria Luiza, before she becomes a visual presence, is already the main subject of conversation when Guigui comes to welcome the bicheiro as he arrives home. They end up quarreling because he shows an interest in that strange rich woman who is devoted to an esoteric religion. Guigui is jealous and makes it clear that she will not accept Boca's involvement with Maria Luiza, although she had accepted his affair with Celeste (she explains that "Celeste is like me"). Considering the specular identification at work in the flashbacks, we can say that the inclusion of this dialogue confirms Guigui's acknowledgment of Maria Luiza's effective meaning in her own life. But one last detail needs to be considered.

In the film, there is a gradual displacement of the figure of the rich woman toward the center of the story. In the first version of events, the play does not mention Maria Luiza, and nothing in the text suggests her presence in Guigui's memory, not even a glimpse of her image. The film features Maria Luiza's fleeting presence in the front yard. The first version brings the first stage of a kind of teleology marked by her gradual movement toward the center of Guigui's consciousness. Her first appearance in the yard cannot be merely a question of verisimilitude, implying that she should be somewhere in the first version in order to be in the living room in the second and third versions. The discrepancies that separate the three versions are greater than this small detail. What counts for the audience is the symbolic meaning of her trajectory from this fleeting presence to her last scene in the film when she enters Boca de Ouro's bedroom to assume her rightful place. It is in his way of shooting her last scene that dos Santos performs his decisive gesture.

In the final version, Celeste has just died, and Boca de Ouro orders Maria Luiza to leave the house. She does not obey him. Instead, she walks to his bedroom and sits on his bed, her desire contrasting with his rage. Watching her image, we notice that we have already seen this same composition before in the film when Celeste, in the first version, entered Boca's bedroom for the first time, following his orders. She sat on his bed and waited when we watched her from the same camera setup that now gives us Maria Luiza's image. In both instances, the camera stays in the other room, where the entire previous scene has taken place, and the woman is visually framed by the bedroom door. This composition creates a sense of a person at someone's disposal, suggesting that the woman is in a cage as Boca de Ouro's possession. The same camera setup highlights an identical symbolic gesture, reinforcing the opposition between the two women: Maria Luiza came to replace Celeste. However, in this scenario, Celeste stands for Guigui, and the deeper opposition expressed by this formal device is that between the rich woman and Guigui herself. The flashbacks succeed in representing what, without Celeste's mediation, Guigui could not fully represent before: her traumatic defeat by her rival. Narration here means liberation, and Guigui's account of Celeste and Leleco's story functions for her as a rite of passage.

In connection with what is suggested by this formal composition, dos Santos introduces a different action in the final sequence to confirm his view. We have already observed that, in contrast to what happens in the play, Agenor and Guigui leave their house and go to the morgue with the journalist, remaining in focus until the last shot of the film (they do not stay at home, forgotten). When they arrive at the morgue, there is a crowd of curious people trying to see Boca de Ouro's body. Surrounded by the crowd, a radio broadcaster comments on the big event. He displays the well-known style of a speaker who wants to get across the sense of drama, to project the prosaic episode onto a mythical realm. But his attitude and words give us a clear sense of kitsch. His naive rhetorical twists produce a humorous effect that, in some ways, affects Boca de Ouro's image. Rodrigues performs, in the text assigned to the speaker, a parody of media discourse, projecting his irony onto the entire cultural milieu that remains under Boca de Ouro's spell. The tone of the sequence suggests the provincial side of Boca de Ouro's legend as created by the radio and the written press. Together with this kind of stylistic irony addressed to Boca de Ouro's world, there is in the film an additional demystification. One member of the crowd succeeds in getting close to the coffin. He looks at the dead bicheiro's face and says very loudly: "Boca de Ouro is a fraud!" Then he shows his own toothless mouth to signal that Boca's golden teeth had gone, and there remains no difference between him and the mythical figure. All this happens while the journalist, after learning that a woman called Maria Luiza had killed the bicheiro, tries to resume his interview with Guigui. He is rejected by the couple who, taking advantage of the confusion caused by the transportation of Boca de Ouro's modest coffin, shake off the journalist and flee, cutting their links with the bicheiro and his affairs. They turn their back on the journalist and on the camera, disappearing behind other passersby, equally unconcerned by the special event in the morgue. Their final gesture of rejection and the last image identifying them with the average city dweller consolidate dos Santos's point of view. He seems to be saying, "Life goes on, let's leave the Boca de Ouro mythical scene and embrace the city that offers us other channels of experience." Guigui's cathartic process is accomplished.

Tentative Expectations

The three-version structure of the play, with its display of contradictory accounts of the past, prevents the spectator from having access to a concrete and undeniable reality. A different reading of *Boca de Ouro* could explore more radically the supremacy of this multiple perspective set by the performance of the unreliable narrator, enhancing the ambiguities and the game of projections, instead of working the flashbacks to suggest a psychological progression and the presence of a liberating process in Dona Guigui's account of the past. Another possible interpretation is that urban life favors a constitution of subjectivity as created by the discourse of others. Although present in the film, this idea does not condemn the main characters to remain entrapped within a circular process of self-estrangement. Nelson Pereira dos Santos refuses the ideas of labyrinth and circularity — akin to a mythical reading of the play — and prefers to glimpse, for Guigui and Agenor, a new life in the future, free from Boca de Ouro's legend.

Rodrigues's parable of resentment and vanity takes Boca de Ouro's tragic defeat as a moral critique of boundless ambition, and it is almost a baroque discourse on vanity. This critique, at the same time, reveals its obverse side. There is a moral weakness that draws people to the charismatic figure whose social strength, on which the media capitalize, contrasts with the precariousness of those who, being poor, see themselves caught in a mediocre family life within a frustrating social context. The play states: "they need this mythical figure and this is perhaps an essential part of their own nature." The film repeats this idea: "they need myth, all this imaginary world built by different means," but dos Santos wants to liberate his characters, albeit tentatively, suggesting that this paradigmatic behavior has a historical dimension and can be overcome.

Endnotes

1. *Bicheiro* is the name given to those who control the *jogo do bicho* or animal game, a very popular illegal lottery which operates in big cities in Brazil. The game is based on the correspondence between numbers and animals.
2. Madureira is a district on the outskirts of the working-class Northern Zone of Rio de Janeiro.

5

María Luisa Bemberg Winks at the Audience: Performativity and Citation in *Camila* and *Yo la peor de todas*

Claire Taylor

The Argentine film director María Luisa Bemberg (1922–1995) is one of the best-known women directors in Latin American cinema. Initially, she started off writing screenplays in the early 1970s, and then directed two shorts and six feature films between the 1980s and the early 1990s.[1] Her work has attracted much attention in recent years: in addition to several articles in both Hispanic and Anglo journals, she was also the subject of a full-length study published in 2000, *An Argentine Passion: María Luisa Bemberg and her Films*. This edited volume brought together a collection of essays that provided a comprehensive overview of Bemberg's life and work, with chapters dealing with each of her films in turn. It is not the purpose of this article, therefore, to repeat what has already been done admirably by King et al. in *An Argentine Passion*, but instead to focus on the issues of performativity and citation, which can be seen as running through two of her films; both within the cinematic dynamics and within the sociocultural production of gender. The two films under analysis here will be *Camila* (1984), and *Yo la peor de todas* (*I, The Worst of All*, 1990), one of Bemberg's later works.

The term *performativity* has been used in a variety of discourses, ranging from linguistic analysis and philosophy to performance studies. In the course of this article I shall be relying upon the plurality in meaning of this term, considering the intricate ways in which images of performance on the screen relate to sociocultural performativity. The notion of performativity has been discussed by several theorists, and, as Andrew Parker and Eve Kosofsky Sedgwick explain it, performativity relates to "the ways that identities are constructed iteratively through complex citational processes."[2] That is, identity is considered not as an essence but as a process, one which is enabled through the citation of previously existing codes. Moreover, as theorists such as Judith Butler have pointed out, this performativity is particularly in evidence in the production of gender identity, where gender is seen as a question of acts rather than of essence.[3] Thus, in addition to the purely theatrical sense of performativity, the performative also functions to enable and install sociocultural constructions, in particular those of gender. This notion proves central to Bemberg's conception of feminine identity in the two films under analysis here, given that in these films, the female protagonists are shown to be involved in role-playing, and the films overall work within a citational dynamic.

Camila

Camila is probably the best-known of Bemberg's films, being the one which gained her the largest audiences, and, according to some, became the most popular film in Argentina's cinematic history.[4] Over 2 million people saw *Camila* in Argentina, the largest audience ever for a national film,[5] and it was the first Argentine film ever to receive an Oscar nomination,[6] subsequently opening in 30 countries around the world. Owing to its timely appearance at the close of Argentina's *Guerra sucia* or Dirty War (1976–1983), the film was read by many as an allegory for the dictatorship that the country had recently suffered, with the parallels between the bloody Rosas regime of the film's 19th-century setting, and the contemporary Argentine situation providing much of the film's interest.[7] Indeed, as John King notes, even the advertising for the film played upon this aspect: the publicity poster for the film carried the tagline (Nunca más "never again"), a term known to Argentines— and subsequently other Latin Americans— being the title of the Truth Commission and its report on the crimes of the regime.[8] The film's plot is based upon the real-life experiences of Camila O'Gorman, a young Argentine woman of the 19th century, and her elopement with her priest and confessor, Ladislao Gutiérrez. As well as this central love story, the film depicts the backdrop to this romance, recreating the oppression and violence of the Rosas regime, and follows the protagonists up until their capture and death by firing squad.[9]

Like several of Bemberg's films, *Camila* is a period piece, and the attention to detail here is minute, yet at the same time, this film is not just a careful reconstruction of a particular period. Rather, it marks itself out as citational from the outset, and simultaneously installs and questions the melodramatic mode in which it functions. I would argue that the critical approach to a period of repressive dictatorship, which clearly drives the film, is not incompatible with the functioning of citation; what Bemberg's film does is to tread a delicate path between the examination of a concrete historical context, and the examination of the performativity underlying the conduct of the protagonists. This citation is evident from the outset, and is confirmed by threads running throughout the film which engage in a presentation of conscious role-playing and performance.

The opening scene of the film clearly recalls the opening to Luis Buñuel's *Belle de jour* (1966), with a series of parallels that function as a citation of Buñuel's earlier work. In Buñuel's film, the opening shot is of a tree-lined landscape across which a path cuts diagonally from the background to front left, whilst the soundtrack is dominated by the sound of horses' hooves, carriage wheels, and the jingling of reins. A coach in the background gradually moves closer as the sound grows louder, finally occupying the foreground and exiting to the left; a second shot is now established, in which the path and coach are directly central to the screen space.

Jean Sorel and Catherine Deneuve in opening sequence of Luis Buñuel's *Belle de jour* (1967).

In the opening to *Camila*, the resemblances to Buñuel's *Belle de jour* as described above are striking. In Bemberg's work, the film opens with the sound of bird song which plays over the image of a gravel path stretching from the background to the front of the screen, flanked on either side by foliage and trees. In a long shot, a horse and carriage are just discernible in the distance and slowly approach, accompanied by the rising sound of horses' hooves, the coachman's cries, and the rattling of the harness. After the carriage has finally reached the foreground of the shot and exited left, there is a brief cut to the assembling of the waiting household, then we return to the carriage, which this time is shown with trees flanking it on either side as it travels directly toward the camera down the center of the shot [see page 112]. It is only after this long establishing sequence that the title *Camila* appears across the screen in red italics.

Clearly, the opening to Bemberg's film works to cite Buñuel's work of some two decades previously, and the effect of this is twofold. First, *Camila* is immediately grounded as a film which, whilst conveying historical events, will also be engaged in the act of citation. Second, and perhaps more problematically, these visual and aural parallels with the opening to Buñuel's work suggest a certain link to *Belle de jour*.

Opening sequence of María Luisa Bemberg's *Camila* (1984).

In terms of any parallels drawn between the content and meaning of *Belle de jour* and *Camila*, the citing of Buñuel's film is clearly problematic in terms of its gender politics; as critics have frequently noted, Buñuel's film risks reencoding the female figure, in the shape of Catherine Deneuve, as object of the gaze. As Evans has noted, for many feminists, Buñuel's film is "beyond the pale, a further example of women's exploitation through stereotype,"[10] indicating that "some scenes in *Belle de jour* can ultimately be regarded as belonging to the sub-genre of pornography."[11] Clearly, the presentation of woman as stereotype and the subgenre of pornography would seem to be far from Bemberg's mind in the citation of Buñuel here, given that *Camila* focuses on a female protagonist who, to a certain extent, defies societal controls and refuses to be the passive object of desire.[12] Rather, Bemberg is less interested in exploring the sadomasochistic elements of Séverine's subconscious that Buñuel's film explored, than in making reference to the broad encoding of Buñuel's opening sequence: that of fantasy. As the scene following the coach sequence reveals to us, the opening sequence to Buñuel's film locates itself not in the realm of the protagonist's waking life and reality, but in her daydreams.

Moreover, whilst the citation of Buñuel's opening sequence is clear here, arguably Bemberg's and indeed Buñuel's depictions in themselves function as citations of an already existing romantic paradigm, the image of the coach ride being encoded, from as early as Gustave Flaubert's *Madame Bovary* (1857) at least, as a romantic trope. The erotic coach ride of Flaubert's 19th-century novel, in which the protagonist Emma rides with her lover Leon through the streets of Rouen, is recalled by Bemberg's version here. Indeed, we learn that the occupant of Bemberg's carriage, Ana Perichon de O'Gorman, is being punished by house arrest for her illicit love affair with the Viceroy, Santiago de Liniers; whilst the lover is not present in the carriage with her, as in Flaubert's version, the carriage ride is nevertheless imbued with overtones of illicit love. Moreover, it is significant that in Flaubert's novel, Emma's desire for romantic attachments is fueled not by some innate sexual drive but by her reading of romantic fiction, suggesting a recursive chain of romantic paradigms through Bemberg, back through Buñuel, through to Flaubert, and finally to the romantic novels so eagerly devoured by Flaubert's heroine. Thus Bemberg's opening sequence is one already heavy with citation and allusion to preexisting types, which sets the tone for the romantic role-playing upon which the film will center.

The notion of citationality and fantasy suggested by this long opening sequence is sustained by the first exchanges of dialogue which follow the arrival of the carriage at the O'Gorman household. After this long opening sequence the grandmother, Ana Perichon de O'Gorman, played by Mona Maris, descends from the carriage and, after a brief exchange with her son, approaches the child Camila. She asks Camila her name, and then inquires: "Do you like love stories?" to which the child Camila replies "I don't know." This exchange is then followed by a freeze frame on Camila's face, after which extradiegetic piano music begins to sound, and the title sequence proper starts. This scene, as Williams notes, implies the link between Camila and the grandmother in that the exchange between them "establishes a love between grandmother and granddaughter."[13] Yet this dialogue is more than just an indication of the growing affection that grandmother and granddaughter will have for each other; it also, clearly, foretells of the "historia de amor" in which Camila and her lover will end up taking the lead roles. The significance of the term *historias*— love *stories* rather biographical accounts— highlights the literary status and indicates the performativity of gender roles: the grandmother does not ask Camila whether she likes hearing about her family, but whether she likes hearing *stories*.

This opening exchange, which significantly comes before the opening credits to the film, is key in the reading of Bemberg's use of melodrama in this film. More than just straight melodrama, this exchange provides a moment of cinematic self-consciousness right at the start of the film; just as much as it is directed to the child Camila, the question is also directed to us, the audience. This question thus functions both intra- and extradiegetically: Bemberg is asking the spectator whether she or he likes love stories, as a preamble to a film that deals with precisely that; the tempestuous love affair between a young woman and a priest. Coming before the opening credits, this citational sequence and the question posed by Mona Maris thus frame the film, making the viewer aware from the start of the self-conscious functioning of this work.

This self-reflexivity returns in a later scene, again focusing on the grandmother and Camila, now a young woman, played by Susú Pecoraro. In this scene, Camila reads out the impassioned love letters that the viceroy had written to her grandmother, adopting as she reads aloud the role of the passionate writer of these letters. Again, this frames the romantic paradigm within the realm of role-playing and performativity; just as the opening scene asked of Camila and of the spectator whether she or he liked love stories, so now we see Pecoraro performing a doubled role-play: the actress plays Camila who is in turn playing the part of the viceroy. It is significant that this scene plays with reality and fantasy throughout, as the actions of the actors and the soundtrack move back and forth across the distinction between the internal reality of the film and the imagined role-playing the two women undertake. The first of these such blendings is evident in the soundtrack, which conveys the sound of a carriage arriving; this arrival is "real" for the film scenario, in that it is Adolfo, Camila's father, arriving, but the grandmother interprets this sound as the guests arriving for an imaginary ball. This play between fantasy and reality is then continued by the characters' actions, as Camila subsequently swaps her role of ardent lover for that of the maid, handing her grandmother her hat in preparation for an imaginary ball; this hat is real and the spectators see it, although the ball for which it is intended is clearly a fantasy. Finally, the third role that Camila assumes in this scene is that of dancer at the ball, asking her grandmother to dance a minuet played by a nonexistent orchestra. Significantly, however, the imaginary scenarios of the characters have, by this stage, invaded the screen dynamics because the minuet to which they dance is indeed heard, albeit faintly, on the film's soundtrack.

Indeed, the earlier overtones to preexisting romantic paradigms, which were sketched in the opening scene, are given greater weight in the conversation between Camila and her grandmother here, as she asks the older woman: "Did you really make love like they do in novels?" In this exchange between the grandmother and Camila it is clear that the passion stemming from books comes to be the first frame of reference for Camila's understanding of romantic relations.[14] That is, what gains primary status here are not some unfettered, primitive sexual urges, but the romantic types— love stories, the grandmother's letters, the complementary roles in a minuet. It is these preexisting types that wield primary status, indicating the performativity of gender roles: The relationship between the two protagonist lovers in this film can never therefore be one of an unmediated inner desire, but rather stems from the reenactment of preexisting codes.

In addition to the significance of these elements of role-play with regard to gender roles, the overt references to performance and role-playing highlight the artificiality of the scenes enacted for us here, and thus reencode the genre of melodrama through which the film works. As has been frequently noted by critics, and detailed extensively by Bemberg herself, *Camila* functions within the realm of melodrama, with some of the most easily identifiable melodramatic elements being evident on the level of plot and audience manipulation. The film plays on the pleasure aroused by seeing repressed sexual relations, with the particular scenario being portrayed here, that of the love of a young woman for a priest who is moreover her own confessor, forming the very stuff of melodrama. The notion of illicit love is one of the mainstays of the melodramatic mode, and the whole state of affairs running throughout the film thus functions in the highly emotionally charged register of melodrama.

In addition to these melodramatic elements on the level of plot, in terms of technique the allegiance this film owes to melodrama is clear. Elements such as costume, lighting, and the use of certain motifs in the film can be allied with the melodramatic style. Bemberg, in a frequently cited quote, has remarked upon her use of melodrama in this film, stating that:

> [M]elodrama is a very tricky genre, because at any minute it can turn into something sentimental, which I detest. So I had all those little tricks, such as the handkerchief, the gold coin, the priest who is sick with love, and the thunder when God gets angry. They're all little winks at the audience.[15]

What is crucial here in Bemberg's comments is the notion of her use of melodrama functioning through a metaphorical winking at the audience in a self-conscious way. In this way, what Bemberg uses are the clichés of melodrama, elements that the audience will recognize as stereotypes; the use of thunder to portray God's anger, for instance, is a pathetic fallacy now so overused that audiences cannot but read it as a conscious citation of a preexisting paradigm.

Thus Bemberg's use of melodrama is double-edged: whilst undoubtedly contributing to the phenomenal viewing figures of the film, the melodrama of *Camila* is never simply just melodrama: at the same time, Bemberg's "winks at the audience" caution us against letting ourselves be carried away by sentimentality. This notion of the self-conscious presentation of melodrama can be seen to be linked to what Williams has noted with relation to Hollywood production values, namely that "*Camila* seeks a close dialogue with classical Hollywood,"[16] yet does not for all this conform to its codes. Rather, Bemberg's film performs a subtle subversion of such conventions. While Williams finds this subversion principally in the reworking of the dynamic of the gaze and its recasting as female, I would argue a subversion can also be found in the encoding of melodrama itself.

Through the instances of role-playing and citation foregrounded by this film it is made clear to the viewer that *Camila* is not a "straight" melodrama, but rather consciously takes up this stereotyped form. Bemberg's subversive use of melodrama lies in precisely these references to role-playing and prior literary or cinematic paradigms which infuse the film. As Pauls has commented, "*Camila* explores the terrain of melodrama, *works its conventions and its rhetoric*; for that reason, it is far removed from that degraded version, the soap opera."[17] That is not to say, however, that *Camila* mocks the melodrama genre or presents it in an ironic tone: this is a film which relies on many of the trappings of the romantic melodrama, whilst at the same time standing back and asking us whether "we like love stories." Herein lies Bemberg's radical reuse of melodrama: the moments of romance within this film are not merely "straight" romance, but, just as with the opening frame, are framed in self-reflexivity. When Camila and her grandmother "act out" the roles of the people at the time, the overt references to performance and literary stories highlight the artificiality of what we see, and for this reason the genre of melodrama too is highlighted in its artificiality. In this way, *Camila* is not empty melodrama, but rather an exploration of this genre, in which it is at once used for its effectiveness and at the same time framed as an already-existing type.

This overall strategy of citation is one that allies Bemberg's impulse with that of her heroine Camila's. In this, Bemberg reworks the tired genre of melodrama just as Camila reworks the clichés of romantic love and elopement. For Camila, her partial rebellion against the laws of the state and the rules of her family lie not in the expression of an unfettered sexuality, but in the assumption of another code, that of romance and elopement with a lover. Similarly, Bemberg does not engage in cinematic aesthetics free from prior encoding — if that were ever possible — but rather situates her challenge in the reuse of the codes of melodrama. Thus Bemberg's and Camila's projects come together in this performative sense of identity formation, signaling identity as process in the reshaping of pre-existing codes.

Yo la peor de todas

Yo la peor de todas is Bemberg's fifth full-length feature film, and, as with *Camila* discussed above, is a period piece. This time the setting is colonial Mexico (known as Nueva España at the time), and the focus is on the life of the 17th-century nun, Sor Juana Inés de la Cruz. Sor Juana was a famous figure in colonial Latin America at the time, and was particularly renowned for her intellect and her writing, producing copious amounts of poetry, plays, and complex philosophical-religious meditations throughout her lifetime. Bemberg's film bases itself, as acknowledged in the opening credits, on Octavio Paz's monumental biographical study of the nun, *Sor Juana Inés de la Cruz, o, las trampas de la fe*, a work of detailed historical research, and which has become the definitive guide to Sor Juana's life.[18] While relatively overlooked for many years, there has been a recent resurgence of interest in Sor Juana and her work, sparked off in part by Paz's informative biography, and also as part of a wider trend in the recovery of women writers from Latin America's past.[19]

In the cases of *Camila* and *Yo la peor de todas* there are similarities in that both works are period pieces, both are based on real-life characters, and both take as their protagonist a female figure who rebels against society's norms. Nevertheless, despite these similarities, these two films work within a different aesthetic. While, as discussed above, *Camila* has been frequently noted by critics to work within the realm of melodrama, *Yo la peor de todas* could be more properly said to have a more symbolic and abstract range. Visually, the differences between the two films are striking: described by Gyékényesi Gatto as a "spartan chiaroscuro,"[20] this film does not indulge in the same rich hues as the earlier *Camila*. Instead, in *Yo la peor de todas* cold blues and gray tones predominate, with colors and contrasts used less to create a sense of historical veracity than for their symbolic importance in conveying a restrictive space in which the protagonist moves.

Similarly, while the historical accuracy of *Yo la peor de todas* has been confirmed by those collaborating on the film,[21] there is much less of the cluttered set of historical realism that we saw in *Camila*. If, in *Camila*, period setting and historical accuracy were paramount in the creating and sustaining of a melodramatic tone, in this later work the sparseness of the set and limited number of props lend themselves to an allegorical reading of the mise-en-scène. The often-cited opening scene, for instance,[22] in which the establishing shot of the wine goblets opens out onto the twin figures of the archbishop and the viceroy, provides a rigid symmetry of image in a geometrically defined space. This film has, therefore, as Verina Glaessner describes it, an "anti-naturalistic style," which differs from *Camila* in that such antinaturalism "sets the film at a distance from the novelettish world of costume drama."[23] Similarly Miller has commented that "Bemberg eschews the lavish *mise-en-scènes* of her former films," deeming the setting of *Yo la peor de todas* an "abstract film set."[24] In this way, this later film of Bemberg's, whilst dealing with a historical period, does not function within the same realist aesthetic of the period drama notable in *Camila*.

Nevertheless, this film also arguably functions through the "winks at the audience" that Bemberg had mentioned in regard to her earlier work, because despite the sparseness of set, the film nonetheless abounds with citational moments, and the performative in relation to gender identity is given close analysis. Just as with the opening of *Camila* and its quotation of *Belle de jour*, so too *Yo la peor de todas* quotes from a range of visual and literary precedents. While the most obvious of these precedents are clearly Sor Juana's own writings, recited at several junctures throughout the film, citation is also apparent in the reference to gender performance.

Thus the citationality in this later film of Bemberg's lies not with the romance paradigm as in *Camila* discussed above, but in the realm of gender identity in the broader sense. The configuration of gender given in this film challenges any notion of a preexisting gendered essence, instead revealing the role-playing and assumption of codes intrinsic to the production of gender. One particular scene which illustrates this conception of gender is the second of the two flashback episodes of the film; in this scene, Sor Juana is tending her sick mother and, as she does, a younger version of herself as a girl enters. The girl Juana is dressed in male clothes, and, addressing the camera as much as the adult Juana, states: "Because I couldn't dress up as a man, I dressed up as a nun." Rather than this episode being an instance of "childish defiance" as Glaessner would have it,[25] it is key to the film and to the conception of gender as role play which can be seen running through *Camila* and *Yo la peor de todas*.

First, the referential meaning of this scene can be seen to have resonances with Sor Juana's own biography: as her autobiographical work, the "Respuesta a Sor Filotea" tells us, Sor Juana takes up the veil not through any religious vocation but from a consideration that this option is the least unpalatable of those available to her.[26] So too Bemberg's scene reveals that the next best thing to becoming a man is becoming a nun, in order to have access to books and learning. Indeed, as can be seen from line 245 of the "Respuesta," the notion of "dressing as a man" is one which Sor Juana expresses in relation to access to the world of learning.[27]

Yet in addition to this referential meaning, this scene is also key in the illustration of the performativity of gender relations, as indicated briefly by Bergman.[28] The notion of "dressing up as a man" provides a reading of gender as performance, suggesting the taking on and the taking off of gender as much as the taking on and off of clothes. This taking on and off of gender is represented both visually and verbally here: concomitant with her words, the figure does indeed dress up in men's clothes. In this way, the young Juana can be seen to be acting out the taking on of masculine characteristics, suggesting that "to be a man" is as much of a "putting on of codes" as a "putting on of clothes." The dialogue here recalls in transposed form de Beauvoir's now famous formulation that "one is not born, but rather becomes, a woman."[29] For Sor Juana, one is not born a man either, but instead gender and sex are assumed. As recent reconceptualizations of de Beauvoir's original statement have argued, the issue of the performativity of gender is brought to the fore in the notion of "becoming" rather than "being" a particular gender. As many subsequent elaborations on de Beauvoir's celebrated phrase have shown, central to this conception of gender is that, far from being innate, gender is a process of the assumption of sociocultural codes.[30]

Moreover, if Bemberg had previously indicated her provocative use of melodrama through the metaphor of the "winks at the audience," then it is significant that in this scene we witness an extradiegetic moment as Juana talks not to her mother, but to the older Sor Juana seated in the foreground, and thus also to the camera. Just as the question regarding a liking for love stories in the previous film was directed to the spectator as well as to Camila, here the gaze of the young Juana and her comment on gender are directed outwards to the spectator of the film.

This key scene in the film offers the possibility of reading this notion of gender roles retrospectively in terms of screen duration, although chronologically toward the future in terms of story duration. Coming before this scene in the film, although several decades later in terms of the chronology of Juana's life, is one of the most erotically charged episodes of the film. This is the scene of the kiss between Sor Juana and the Vicereine, in which, significantly, the moment of the kiss is preceded by a type of striptease. This scene, it could be argued, functions as the counterpart to Juana's expressed desire of "[dressing] up as a nun" of the flashback scene, in that here, the layers of ecclesiastical clothing are literally stripped away. The Vicereine demands that Sor Juana remove her veil, and the subsequent process, lasting for 45 seconds, is a slow removal of layer after layer of several strips of fabric wound numerous times around Assumpta Serna's head. First, Serna removes her black outer veil, followed by a white scarflike garment, then the entire hood, and finally the small mobcap underneath these outer layers. Once this process of undressing is complete, the Vicereine kisses Sor Juana, taking her face into her hands and turning it toward her, away from the camera.

To a certain extent, this scene can be read as a taking off of codes, and, as Denise Miller notes, gives another dimension to Bemberg's stated aim in this film as attempting to "denun" her film.[31] Yet this scene is more than just a taking off of clothes and of codes; rather than being a revelation of the naked truth of Sor Juana's sexuality, this scene is encoded as a further performance, that of striptease. This moment of unveiling is still clearly a performance in that its enactment through slow and deliberate motions clearly mimics the deferment of desire central to striptease. If the episode recalling the decision to become a nun, therefore, reveals gender identity as a performance, this episode portraying desire is no less performative. In this way, these examples of gender and desire are just as much a part of the performative as the more overt examples of performance which pervade this film, such as the rehearsals for plays and the recitations of poems.

In conclusion, both films show gender identity to be a process rather than an essence, and both locate their heroine's rebellion not in a space free from societal encoding, but in the reworking of existing codes. Arguably, this partial rebellion can be seen to be reflected in Bemberg's cinematic technique itself, in that she too reworks codes such as that of melodrama. Bemberg does not eschew what is often seen as an "ideologically suspect" genre, such as that of melodrama, in favor of an antirealist attack on its codes, but instead reworks its terms, just as her protagonists rework existing gender codes in order to fashion a tentative space for self-affirmation.

Endnotes

1. Bemberg's feature films are as follows: *Momentos* (*Moments*, 1980); *Señora de nadie* (*Nobody's Wife*, 1982); *Camila* (1984); *Miss Mary* (1986); *Yo, la peor de todas* (1990); and *De eso no se habla* (*I Don't Want to Talk About it*, 1993).

2. Andrew Parker and Eve Kosofsky Sedgwick (eds.), *Performativity and Performance* (New York: Routledge, 1995), p. 2.

3. See for instance Butler's contention that "the gendered body is performative ... it has no ontological status apart from the various acts which constitute its reality": Judith Butler, *Gender Trouble: Feminism and the Subversion of Identity* (New York: Routledge, 1999), p. 173.

4. Jorge Ruffinelli, "De una *Camila* a otra: historia, literatura y cine," *Foro Hispánico* 10 (1996), p. 11.

5. See John King who notes that over 2 million Argentines saw the film, and that "for several months, the film out-grossed the main Hollywood features, *E.T.* and *Porky's*": John King, *Magical Reels: A History of Cinema in Latin America* (London: Verso, 2000), p. 96.

6. Zuzana M Pick, *The New Latin American Cinema: A Continental Project*. (Austin: University of Texas Press, 1993), p. 82.

7. Juan Manuel de Rosas became governor of Buenos Aires in 1829, and in effect became dictator of the whole country, running a violent and repressive regime until his fall from power in 1852. As Ruffinelli notes, for the audience the story of Camila was "easily projected onto the present because the historical context referred to another tyranny" (our translation): Ruffinelli, "De una Camila a otra," p.11. Similarly, King comments that "the film is ... transparently clear in its use of history as a commentary on recent events": John King, "Assailing the Heights of Macho Pictures: Women Film Makers in Contemporary Argentina," in Jennifer Lowe and Philip Swanson (eds.), *Essays on Hispanic Themes in Honor of Edward C. Riley* (Edinburgh: University of Edinburgh Press, 1989), p. 369.

8. The title *Nunca más* (Never Again) was given both to the committee and its report on their findings into the human rights abuses of the Argentine dictatorship, with the published report carrying the full title, *Nunca más: informe de la Comisión Nacional sobre la Desaparición de Personas* (*Never Again: A Report by Argentina's National Commission on Disappeared People*) (Buenos Aires: EUDEBA, 1984). Subsequently, other works dealing with cases in Chile, Uruguay, Guatemala, and Bolivia, amongst others, have used the phrase *nunca más* in their titles as shorthand for an investigation into human rights abuses.

9. Several critics have documented the various historical sources for Bemberg's film:

see the opening page of Bruce Williams, "In the Realm of the Feminine: María Luisa Bemberg's *Camila* at the Edge of the Gaze," *Chasqui*, 25:1 (1996), pp. 62–71, for details of the various versions of Camila O'Gorman's story, both cinematic and novelistic, which have been produced in Argentina over the years.

10. Peter William Evans, *The Films of Luis Buñuel: Subjectivity and Desire* (Oxford: Clarendon, 1995), p. 152.

11. Ibid., p.153.

12. Critics have frequently commented on the portrayal of Camila as an independent woman who challenges social conventions: see for instance, Pick, who notes that the film sees "desire as a liberating element" in Camila's actions (*The New Latin American Cinema*, p. 83), and Morris who highlights Bemberg's technique in making Camila into the subject who "expresses the force of her sexuality in her gaze": Barbara Morris, "Two Faces of Woman: Filmic Discourse in Bemberg's *Camila* and *Miss Mary*," in Douglas Radcliffe-Umstead (ed), *Sixth Annual International Film Conference* (Romance Languages Department, Kent State University, 1988), p. 75.

13. Bruce Williams, "The Reflection of a Blinded Gaze: María Luisa Bemberg, Filmmaker," in Marjorie Agosín (ed), *A Woman's Gaze: Latin American Women Artists* (New York: Pine, 1998), p. 179.

14. As has been frequently noted by critics, Camila takes great pleasure in reading romantic fiction: see Alan Pauls, "On *Camila*: The Red, the Black and the White," in John King, Sheila Whitaker, and Rosa Bosch (eds), *An Argentine Passion: María Luisa Bemberg and her Films* (London: Verso, 2000), pp. 110–121 (p. 119), and Morris, p. 79.

15. Bemberg, cited in Pick, *The New Latin American Cinema*, pp. 83–84.

16. Williams, "The Reflection of a Blinded Gaze," p. 177.

17. Pauls, "On *Camila*," p. 110.

18. Octavio Paz, *Sor Juana Inés de la Cruz, o, las trampas de la fe* (Barcelona: Seix Barral, 1982); Octavio Paz, *Sor Juana: Her Life and World*, trans. Margaret Sayers Peden (London: Faber, 1988). Much has already been written comparing Bemberg's film to Paz's text, so I shall not dwell on the issues of adaptation here: for an excellent study of this, see Denise Miller, "María Luisa Bemberg's Interpretation of Octavio Paz's *Sor Juana*," in King et al, *An Argentine Passion*, pp. 137–173; see also Nora B Forte and Raquel Miranda, "Literatura y cine: desplazamientos y transposiciones en *Yo, la peor de todas* de María Luisa Bemberg," *Anclajes*, 4:4 (2000), pp. 57–74, and Susan E Ramírez, "*I, the Worst of All*: The Literary Life of Sor Juana Inés de la Cruz," in Donald F Stevens (ed), *Based on a True Story: Latin American History at the Movies* (Wilmington, DE: Scholarly Resources Books, 1997), pp. 47–62.

19. See, for example, recent works such as Stephanie Merrim (ed), *Feminist Perspectives on Sor Juana Inés de la Cruz* (Detroit, MI: Wayne State University Press, 1991); Carmen Beatriz López Portillo (ed), *Sor Juana y su mundo: una mirada actual* (Mexico City: Fondo de Cultura Económica, 1998); and the selection of articles on Sor Juana in Mabel Moraña (ed), *Revista Iberoamericana: Número especial dedicado a la literatura colonial: sujeto colonial y discurso barroco*, 61:172 (1995).

20. Katherine Gyékényesi Gatto, "Representing the Silence of Conversion in Octavio Paz's *Sor Juana, or, The Traps of Faith* and María Luisa Bemberg's *I, The Worst of All*," *Monographic Review/ Revista Monográfica*, 16 (2000), p. 306.

21. Historian and researcher Nina Scott was approached by Bemberg to read the script prior to the filming of *Yo, la peor de todas*, and has commented on the "historical accuracy of details in the film": Nina Scott, "Sor Juana and Her World," *Latin American Research Review*, 29:1 (1994), p. 152.

22. See Miller's analysis of the scene: "María Luisa Bemberg's Interpretation of Octavio Paz's *Sor Juana*," pp.145–146.

23. Verina Glaessner, "*Yo, la peor de todas (I, the Worst of All)*," *Sight and Sound*, 1:7 (1991), pp. 64–65.

24. Miller, "María Luisa Bemberg's Interpretation of Octavio Paz's *Sor Juana*," p.140.

25. Glaessner, "*Yo, la peor de todas (I, the Worst of All)*," p. 65.

26. Sor Juana Inés de la Cruz, *A Sor Juana Anthology*, trans. Alan S. Trueblood (Cambridge, MA: Harvard University Press, 1988). Sor Juana's "Respuesta a Sor Filotea" ("Reply to Sor Philotea") first appeared in 1691 in response to criticism of her work written under the pseudonym of Sor Filotea. In her reply, Sor Juana defends her right to study, and also provides a wealth of biographical details illuminating her motivations for learning. For the motivations behind her decision to become a nun, see lines 271–273 of the "Respuesta," which read: "given my total disinclination to marriage, it was the least unreasonable and most becoming choice I could make," p.212.

27. The episode describing her request as a child to be allowed to study at Mexico University reads as follows: "I began to deluge my mother with urgent and insistent pleas to change my manner of dress and send me to stay with relatives in the City of Mexico so that I might study and take courses at the university" (ibid., p. 211). While the expression "change my manner of dress" is not immediately specific to gender, in the context of Mexico University, at the time a male-only institution, the connotation is clearly that she would have adopted men's clothes.

28. Emilie Bergmann, "Abjection and Ambiguity: Lesbian Desire in Bemberg's *Yo, la peor de todas*," in Sylvia Molloy and Robert McKee Irwin (eds.), *Hispanisms and Homosexualities* (Durham, NC: Duke University Press, 1998), p. 231.

29. Simone de Beauvoir, *The Second Sex*, trans. H. M. Parshley (New York: Vintage, 1989), p. 267. The influence of de Beauvoir on Bemberg's thought has been commented on by Bemberg in her interview with Trellez Plazaola where she notes the impact upon her of reading *The Second Sex*: Luis Trelles Plazaola, "María Luisa Bemberg," *Cine y mujer en América Latina: directoras de largometrajes de ficción* (Río Piedras: Universidad de Puerto Rico, 1991), p. 109.

30. Indeed, theorists such as Butler have gone even further than this, suggesting that sex itself is a construct just as much as the sociocultural construction of gender which purports to name that sex. See for instance Butler's chapter on Wittig, "Monique Wittig: Bodily Disintegration and Fictive Sex" in her *Gender Trouble*, pp. 141–163.

31. Miller, "María Luisa Bemberg's Interpretation of Octavio Paz's *Sor Juana*," p. 152.

6

Nelson Rodrigues into Film: Two Adaptations of *O beijo no asfalto*

Stephanie Dennison

Introduction

One area of cultural studies in Brazil that is increasingly attracting attention is the work of playwright and journalist Nelson Rodrigues, who is currently enjoying a timely revival.[1] As a consequence, research is beginning to be carried out on the film versions of his works of fiction. A total of 20 films make him Brazil's most adapted writer for the big screen. The so-called Cinema Rodrigueano boasts critical successes (Arnaldo Jabor's *Toda nudez será castigada* [*All Nudity Shall be Punished*], 1973) box-office smashes (*A dama do lotação* [*Lady on the Bus*), 1978), the odd flop (the first adaptation, *A mulher sem pecado* [*Bound For Sin*], disappeared without a trace when it was released in 1952) and even remakes (*Boca de Ouro*, a 1990 remake of Nelson Pereira dos Santos's 1962 neorealist original, among others). The latest adaptations to be released, *Traição* (*Betrayal*, 1998) and *Gêmeas* (*Twins*, 1999), owe a certain debt of gratitude to this vast body of work produced since 1952, as do countless other films which have been inspired by Nelson Rodrigues's unique vision of the world and its celluloid interpretations. This chapter will compare two stylistically very different celluloid interpretations of Rodrigues's most successful play, *O beijo no asfalto*, which was first staged in 1961, and it will consider in particular the ways in which each film treats (or fails to treat) the subjects of politics and sexuality.

In the play and two film versions, action begins when a man is knocked down by a bus in Rio de Janeiro, and as he lies dying, he asks a passer-by, Arandir, for a kiss. Arandir, moved by the dying man's request, responds. A reporter, desperate for a story and knowing that "homosexuality sells papers like hot cakes," colludes with an unscrupulous police detective and invents a homosexual scandal in broad daylight, which later develops into an accusation of murder. The entire city, Arandir's wife included, start to believe the fabricated tale. Only his sister-in-law defends him, and sees in her own father's promotion of the fiction a jealousy of his other daughter provoked by unnatural feelings of love for her. She is wrong, however, and the homosexual of the play is the father, secretly in love with Arandir, whom he kills at the end.

This play in many ways is typical of Rodrigues's literary production. The big themes of love and death are present in all his work, and much of what he produced was deliberately melodramatic. Incest is never far from Rodrigues's mind: all his work reveals a determination to offend, or at least to provoke a strong reaction from his audience or readership. He spent his life deliberately courting controversy, coining oft-repeated phrases such as "all women like to be beaten."[2] In his recent work on sexuality and Brazilian cinema, David Foster describes Rodrigues's work in the following terms:

> Rodrigues's interest in sexual issues concerns principally the intersection between the hegemonic criterion for bourgeois decency, which basically means an endorsement of compulsory monogamous and reproductive heterosexuality, and the contradictory realities of lived human experience, where such a hegemonic criterion is both difficult to adhere to and, as the source of both comedy and pathos, essentially impossible to enforce.[3]

In the case of the plays released in the 1950s and 1960s, it did not take much to offend everyone.[4] Left-wing critics rallied against him for the lack of emphasis on the sociopolitical context and the supposedly morally conservative underlying messages of much of his work. Conservative elements took umbrage at, in particular, the way sex and sexuality were openly portrayed in his work; for example, teenage prostitution in *Perdoa-me por me traíres* (literally: Forgive me for your betrayal of me) from 1957, a teenage pregnancy in *Os sete gatinhos* (The Seven Little Kittens) in 1958, and a gang rape organized by the young victim for her own pleasure in the 1962 play *Bonitinha mas ordinária* (Cute but Vulgar). These three examples in fact seem tame alongside the 1947 play *Álbum de família* (Family Album), banned for almost 20 years, in which every member of a respectable middle-class family was in love or having an affair with at least one other member.

There is one element, however, found in *O beijo no asfalto* which distinguishes it from other plays seemingly on a similar moral crusade: the main character is neither revealed to be hiding a deep and shameful secret, nor is he forced away from a life of virtue to one of vice. In essence, and unlike many characters in Rodrigues's work, he is not morally bankrupt. Rodrigues loved to suggest in his work that innocence and purity do not exist in lower-middle and middle-class families in Rio. If it looks too good to be true, you can be sure it is; for example, Sabino's abstinence from sex in *Toda nudez será castigada*, the virtuous teenager in *Os sete gatinhos*, the rape victim Maria Cecília in *Bonitinha mas ordinária*, and so on.

According to Rodrigues, the play was written in 21 days toward the end of 1960. It was inspired by the true story of a reporter from *Globo* newspaper, Pereira Rego, who had been knocked down by a bus in Rio. The reporter, as he lay dying, asked a passer-by, who had knelt down to help him, for a kiss. The passer-by, as it happened, was a young woman. Rodrigues rewrote the ending of this true story to increase dramatic effect. At the end of the play, he ironically uses a gay man to carry out the "necessary" exercise of patriarchal justice, and therein lies his own attack on sexual hypocrisy and stereotypes of masculinity. Of course, far from writing his first politically correct play, what Rodrigues really had in mind when preparing *O beijo no asfalto* was an attack on those whose rigid political ideologies had forced him into isolation in artistic circles at the time. These so-called ideological patrols were, as he saw it, hypocritical, in that while he was labeled retrograde, he was the only author in the early '60s to be producing sufficiently socially challenging material, and the only author in Brazil to be censored.[5] The similarities to Kafka's *The Trial* are surely more than coincidental.[6]

Flávio Tambellini's O beijo

Turning to look at the first adaptation of *O beijo no asfalto*, Flávio Tambellini's first feature-length film, *O beijo*, was released in 1966. In terms of adaptation, the most striking change to Rodrigues's play made by Tambellini and his screenwriters is to the character of the reporter, who takes on a central role in the film. The reporter is given a past, a deep secret that is gradually revealed symbolically (scenes of the seashore, crashing waves) and then within the narrative of the film. A woman at a nightclub reveals to a friend that the reporter had watched his young son drown in the sea and had not saved him. His body had never been recovered. Hence his desire to destroy Arandir, who had selflessly given "a merciful kiss" to a dying man.

Tambellini in his adaptation had notably been inspired by an analysis of Rodrigues's play written by the dramatist's good friend Hélio Pelligrini, a literary critic and qualified psychoanalyst. Despite Rodrigues's well-known suspicions of Freud, he delighted in the fact that Hélio was capable of elevating, as he saw it, his work from popular drama to highbrow art simply by arguing for a psychological explanation for the dastardly deeds of his characters. Hélio famously wrote of *O beijo no asfalto*: "Arandir, on kissing the dying man, 'kissed death on the mouth,' became contaminated with death, and assumed, symbolically, the impenetrable finitude of us all."[7]

Tambellini seems to have kept this phrase in mind when filming *O beijo*, particularly with regard to the morbidity with which the actors go about their business. Gnarled and distorted gargoyles crop up frequently in outdoor shots; the staring eyes of Arandir's assassin (his father-in-law) in close-up at regular intervals; the constant references to the death of the reporter's son, and so on. Textbook expressionism, but overdirected to the point of almost being a parody of an expressionist movie.

The motivation behind the reporter's victimization of Arandir, and the eventual accusation of murder which he makes against him, is guilt, as the reporter needs to create in Arandir an image as vile as the one he has of himself. He had to accuse Arandir of murder to forget his own guilt. The whole notion, therefore, of the power of the media to control people's lives, and the concept of the sleazy hack without scruples, which are present in and ultimately dominate the play, are absent from this version. The sociopolitical context to the story is further avoided in this film by minimizing the importance of homosexuality. Explicit references to homosexuality and bisexuality, which make an admittedly occasional appearance in the play, are absent. The closing scene of the play, when the repressed homosexual father-in-law kills Arandir and embraces him, in a replay of the opening scenes, is missing too. In Tambellini's version, Dália, the sister-in-law, substitutes her father in the scene.

Tambellini chooses an interesting way to get round the apparent lack of courage to deal with what was still very much a taboo subject at the time. Once again, the transformed role of the reporter in the film is the key. In the film we witness the reporter's gradually deepening personal crisis through a series of signposts. He smashes a couple of mirrors, for example, and stares at the fragmented pieces of his reflection. At one point he mutters: "I can't be sure of anything." He violently forces himself upon Arandir's wife, Selminha, during an illegal police interview, after she defiantly screams that her husband is a real man. The signpost that links in with the subtext of homosexuality is a peculiar scene that takes place in a nightclub. Alone in the audience, the reporter is entertained by a dancer/stripper, played by a young Betty Faria. The stripper begins her dance dressed as a man (and a clichéd image of masculinity to boot: dressed in bowler hat, raincoat, and shirt and tie, she is reminiscent of the cross-dressing entertainers in *Cabaret*). The dancer whispers to the reporter: "This one's especially for you." The stripper's motivation for the dance is that, if her observer is capable of elevating the status of a mere kiss in his newspaper, just think what he could do for her career. The fetishization of the kiss is thus reinforced by the scene, as is the sexual insecurity of the reporter as another source of his hatred of Arandir.

By not referring openly to homosexuality in *O beijo*, and by equating it with the reporter's vile secret (a dark and unspeakably nasty thing to be hidden from view), Tambellini's adaptation is ironically more morally conservative than the play on which it is based. Also, by suggesting that fate led Arandir to the roadside at the precise moment that the road victim was knocked over,[8] Tambellini manages to condone the ritual victimization that takes place in the film, therefore stripping the film of its power to reflect on the sociopolitical status quo.

Bruno Barreto's O beijo no asfalto

The second, more interesting version of the play, which retained the play's full title, was directed by Bruno Barreto and released in 1981 with resounding box-office success. Barreto's version is more faithful to the play, but there are some modifications to the original that inform the political and sexual tone of the film.

First of all, Arandir is not portrayed as being clearly innocent of accusations of homosexuality. Barreto plants his seeds of doubt partly in his choice of actor to play the part of Arandir. By 1981 Ney Latorraca would have been known to most film and TV audiences as gay, despite frequently playing straight roles. Latorraca's interpretation, at times, borders on camp, particularly in the scenes where he is revealed as being more sensitive than the average man. This is the only evidence that the spectators have to go on in this mystery; those who are swayed by it discover to their horror that the father-in-law Tarcísio Meira, that icon of manliness and one of TV Globo's principal *galãs* or leading men at the time, is the homosexual of the piece. The seeds are therefore sewn to increase the dramatic impact of the denouement, and to reinforce the notion of collective participation in the witch hunt.

In this work, the audience's revulsion is not, as is often the case with Rodrigues's work, aimed at the array of gradually morally fading characters on stage (the police chief and journalist are identified as evil from the outset, so they do not count), but the anonymous mass of people who inhabit their world. Barreto captures this rather effectively, by offering us numerous fleeting glimpses of ordinary people going about their routines in the big city: the man selling sugar-cane juice, the prostitute and her sailor client, kids playing soccer in the street, and so on. The director takes this idea of unanimity one stage further by allowing the story of the homosexual scandal to transcend the newspaper offices and infiltrate the visual media. A television journalist carries out a vox pop, posing the question: "Would you have kissed him?" Amid the almost expected negative responses appears a sound bite from the textbook feminist/psychoanalyst/left-wing intellectual (Rodrigues's nemesis?), and the contrast between her measured and sensible response and that of the public at large could not be more marked. This is a key moment in Barreto's film. He seems to want to emphasize this gap between the ideal that intellectuals and cultural commentators in Brazil work toward, or to put it another way, the official version of the nation (an intellectually mature and tolerant nation, with no torture, and not a proper dictatorship—congress was only closed once in how many years, after all?), and the other version, symbolized by the people who crop up in Barreto's film as previously mentioned (such as the man selling sugar-cane juice). This gap, in fact, is well illustrated by film reviewer Sérgio Augusto's remark that the treatment of homosexuality in the film is "as up-to-date as a chastity belt."[9] Barreto suggests otherwise—as incredible as it might sound, this could still happen.

This gap is further illustrated by one of the most striking segments of Barreto's film: the harrowing sexual assault on Arandir's wife carried out by the journalist. In the scene, which happens offstage in the play, Selminha is forced to lift her skirt and remove her underwear in front of the journalist (with the detective looking on in the background), while the journalist's fist and cigar are alternately placed between her legs. One respected film critic bizarrely pointed to the tasteful eroticism of the scene, apparently incapable of distinguishing between it and an earlier scene where we see the sister Dália, played by the pin-up of the moment, Lídia Brondi, taking a shower.[10] And surely that is the point that Barreto is trying to make here. His film is dotted with the clichés of the *pornochanchada*[11] (which, of course, would normally have been played for laughs as well as titillation): for example, the young and beautiful girl unwittingly observed taking a shower, young and beautiful girl undressing to seduce sexually frustrated man, young girl loses her underwear. The film appears to be stating that the real effect of *pornochanchada*, rather than getting Brazilians to watch national cinema after the demise of the *chanchada*, as

Selminha (Cristiane Torloni) returns home to discover the word *queer* daubed on her house in Bruno Barreto's *O beijo no asfalto* (1981) (courtesy of LCB Produções Cinematográficas).

the same critic suggests, is that from then on any kind of nudity, regardless of the context, would be interpreted as being there on purpose to excite the audience. *Pornochanchada* (and the dictatorship's tacit approval of it) confirmed that it was acceptable to be a voyeur. And this is exactly what we the spectators are in the sexual assault scene. The camera angle is such that it views for us as if we were participating in the act, mirroring the detective's colluding gaze. We share the responsibility for both sexual and political oppression, for refusing to believe what is going on around us, for suspending disbelief just as we do when we go to the cinema, and for seeing purely what we want to see. To put it another way, we have lost the ability to distinguish between gestures such as a merciful kiss and a sexual one, given the context of *pornochanchada*, and more widely perhaps, of dictatorship.

As *O beijo no asfalto* was released in 1981 (post-*abertura*),[12] it is easy to think of the police violence in the film as being a comment on the evils of the recent past: the detective in cahoots with the journalist to victimize an innocent man, an incident that is related by one of the characters whereby the same detective kicked a pregnant woman in the stomach causing her to miscarry, the journalist who forces Arandir's wife to undress as the detective looks on, and so on. But all of these elements are present in the original play, written in 1960 by a writer who would later support the military dictatorship, declared in 1964.[13] Police violence and torture pre-date military rule, as Brazilian audiences would know only too well. That is not to say that the subject matter of the film (the persecution of those who have done nothing wrong, and the quick acceptance of society in general of a reality constructed by the media), does not bring to mind the full-scale political oppression and censorship of only a few years earlier.

There is, however, another way of understanding Barreto's depiction of politics, nudity, and homosexuality in *O beijo no asfalto*, which has more to do with the desire to entertain than to subvert or inform. Despite the director's evident attempts to rethink sexuality, and more explicitly masculinity, Arandir's death at the hands of his lying, murderous, and gay father-in-law merely reinforces same-sex patriarchal discourse, just as Rodrigues's original play had done. As David Foster puts it: "gayness as a negative social marker is deftly and suddenly shifted in a definitive manner from Arangir [*sic*] and placed on the shoulders of someone else, who, as a murderer, remains negatively marked."[14]

Foster goes one stage further in his unraveling of the latent homophobia, despite Barreto's good intentions, in the film:

> Since the homophobic mind often associates mental instability and criminality with the homosexual, the shooting confirms a powerful stereotype. And since there is no opportunity, with the quick closure of the film, to explore how violence, even murderous violence, is the consequence of the violence of the closet within which homophobia confines the father-in-law, the spectators ... [can] leave the theater thinking that violence is, after all, the birthright of the homosexual.[15]

Ismail Xavier has described the style of the large number of nominally political films such as *O beijo no asfalto*, which were released in Brazil after 1979, as lukewarm "*abertura* naturalism films."[16] The term *abertura naturalism* denotes films that deal with sex and violence and repressed political experience of the last two decades of dictatorship.[17] One critic described Barreto's film as being a slick but straightforward copy of the unadventurous American police thrillers of the 1950s.[18] In other words, the painful political context of the film has little to do with historical memory and more to do with taking advantage of changes in the political climate to use formulas familiar to an audience mad on Hollywood, with the simple goal of increasing box-office returns. The same could easily be said of Barreto's depiction of nudity and female sexuality in the film: there is little doubt that the displays of nudity (regardless of the context) of Cristiane Torloni and Lídia Brondi provided one of the film's main attractions. Just as many directors of Rodrigues's work had done before and would do after him, Barreto both condemns and enjoys the benefits of the exploitation of female bodies, in the wake of the officially sanctioned ascendancy of the pornochanchada.

Endnotes

1. Since the early 1990s, Nelson Rodrigues's work has been very much in vogue in Brazil. His nondramatic fiction has been reedited by Companhia das Letras and is selling well. The hit miniseries *A vida como ela é,* based on Rodrigues's newspaper column of the same name, was a success for Globo Television. His plays are once again being staged regularly: Marco Antônio Braz's *Boca de Ouro* (1997) and *Perdoa-me por me traíres* (1999), and Moacyr Goés's *Toda nudez será castigada* (1998) are three major productions. For examples of scholarship on Nelson Rodrigues, see the journals *Range Rede* (no. 4) (Rio de Janeiro: UFRJ, 1998) and *Travessia* (no. 28) (Florianópolis: UFSC, 1994).

2. For more on Rodrigues and his well-known sayings, see Rui Castro's anecdotal and entertaining biography: *O anjo pornográfico: a vida de Nelson Rodrigues* (São Paulo: Companhia das Letras, 1992).

3. David William Foster, *Gender and Society in Contemporary Brazilian Cinema* (Austin: University of Texas Press, 1999) pp. 129–130.

4. For more information on the press reaction to Rodrigues through the years, see Stephanie Dennison, "Critical Responses to the Screening of Nelson Rodrigues," *Studies in Latin American Popular Culture* (2000), pp. 129–144.

5. Castro, *O anjo pornográfico,* p. 321.

6. The kiss of the title triggers a journey of self-discovery, similar to K's in *The Trial,* where Arandir discovers the real meaning of his relationship with his wife, his sister-in-law, his colleagues, his father-in-law, and so on. There are features of Tambellini's film that suggest that the director had been inspired by Orson Welles's 1961 film version of Kafka's novel. First of all, Welles's use of a cartoon to open the film and supply the underpinning message. In the case of *O Beijo,* the opening credits are rolled over a backdrop of a painting, in the expressionist style, of Christ carrying a cross, which is animated by the voices of grotesque onlookers whispering about the lack of innocence of the kiss, thereby forging a link with Christ's betrayal and crucifixion at the behest of the community at large, and in a sense reinforcing the link between Tambellini's interpretation and Kafka's novel. K, the sacrificial character in *The Trial,* was unaware of his crime. He enjoyed freedom and as Welles's film version emphasized in the cartoon opening, he unconsciously consented to the trial and thus implicitly accepted his guilt. Arandir's guilt was not about being gay but daring to stare death in the face. Our guilt is to condemn purity and innocence wherever we find it.

7. Hélio Pelligrini, "A obra e *O beijo no asfalto,*" transcribed in Nelson Rodrigues, *Teatro completo,* Vol 4 (Rio de Janeiro: Nova Fronteira, 1989), p. 368 (our translation).

8. Tambellini juxtaposes shots of both the accident victim as he steps off the sidewalk and Arandir checking their watches. The scene could of course also be interpreted as playfully hinting that the two men did, after all, have a prearranged meeting, in order to reinforce the notion that we are easily fooled by appearances.

9. Sérgio Augusto, *Isto é* (São Paulo: June 3, 1981).

10. José Carlos Oliveira, "Um beijo bem dado," *Jornal do Brasil* (Rio de Janeiro: March 27, 1981).

11. *Pornochanchada* was the derogatory term used to describe the popular soft-core

comedies that dominated domestic film production in Brazil during the 1970s, which would later develop into hard-core from 1982 onwards. The term is derived from the word *chanchada*, used to describe the popular musical comedies that had a huge following, particularly in the 1940s, and about which film critics were equally condescending.

12. *Abertura*, or political opening-up, refers to the period that roughly encompasses 1976 to 1984, when the Brazilian military's hold on government, and the methods they had used to keep that hold, such as political oppression and censorship, gradually began to diminish.

13. One interesting addition to the more or less faithful reproduction of dialogue from the play are the words, uttered by the police chief: "There's no torture in this precinct" (our translation). The addition is highly ironic: after the so-called coup within the coup of 1968, which ushered in a period of severe political oppression, Nelson Rodrigues had a reputation for denying that torture existed; that is, until his own son, a member of an underground opposition group, was captured and tortured.

14. Foster, *Gender and Society*, p. 316.

15. Ibid., pp. 316–317.

16. Quoted in Fernão Ramos (ed.), *História do cinema brasileiro* (São Paulo: Arte Editora, 1987), p. 316.

17. Robert Stam, João Luiz Vieira and Ismail Xavier, "The Shape of Brazilian Cinema in the Postmodern Age," in Randal Johnson and Robert Stam (eds.), *Brazilian Cinema* (New York: Columbia University Press, 1995), p. 412.

18. Ronaldo de Noronha, "Cadáveres insepultos," *Estado de Minas* (Belo Horizonte: June 17, 1981).

PART III

Nation and Identity

7

Born at Last? Cinema and Social Imaginary in 21st-Century Uruguay

Keith Richards

Uruguayan cinema occupies a curious position, in terms both of Latin American film and of national culture. The title of this chapter refers to a widespread perception, almost a commonplace, regarding the periodic "birth" or "rebirth" of the Uruguayan film industry, a recurring myth that derives from film publicists and critics alike. A convenient tag for promoters eager to stress the uniqueness of the occasional national product, it is often repeated in derisive fashion in Montevideo film reviews. It is the fate of almost every Uruguayan feature film to be heralded either as the first of its kind or as a sign of the renaissance of the national industry. Uruguay is a small nation, in both geographic and demographic terms, but its disproportionately high cultural profile suggests that the paucity of its film production is a phenomenon due more to sociopolitical and economic factors than to purely aesthetic ones. There are signs, however, that at the beginning of the 21st century Uruguayan cinema had at last begun to take itself seriously and respond to the country's circumstances on national, regional, and global levels. Calls for a coherent body of film production have accompanied the clamor for coherent and supportive legislation for well over a decade, as scholars such as Luciano Álvarez advocate administrative and aesthetic strategies that recognize the crucial coexistence of the medium's industrial and artistic elements.[1] The imperative for a country of such modest resources is to meet the daunting challenge of becoming integrated into a much broader network of production and distribution whilst resisting the homogenizing effects of globalization and the centripetal pull of far larger neighbors in Brazil and Argentina.

In the first part of this chapter I propose to look at the history behind this situation, asking why so few films have come from a country with such an impressive tradition in the arts, particularly literature, and examining the upturn in Uruguayan film production in the late 20th century. The lack of resources and infrastructure goes some way toward an explanation; but Uruguay suffers less economic hardship than other Latin American nations and offers a modest, but significant, cinematic output. One might also ask what kind of contribution can be expected from cinema to a social imaginary debilitated by factors such as amnesia or the rupture of collective memory, the interruption of democratic development, and the exile or liquidation of artists and intellectuals. Uruguayan national identity is a fragile commodity, as with most Latin American countries, the foundations of national discourse having been questioned by numerous intellectuals and artists since the 1950s. I will proceed to look at a number of films from the 1990s and the early 21st century in relation to the staples and clichés of Uruguay's self-image. I will examine the extent to which these provide a valid and coherent response to the crisis of self-conception that is discussed daily in the nation's media.

In addressing these questions it is necessary to view Uruguayan filmmaking as part of the continuing debate over the creation of national cultural identities in Latin America, and the role of the state in this process. I also intend to look at the praxis of building a film industry in the face of the global economic situation: how do financial concerns, combined with these social and historical conditions, act upon the cinematic end product? Uruguayan cinema suffered from neglect and a lack of coherent policies both before and during military rule. Since the early 1990s or so, however, there have been signs of a will to promote film from both the public and private sector. There are also a few imaginative and resourceful filmmakers prepared to draw financially from both sectors, and aesthetically from popular and literary sources. Within the context of the debate over responses to the global market, the difficulties experienced by the nation-state, the possibility of cultural autonomy, and the position of Latin America as "subaltern" or "postcolonial," there appear to be emerging the seeds of some valid responses to the predicament of small nations.[2] Some of these productions also reflect Jesús Martín-Barbero's notion of new cultural hybrids stemming from "mediations" between high culture and popular culture.[3]

The difficult gestation of Uruguayan cinema is too convoluted a tale fully to be told here, but the point can be illustrated by citing just a few instances. As is noted by Guillermo Zapiola, *Dos destinos* (Two Destinies) was introduced in 1936 as "the beginning of a new film industry in

Uruguay."[4] In 1946 *Los tres mosqueteros* (The Three Musketeers) was greeted optimistically: "Uruguayan cinema takes its first step with this film."[5] Zapiola further notes that shooting for *El lugar del humo* (The Place of Smoke), as late as 1979 when the country had already produced some 20 films, was misrepresented as follows: "soon shooting will begin on the first national full-length feature."[6] The absurdity of this is by no means lost on Uruguayan observers of their own film culture, but it also reflects the reality of a country where historical and social processes have often been truncated or even reversed.

The state of cinema in Uruguay can be seen against a background of what Juan Rial has termed Utopian political myths: a social imaginary that leaned heavily on the legacy of the welfare state and other reforms instituted by José Batlle in the early 20th century to mask subsequent failures to maintain the social achievements and national profile established during that time.[7] Despite the enlightened nature of the *batllista* period, the myth of the "Happy Uruguay" that it engendered was to become a hindrance when the nation encountered less fortunate times. The second half of the 20th century saw enormous changes in national identity (the mere definition of which has become increasingly problematized) and social imaginary on a global level. In the Uruguayan context there has been what Hugo Achugar has termed "the sequence of 'democracy-dictatorship-restoration' through which the recent history of our country has been organized."[8] These seismic changes have caused fissures in the nation's self-perception that require urgent attention. This is hardly simplified by the current situation of postmodern or postnational flux, and the effects of globalized imagery upon previously stable notions of allegiance, belonging and identity.

Rial cites four Uruguayan central "myths," categories of social imaginary also discussed by Achugar and Jorge Ruffinelli among others.[9] They can be outlined as follows: first, *consensus* or the rule of law, the notion of a convivial sharing of space between classes and observance of social rules. The second myth, of a *cultured citizenry* reflects the literacy and education programs of the Batlle years, but also a somewhat pretentious intelligentsia termed *culturosos*, providing no threat to the social order. The third myth is that of *averageness* (which might be read, according to Rial, as "mediocrity"), a collective self-restriction that discouraged flamboyance or individual brilliance. Finally there is *uniqueness*, which did not connote superiority; rather it reflected the conception of Uruguay as the "little country" or "paisito," a land modest in more than just geographical terms. With the deterioration of these mythical elements in mind, one can identify three salient geopolitical and social circumstances that have conditioned Uruguayan cinema, as outlined below.

Expectation versus Output

First, one can point to the disparity between film literacy and national production, a by-product of the relatively high standard of education achieved under Batlle and the effect of creating what was considered a society of "cultorosos," with a keen interest in aesthetic questions. This term *culturoso*, as explained above, connoted a certain pretension, yet was adopted with good grace as it vouchsafed an acceptance of mediocrity facilitating a process of bonding between social classes. A film public, which had come to discern and criticize, became ever less indulgent of poor quality home produce. Local journalists encouraged this reaction on the part of the audience: Homero Alsina Thevenet has pointed to a strong tradition of cultural journalism that began with the "*Generación del '45*" (Generation of 1945) and lasted two decades.[10] Uruguay famously became a land of film critics with practically no national cinema. As early as 1928, the writer Horacio Quiroga was moved to comment that the nation's critical faculties were outstripping its production: "the public taste — that of the metropolis, at any rate — has today reached a level that no national film would dare challenge, at the risk of being greeted with endless mockery."[11]

The critic and director of the National Film Archive (Cinemateca Nacional) Manuel Martínez Carril points out that, in 1950s Montevideo, there was a cinemagoing population of 23 million spectators annually, equal on average to each inhabitant seeing almost one film each month.[12] In the more straitened economic circumstances of the late 1990s, cinema had become a relative luxury and attendance had, due to this and a number of other factors, declined considerably (to 700,000 in 1997). Yet even today the Cinemateca Nacional is one of the most enterprising in Latin America. Its journals *Cinemateca Revista* and *Otrocine* show a degree of awareness and discernment quite disproportionate to the country's level of film production. Uruguay has produced a number of respected critics and holds an important annual festival at Punta del Este. However, this is a double-edged sword: the level of public awareness, as Quiroga pointed out, long ago outstripped national output and has even come to fuel a sense of inferiority. The syndrome is, according to the renowned documentary maker Mario Handler, by no means helped by national film criticism: "All it has done is create pot-bellied spectators. I don't know why Uruguayan critics have misunderstood national cinema. It's just too exaggerated, almost an insult. Uruguayan filmmakers in the outside world have always been ignored."[13] Handler, who himself spent many years in exile, is voicing a common grievance — one also expressed by Gabriel Peveroni, who complains of "the foolish argument that 'they should have filmed this, that or the other,' usually offered by a number of local critics."[14]

Crossing the River

Second, one can point to the position of Uruguay between two giants, Argentina and Brazil. These cultural worlds, and in particular the metropolis of Buenos Aires, have exerted enormous pull on their "buffer state" in more than just cultural terms. In the context of regional cinematic production, Argentina, with its cultural similarities, has tended to have a particularly powerful, if ambivalent, influence on its smaller neighbor. There has been the dual effect of stimulation in employing Uruguayan talent, locations, and expertise but also stultification in effectively discouraging the development of a true film industry in Montevideo. The temptation has always been to work in nearby Buenos Aires rather than build an industry in Montevideo. Guillermo Zapiola, for instance, talks of coproductions with Argentina as "a possibility of obtaining capital and broadening the market"[15]; but he argues that this apparent convenience nonetheless had a debilitating effect on Uruguayan cinema, above all during the 1930s and 1940s, leading to "a rudimentary and precarious cinema, unsustainable even according to the most benevolent criteria."[16]

This state of affairs is further complicated today by the existence of Mercosur, the economic bloc that also includes Paraguay. The first Mercocine film festival was held in Punta del Este in February 1999 and also featured films from Bolivia and Chile. Whether this will bring about an enduring film distribution network between the countries concerned is still a matter of speculation. Perhaps there is cause for a little more optimism than has been shown by some observers: it is possible that awareness is growing of the value, in terms of international prestige, of a viable cinema industry as well as the long-term effects on employment and the economy.[17]

It may well be asked whether Uruguayan identity, in its cinematic manifestation at least, has been conditioned by the Argentine influence. Many films and audiovisual projects have crossed the River Plate — both literally, and in the fictional sense of film content. As well as lower production costs, Uruguay has relatively untouched historic locations to offer Argentine cinema. Colonia, a small town on the Plate opposite Buenos Aires, offers a well-preserved architectural heritage that is visible in Héctor Olivera's *El muerto* (The Dead Man, 1975), María Luisa Bemberg's *Camila* (1983), Eduardo Mignogna's *El faro* (The Lighthouse, 1996), and several other productions.

Uruguay, and in particular the city of Montevideo, has long had a special role as a place of escape, whether physical or existential/philosophical, in Argentine lore. Smaller neighbors tend to permit a chimerical sense of superiority in terms of intellect or material progress. In this case, however, the smaller country is also the repository of a metareality that the larger has lost (or perhaps never had). As parallels we might look at the ambiguous view of Ireland taken by the English, or of Mexico by North Americans. Uruguay is often seen, somewhat romantically, as "la orilla mágica" (the magical shore), bound neither by mundane rules nor even earthly laws. The ethnic and cultural links to Argentina make this all the more poignant, and this perception emerges in many aspects of cultural life other than cinema. The famous tango singer Carlos Gardel claimed to be Uruguayan to hide his illegitimacy. Among several of Jorge Luis Borges's short stories set in the Uruguayan province is "Funes el memorioso" (Funes the Memorious), with its hyperbolic examination of memory. Montevideo was visited by Argentines seeking banned literature during various periods of political repression. Returning to cinema, the Argentine Eliseo Subiela's 1996 film *El lado oscuro del corazón* (Dark Side of the Heart) presents the Uruguayan capital as a city offering sexual and amorous liberation to a young poet (based upon the Argentine Oliverio Girondo). A similar image of abandon, though somewhat less whimsical and bohemian, can be found in the Uruguayan Diego Arsuaga's *Otario* (Idiot), discussed below.

The possibility of Uruguayan–Argentine coproductions was opened with *Patrón* (Boss), directed by Jorge Rocca in 1995. This collaboration between Argentine and Uruguayan producers (Aleph and CEMA, respectively), alongside the Argentine Film Institute, was shot in black and white with almost no dialogue and tells of an arranged marriage between a young woman and a far older landowner who uses her to bear his son. The wife exacts a novel form of revenge reflecting her abuse as a purely childbearing object. *Patrón* rarely makes specific mention of its setting and might equally effectively have been made in Argentina. However, it showed a possible way forward, far more honorable than the attempted appropriation of the Argentine production *Un lugar en el mundo* (A Place in the World). Adolfo Aristarain's work was entered as the "Uruguayan" nomination for the foreign-language Oscar in 1993, a move heavily criticized at home as a transparent falsehood symptomatic, once again, of Uruguayan dependency.

Dictatorship and Denial

Third, and by no means least in importance is the period of political upheaval and repression lasting from 1973 to 1985, and its effects on social development. The legacy of this traumatic period of military rule was an array of shocked reactions: collective and official amnesia, withdrawal into private nostalgia, and alienation. Unlike Argentina and Chile, where several films have dealt with the effects of disappearance and discontinuity, there has been little evidence of this in Uruguay. However, as we will see, there are examples of oblique metaphorical approaches to the problem or even unconscious references to it.

Uruguay moved away from being the "Switzerland of South America," as it was known in the early decades of the 20th century, a period of optimism and social reform. The fading of a self-image based on the notion of uniqueness was fed by thinkers like Rodó, with his emphasis on the benefits of "Europeanization" whilst maintaining a separate national ethos. This legacy gradually receded, and by the 1950s a form of counterimaginary was operating, in accordance with new and harsher realities. Instead of the affectionate diminutive "paisito," consecrated by sayings like "Como el Uruguay no hay" (There's no place like Uruguay), in the final decade of the 20th century, the country was often viewed in terms of what it had lost. In an article prompted by the 1999 presidential election, Mario Benedetti wryly observed that Uruguay is not an underdeveloped country, but "a country in the process of underdevelopment."[18] The disillusionment at loss of status, after the disappearance of economic and social advantages over previously worse-off Latin American neighbors, is palpable here.

Ruffinelli, referring to Uruguayan literature, has highlighted the effects on the social fabric not only of exile but what has been termed *insilio* (which would have to be translated into English as "insile").[19] This refers to a form of personalized exile brought into being by internal repression and ostracism directed at those who did not escape or go into exile. In Benedetti's view this remains today as the military's "legacy of mean-spiritedness and fear."[20] This self-perception of cowed petty individualism and abdication of responsibility was in urgent need of confrontation and resolution.

A number of Uruguayan commentators have pointed to the need to construct a new body of social imagery after the dismantling of the "Happy Uruguay" myth during the long process toward the 1973 coup. This was an image distilled from the Batlle years and their legacy, replaced by disillusionment and even despair: a condition perhaps best expressed by Rial's application of the term *autism*. Mario Benedetti's almost untranslatable neologism *sobremorir* is a play on sobrevivir (to survive), replacing vivir (to live) with morir (to die).

Rial points to changes in the ordering and perception of time, and a new interplay between objective chronos and subjective *kairós* that had been effectively suspended. Since the restoration of democracy, he suggests, a "new magma of social meanings" is in existence, but is yet to become clearly defined.[21] Carina Perelli, whose focus is on the social role in Uruguay of collective memory, looks at ways of manipulating the "symbolic sphere"— assimilating and making bearable the legacy of military rule or the "década infame" (infamous decade)— through a process of "resignification."[22]

The question of the validity of state intervention in culture is an ongoing debate not limited to Uruguay or even to Latin America. The difference between Uruguay under dictatorship and since the restoration of democracy is partly visible through the changes in official cultural policy. Under the military, says Rial, there was little or no effort to form a new imaginary — simply a program of repression.[23] Jorge Abbondanza, in 1982, was already talking about a crisis in national culture — one of the symptoms of which was an "abundant blessing of ... mediocrity."[24] Abbondanza even talks in terms of "impunity" for the perpetrators of this cultural malaise and promoters of sterile nostalgia, advocating war against the evils of sclerosis, stagnation, and imitation.

In the same year, Manuel Martínez Carril was lamenting the overall quality of both film production and promotion, with reference to four productions from the late 1970s and early 1980s.[25] *El lugar del humo* (1979) was, as mentioned above, one of many "first Uruguayan films" and fell foul of the discrepancy between its promotion hype and artistic quality. The coproduction *Gurí* (Kid, 1980) was a modest but uninspiring attempt at a gaucho western, whilst *Sábado disco* (Saturday Disco, 1981) was generally considered a failure on all levels. Juan C. Rodríguez Castro's examination of a key moment of Uruguayan 19th-century political history *Mataron a Venancio Flores* (They Killed Venancio Flores, 1982) was a very different case: widely praised for its cinematic quality, the film nonetheless failed to capture the public imagination. Martínez Carril was moved to comment on the futility of government subsidy for "a cinema unable to fend for itself" and saw an urgent need for the cinema not only to address the real needs of its audience, but to decide, and quickly, what that audience was to be.[26] Rodríguez Castro was frustrated in his aim to find a point of departure for cinematic creation on a national level. However, his comments on the possible future for Uruguayan cinema, maximizing the country's resources in collaboration with other Latin American communities, have already been borne out.[27]

Toward the end of the 20th century, there appeared signs of sustained support and stimulus for worthwhile film production in Uruguay. The 1990s saw a modest but significant output of films and video produc-

Walter Venencio in *Mataron a Venancio Flores* (Juan C. Rodríguez Castro, 1982) (courtesy of the Cinemateca Uruguaya).

tions, reflecting current realities and addressing gaps in social and national imaginary, as well as providing an improvement on previous Uruguayan productions in terms of entertainment value reflected at the box office.

A look at some of these 1990s films and their public and critical reception may give a clue as to the nation's current self-image. They evidence two separate tendencies: Diego Arsuaga's *Otario* (1997) and Alvaro Buela's *Una forma de bailar* (A Way of Dancing, 1997) were both shot on video and transferred to 35mm, and display relatively modest artistic and discursive aims. Critical and public praise for these certainly worthy efforts appears to indicate a general wish to avoid not only overt political content but also any pretension to artistic breadth; however, neither is without its element of social content. The same may be said of Beatriz Flores Silva's *La historia casi verdadera de Pepita la Pistolera* (The Almost True Story of Pepita the Gangster, 1993) and Carlos Ameglio's *El hombre de Walter* (Walter's Man, 1995), which nonetheless is far more thematically abstruse. Ameglio's project, however, did not also take financial risks, which is the charge made against two feature films produced during the decade in question. Pablo Dotta's *El dirigible* (The Zeppelin, 1993) and Leonardo Ricagni's *El Chevrolé* (The Chevrolet, 1997) shot on 35mm, were more ambitious projects both in terms of budget and discursive scope. Both were funded partly from abroad and given ample promotion. Largely as a result of this apparent audacity they both received an ambivalent public and critical response. They fared well enough at the box office, yet were widely charged with pretension and of wasting funds and opportunities.

These are films conceived, in far more overt a manner than Buela's or Arsuaga's works, to open a debate on the subject of Uruguay's current condition. There is a reminder here of the "myth" of averageness: a tendency to punish excessive ambition in a country that distrusts any whiff of grandiloquence or pretension amongst its own, whilst indulging the same tendencies in European, North American, or other foreign productions.

El hombre de Walter is a 50-minute video production written and directed by Carlos Ameglio. Inspired by the 1940s experiments of the pioneering robot scientist Grey Walter, it is by turns (and even simultaneously) amusing, grotesque, dreamlike, and curiously erotic. It reworks some of Walter's findings with regard to the automatism of living organisms and their possible reproduction by artificial means. However, the end product shows the influence of Buñuel, along with that of Lewis Carroll and of sci-fi and horror films in general.

The protagonist is the apparent master of a large, elegantly furnished house, but is almost constantly either locked in or locked out. The difficulty he finds in navigating his own property forms a parallel with his own sexual frustration and exclusion, as a series of women refuse his advances. The man strides across spacious interiors, blunders through tentacle-infested subterranean labyrinths, or follows a young girl (Alice?) around the garden. The desired sexual encounters are all aborted when the four women concerned use, as an excuse for postponing union, the imminent arrival for a social gathering of "el Presidente." One of them explains that the party is an excuse to facilitate a political agreement of great benefit to the nation. Ameglio's film defies rational analysis but its allusions to a stultifying political legacy are clear enough.

In Diego Arsuaga's *Otario*, the eponymous stooge (*otario* is unflattering Uruguayan slang for *fool* or *idiot*) is led a dance between the Argentine and Uruguayan capitals, having been hired by a rich Spanish wife to keep track of an errant husband in a story of fraud, self-deceit, mistaken identity, and existential perdition. The film is persuasive and consummately executed as a film noir pastiche, but has broader ambitions than this. Its protagonist is Souto, an ex-policeman turned private detective from Buenos Aires, sent to Montevideo by the Spanish woman anxious to track down the husband whom she has been maintaining financially for some years. This seemingly straightforward task proves impossibly complex once the reality of the situation is encountered. The *porteño* (native of Buenos Aires— seen as presumptuously sophisticated or streetwise in regional lore) meets duplicity and corruption beyond his imagination: worst of all, he falls for and attempts to "save" the abused and masochistic Lucy, a woman as addicted to morphine as she is to the club owner

Quirós. Souto's musings on his fate, in the form of voice-over interior monologue, take place during his repeated crossings on the River Plate ferry. The muddy waters of the estuary appear as a metaphor for the bottomless intractability of this Montevideo demimonde: the nightclub-brothel run by the "husband" and its cast of fascists, child molesters, and drug smugglers. The irony of the club's name, *El Paradise*, is also to be found in Souto's opening line, "those weren't bad times." The Uruguayan capital is seen once more as a kind of poetically depraved alter ego for the Argentine; the difference here, though, is that the fundamental viewpoint is Uruguayan. *Otario* is close in some ways to the aforementioned Héctor Olivera film *El muerto*, based on the eponymous short story by Jorge Luis Borges in which the presumption of an Argentine interloper in attempting to replace a Uruguayan estancia or ranch owner is ultimately confounded and punished. An Argentine review of *Otario* supports the notion of a Uruguayan self-image reflected back from Buenos Aires:

> There is a lightness of tone, a convoluted plot line and some mordant dialogues, spoken *sotto voce*, as if corresponding to the idea we have of the "little country." The Uruguayan intonation is a delight, except in the case of the protagonist ... who is Argentine. But this is the Idiot himself, who understands nothing of what is happening around him and there's no doubt they came to these shores to mock those of us from Buenos Aires.[28]

Álvaro Buela's *Una forma de bailar* sets itself an apparently modest task, that of narrating a tangled but not outrageous love triangle. Esteban gives a temporary home to his best friend Roberto, thrown out by his wife, Laura, for being an incorrigible Don Juan. Esteban and Laura, however, find a mutual attraction and empathy that had been unspoken for years. Through this story of long-thwarted love the film creates a pervasive feeling of nostalgia, regrets at lost opportunities and vanished youth. The sense of loss is conveyed visually by several means: the ghostlike illustrations of verbally evoked memories in voice-off; interior traveling shots that dwell on photographs revealing self-delusion; the reflected image on the video screen of Laura and Esteban having switched off the party tape in which they have accidentally caught up with a painful truth. A judicious use of music, especially by Roberto Musso, heightens this atmosphere, in which personal ghosts have to be identified and, eventually, exorcised. The well-intentioned but timid protagonist, Esteban, is a faint echo of the autism (if not mediocrity) spoken of by Rial and other commentators. The rather facile theories offered by his sister, a psychology student, are of no more help than the possessive attentions of his mother nor his own unconvincing protestations that "soy lo que quiero ser" ("I am what I want to be"). The overriding idea is that of reaching manhood or maturity through a denial of the recipe given to Esteban by his father: by losing rather than acquiring restraint and inhibitions. To dance is to finally make contact with one's intuitions. Buela's film struck a chord with Uruguayan audiences, who could readily identify with Esteban's generation. Virtues were noted in the very lack of scope of the film, which handles actors, narrative, and finances with equal economy and facility. Perhaps just as important as the personal solutions it presents are the possibilities of creating in audiovisual media without outside funding or financial disaster. Buela coproduced with the television Channel 10, which also broadcast the film; this did not prevent its strong performance at the box office.

Among the criticisms leveled at *Una forma de bailar* were a lack of breadth in its social vision. Fernando Gago talks about exclusion in the social milieu of Esteban and in the character's self-absorption: "his concerns go no further than the merely sentimental."[29] For Gago, the audience learns little or nothing about the occupations or backgrounds of any of the characters. Surrounding realities are not questioned, and although their economic situations are apparently fairly comfortable, we never find out why. Gago also complains of the lack of exterior shots, which only serve to link the interiors: "it's a film with no surprises, no spectacle, no risks and no tears."[30] However, this film does not seek to present a cross-section or any kind of social-realist analysis. Its minimalist focus is more synecdoche than microcosm. Gago also comments on the narrative strengths of the film, the effortless facility with which it tells its story. This might appear frivolous in a different context, but such competence is no small achievement if contrasted with a perceived series of pretentious failures.

Uruguay's foremost woman filmmaker, Beatriz Flores Silva, trained in Belgium and became the first director of Uruguay's first national film school, the Escuela de Cinematografía, in 1995. Her portfolio now includes two feature films; *La historia casi verdadera de Pepita la Pistolera*, shot on video in 1993, tells the unlikely story of a woman driven by poverty and despair to rob several currency exchange houses "armed" with an umbrella handle. The script is nonetheless based on real events that occurred in 1988 — although, as the title suggests, there is a certain skepticism toward notions of truth that allows an interrogation of social categories as well as permitting comic empathy. The strategy reappears in *En la puta vida* (Tricky Life, 2000), Flores Silva's second feature. Again the film uses an essentially true story based on a book by journalist María Urruzola, but this time the focus is the international traffic in Uruguayan women as prostitutes. Mónica Lettieri explains the construction of the scripts around "eye-witness" reports projected by the news media:

> Both films question the processes by which society defines those who stray from its norms. The images and the script show these characters categorized according to their deviations and anomalies, described and recognized by labels charged with negative connotations [thief, criminal, prostitute, danger to society]. These labels, which impose the isolation of the deviant in jails, asylums and psychiatric wards, construct a lamentable paradox: the very same social institutions [police, law, radio and television] that exist to control the deviations are responsible for their initial exaggeration.[31]

En la puta vida capitalizes on a story line that brings together European and Uruguayan interests; the subject matter, however murky, is offset by moments of humor. A coproduction involving Spain, Cuba, and Belgium along with Uruguay, *En la puta vida* attracted 135,000 spectators in 15 weeks of exhibition in Montevideo.

Dotta's *El dirigible*, which apparently did not manage to dodge the pitfall of excessive ambition, came off worst with the critics and the public. One graffito spotted in Montevideo ironically proclaimed "¡*Yo entendí* El

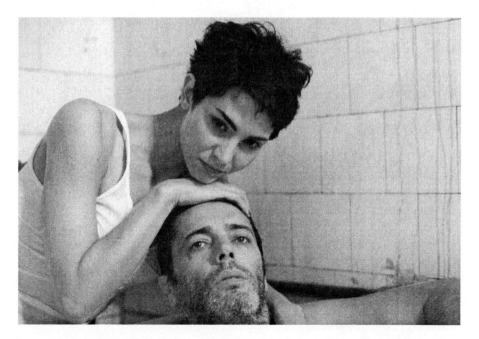

Mariana Santangelo and Silvestre in *En la puta vida* (Beatriz Flores Silva, 2000) (courtesy of the Cinemateca Uruguaya).

Dirigible!" (I understood *El dirigible*!) but was apocryphally signed "José Feliciano."[32] The near-vilification of this film seems to be due to its failure to satisfy the considerable expectations it raised as, once again, the specter appeared of the birth of Uruguayan film. (In the U.K., before Channel Four's television première, it was announced as "the first film to come from Uruguay in forty years"). Dotta's effort disappointed an eager public with its departure from linear narrative and unity, incursions into cinematic montage that brought charges of hermeticism, and free use of literary references. Dotta gives the work and persona of Uruguay's most famous novelist, Juan Carlos Onetti, an integral role in the narrative, incorporating his famously jaundiced view of Uruguayan national identity. The characters quote liberally (in the view of some critics, gratuitously) from Onetti and the poet Delmira Agustini. In this way *El dirigible* sacrifices verisimilitude in favor of a semiotically charged allegorical approach to the condition of Uruguay. The film's depiction of Montevideo recalls Cristina Peri-Rossi's allusion to a "literary city where words are worth more than images."[33] However, the very absence of images is at the heart of the problem: this is a society that has forgotten how to look at itself. Overall, the view presented in *El dirigible* reflects that of Onetti:

> The antidote to the shiny official image of middle-class Uruguay. An Uruguay of thieves and brothels; its defeated characters, flawed and cynical, seen in the light of winter. Cheap lodgings, snippets from gloomy newspapers and despised streets: a Uruguay without caste, devoid of history and lineage that, at a certain point, can be summed up in these words: "What is there behind us? One gaucho, two gauchos, thirty-three gauchos."[34]

The above quote from Onetti's famous story *El pozo* (The Pit) is repeated in Dotta's film, which presents a similar social landscape. Petty crime, social disaffection, and a taste for scatology coalesce in the figure of a young thief, Moco (Snot), who has apparently stolen a taped interview with Onetti. There is the suspicion, however, that the woman journalist who claims to have conducted the interview (and who also claims to be French) was in league with the thief all along. Moco, who may have stolen the woman's bag on demand, mocks the bourgeois anxieties of those desperate to retrieve the cassette without possibly being sure that it even exists. Onetti's much-publicized refusal to return to the homeland he termed nonexistent seems to have been respected: this trace of his existence has disappeared, thanks apparently to Moco, a member of the underclass he made central to his work.

El dirigible, whatever its perceived shortcomings, called into question the state of the Uruguayan nation and the imagery required to express

In foreground, Gonzalo Cardoso (left) and Marcelo Bouquet, with cast of extras in background, in *El dirigible* (Pablo Dotta, 1993) (courtesy of Tornasol Films).

its posttraumatic reality. Not all reception of this film was negative, but the public response was generally one of disappointment: "me hubiera gustado que me gustara" ("I'd like to have liked it"). The image presented is certainly a less than flattering one: its reception, however, evokes the common perception that this is a public unused to seeing itself depicted on screen.

The film foregrounds one crucial event in Uruguayan 20th-century history — the death of deposed President Baltasar Brum, who committed suicide when confronted with an imminent coup in 1933. The coup was to usher in a period of harsh conservatism after the Batlle years of social reform, and significantly this was an event of which no photographic image exists. Dotta suggests a parallel between the politician and Onetti, who also took a stand against political repression — albeit far less dramatic and even unacknowledged. Tellingly, the final song, by Fernando Cabrera, which opens with the lines "There's no time, no hour, no clock/There's no before nor after nor maybe" is evocative of Rial's comments on subjective and objective time. *El dirigible*, which uses the image of the Zeppelin flying over

Montevideo as a reminder of the scarcity of visual information in this country, makes an appeal to collective memory in what Oribe Irigoyen calls its "permanent allusion to Montevideo's memory, its lacunae and its empty spaces."[35]

El Chevrolé, Leonardo Ricagni's first feature film, uses as its source a play by Mauricio Rosencoff, *El regreso del gran Tuleque* (The Return of the Great Tuleque). Rosencoff is a well-known and widely respected figure in Uruguay, not only for his writing but also for his involvement with the Tupamaros urban guerrillas, as a result of which he spent 13 years in prison. *El Chevrolé* places Rosencoff's work in a mainstream context, but makes significant changes to the original vision. The film incorporates a soundtrack using contemporary rock music in order to enhance its marketability. It also creates a mystique surrounding the central character, identifying him with a caricatured Montevideo that was decried by the critic Gabriel Peveroni: "A place in which 'Magic Realism' cohabits with a highly picturesque underground, where one is simultaneously in heaven and hell."[36]

Ricagni spent several years in Europe, where he worked in advertising, and is more than aware of the pragmatics of film financing in a global context. Asked whether he had set out to present a portrait of Uruguay, or at least one of the country's faces, the director gave an ambiguous reply:

> On the one hand, the film does not set out to portray Uruguay, but on the other hand it does show the country absolutely ... I'm not at all interested in showing a folkloric Uruguay, but rather — and I emphasize this— I'm interested in showing a Uruguay that might be a blueprint of a kind of Latin America, what might be the vision of a foreigner in Uruguay.[37]

Ricagni's film certainly avoids any folkloric depiction along classic gaucho lines. He makes use, however, of a lesser-known element of Uruguayan tradition, the candombe carnival parades in which Montevideo's black community pays annual homage to the sea goddess Yemanyá. This is actual footage rather than reenactment, and is processed into the narrative through skilful editing and sound engineering. The above quotation, which may appear to be self-contradictory, refers to an attempt to channel popular culture into a self-affirming role rather than merely exotic detail. It is largely from the candombe ritual that El Tuleque and his band ultimately draw strength and efficacy.

This is the closest Uruguayan film to a "cine de desaparecidos" or cinema of the disappeared, of which there are a number of instances in Argentina and Chile. A framed musician, El Tuleque, is released from jail in the opening scene. This image is used to establish the protagonists of a number of other late 1980s and 1990s productions: Subiela's first two features, for example, or Alejandro Agresti's *Boda secreta* (Secret Wedding, 1988), Eduardo Calcagno's *El censor* (The Censor, 1995) and even Gonzalo Justiniano's *Amnesia* (1994). The difference is that El Tuleque has a vital role to play: he is called upon to help save a sacred water source threatened by a new hotel development earmarked to replace a marginalized neighborhood. This plot line allows identification of a more insidious adversary than the military, no longer a merely local threat and with global finance instead of weaponry. The response is a cultural reaffirmation of values buried during the dictatorship: El Tuleque rounds up the former members of his band, Los Chevrolés, to enter a competition and win the funds needed to save the site.

This film's use of the cityscape, like that in *El dirigible*, is expressively dystopian: but whilst Dotta uses a parodic view of Montevideo's self-importance and faded grandeur, Ricagni presents a ravaged quasi-void, which the released and revitalized El Tuleque and his band are able to invest with new meaning. This is a "feel good" film that makes use of contemporary cultural trends: young rock bands in Uruguay are included as well as older ones. There is an awareness, too of the continuing prominence, albeit symbolic, of ex–Tupamaros urban guerrillas in public (political and cultural) life. *El Chevrolé* has an eye to international markets, with its Spanish costar Pastora Vega and a version with voice-over narrative in English. Ricagni seems to perceive a need, also expressed by Handler, to make films for the wider world, but from a Latin American standpoint.[38] As has been pointed out by Victoria Ruétalo, *El Chevrolé* uses an aesthetic of regeneration in addressing the local through the global: the use of the port of Montevideo in itself is an internal and external communication.[39] The eponymous Chevrolé is the recycled and resignified front end of an old car, pulled by El Tuleque like a rickshaw. Similarly, there is the "reuse" of almost discarded humans, such as the ex-members of the band. Improvisation and inspiration are powerful forces in this urban wilderness that can yet be restored.

The final years of the 20th century witnessed more Uruguayan features seeking to tap into the youth market with their themes and use of rock soundtracks: *25 watts*, directed by Pablo Stoll and Juan Pablo Rebella, was criticized for its focus on the vacuous and aimless life led by a section of Montevideo youth. That this tableau of boredom and self-indulgence might also be seen in Buenos Aires and many other cities only increased the critical feeling toward the film, which was considered derivative of Argentine productions investigating similar themes. An example is *Pizza, birra, faso* (Pizza, Beer, Smokes, 1999) by Bruno Stagnaro and Adrián Caetano, which adopted a fictional approach to the street lowlife seen in the earlier documentaries of Caetano (himself a Uruguayan). Raúl Perrone's *Labios de churrasco* (Beef Lips, 1994) is another example of this tendency, closer to Stoll and Rebella's film in that its chosen subjects do not indulge in illegal activities (or practically any other). The box-office success of *25 watts*, which confounded critics, has been attributed to the film's by now global theme of youthful disorientation, its characters scrutinized, but not without humor and compassion. For once, the success of a Uruguayan film extended beyond the home market: *25 watts* drew 10,000 spectators in Buenos Aires (a record for a Uruguayan film in that city), and has been well received at numerous international festivals. In a similar vein, Marcelo Bertalmio's *Los días con Ana* (Days with Ana, 1999) takes a sympathetic look at a group of young people whose lives are as predictable, if somewhat less moronic, as those of the friends portrayed in *25 watts*. Bertalmio's film focuses upon an enduring problem in Uruguayan society and across Latin America: the attraction for educated people of more prosperous countries with greater career possibilities. Ana's decision to leave the country disrupts the complacent balance of her circle of friends, who are forced to come to terms with their situation. *Los días con Ana* was well received by both critics and the public, who welcomed its persuasive humor and the youthful promise of all those who contributed to the project.

The content of Esteban Schroeder's 1999 film *El viñedo* (The Vineyard) is well-known to national audiences, who were moved by this true story of murder, corruption, and concealment when it emerged only two years previously. The killing of a young man by his boss in the eponymous vineyard allows for a proportion of social comment as well as personal tragedy and empathy, brought to the film by the narrative device of an investigative reporter. Schroeder and Pablo Vierci, who coscripted this film, make a virtue of the story's simplicity and its accessibility to a public eager to see the transposition from newsprint to celluloid. Schroeder's production crew was praised for the fluency of the final product by Guillermo Zapiola, who sees in this film definitive proof of the viability of an audiovisual industry in Uruguay.[40]

Despite its having been conceived as the pilot for a television series, and shot on video and transferred to 35 mm, *El viñedo* broke box-office records in Uruguay (which have since been bettered by Flores Silva's *En la puta vida*). However it was found to lack interest for outside audiences, enjoying little commercial success in Argentina and creating minimal impact at festivals elsewhere.

Luis Nieto's *Estrella del sur* (Southern Star, 2002) is another film that takes up a theme of national concern, despite being a coproduction with

Spain, France, and Argentina. Nieto had already made two features dealing with Uruguayan dilemmas; *Su música suena todavía* (His Music Plays On, 1999) and *La memoria de Blas Quadra* (The Memory of Blas Quadra, 1999). With *Estrella del sur* he moves into the realm of political action and its aftermath: Gamboa, a former Tupamaro rebel, returns from exile with his son to find that his plan to begin afresh is beset with difficulties. The Mallorca-born son has almost irreconcilable notions from those of his father concerning Uruguay (which the former considers the end of the world) and in relation to direct political action. Nieto, whose own life experience is not dissimilar to that of his protagonist, prefers to emphasize the film's relevance to Uruguayan society in general than to his personal biography. As with his first two films, with their focus on aspects of civilian political responsibility, *Estrella del sur* examines the breach between generations and social sectors resulting from the era of military dictatorship. The ideological divisions still exist, but now so do others: those on the left who stayed behind, the exiles, the children born abroad, all offer distinct and valuable perspectives.

The other important film released in 2002, Diego Arsuaga's *El último tren* (The Last Train, also known as *Corazón de fuego* or Heart of Fire) was coproduced with Spain and Argentina and shot in Uruguay. Its theme, that of the "rescue" of an old steam train due to be sold to a U.S. film studio, offers a clear enough political analogy: the cultural patrimony defended by three senior citizens could be seen to represent the economic fate of both Argentina and Uruguay at the hands of capitalist interests from the same superpower. Here again a generational conflict is visible in the contrast between direct action, on the part of the three older men (famed Argentine actors Pepe Soriano, Héctor Alterio, and Federico Luppi) and the younger characters' complacent acceptance of the omnipotent dollar. The train might also represent a receding past, the legacy of the Batlle reforms discussed above, apparently obsolete in the face of globalization and neoliberalism. However, the three men's gesture generates some unexpected support and raises the prospect of further actions of that kind.

The list of productions from 2003 includes *Whisky*, a second feature by Stoll and Rebella whose script won a prize from the Sundance Institute. Leonardo Ricagni also released a second film, and although it can hardly be considered an example of Uruguayan cinema, his crime picture *29 Palms*, shot in the United States with North American actors, at least offered the director a further opportunity to ply his trade. Meanwhile, the release of Guillermo Casanova's *El viaje hacia el mar* (Journey toward the Sea) provided another encouraging sign that Uruguayan public interest in domestic production remains undimmed: this coproduction with

Argentina, which nonetheless uses a Uruguayan literary source (a short story by Juan José Morosoli) and mostly national crew and cast, outperformed Hollywood products like *Charlie's Angels* at the box office. The film's welcome was by no means limited to its home audience; it won first prize at the 2003 festival of Latin American cinema in Huelva, Spain. Casanova's film has in common with that of Rebella and Stoll an intimately comic, minimalist focus upon ostensibly insignificant and somewhat quixotic characters: respectively, five men who set out to travel to the coast in an old van, and a factory owner attempting to camouflage his lifestyle so as not to feel belittled during a visit from his more successful brother.

The future for Uruguayan film is of course by no means clear; there is still severe criticism of what is widely seen as inadequate support for film in official cultural policy. However, there are initiatives that indicate a new optimism alloyed with the flair and pragmatism seen in the productions mentioned above. Álvaro Casal strikes an optimistic note, inspired by the relative boom in production during the first years of the 21st century, in declaring that Uruguayan cinema has finally shaken off the poverty, in both economic and human terms, with which it was always associated.[41] These most recent films are all contributions to an imaginary which may accommodate both of the tendencies outlined above: on the one hand modesty, caution, and a sense of humility that might seem to hark back to the "averageness" posited by Rial. As a balance to this can be found a more exuberant and ambitious kind of vision, courting charges of pretension. Carina Perelli, whilst warning against efforts to force this imaginary into too didactic and specific a form, reminded us in 1993 that:

> We Uruguayans did not experience a single reality. Besides the geographical distances imposed by exile, imprisonment, and "insile," there were temporal distances [time experienced subjectively, or as that of others]; thus, dissimilar realities existed even for those whose lived experience was the same. Those differences are what underlie attempts to reconstruct our collective memory and manipulate it for political purposes.[42]

Perelli went on to suggest that, if the breakdown of collective memory occurs, there is no guarantee that the social imaginary will not break down as well.[43] To quote Mario Benedetti once more, "De-exile is no easy task."[44] The connection between collective memory and cinema, the capacity of this medium to create a semiotic or symbolic system at national, infranational, or supranational levels was demonstrated throughout the 20th century. For Uruguayan filmmakers there seems to be a multiple challenge: the avoidance of essentialist clichés and redundant myths of national identity while continuing to affirm a cultural autonomy that enlists literary as well as popular culture. There are the possibilities, either of becoming swamped or exoticized by the global market, or of appropriating the terms and conditions of that market and contributing to a new mythopoeia.

To conclude, it is worth remembering an expression, sometimes cited as a response to difficult times, from Obdulio Varela, captain of the Uruguay soccer team in the 1950s. Having just led his side to a stunning win over World Cup favorites Brazil in the 1950 maracanazo final in Rio de Janeiro, the phlegmatic and self-effacing captain spoke of the need to "empatar con la realidad" (tie, or level, with reality) in order to maintain clarity. Although it can boast no cinematic equivalent to this sporting triumph, Uruguay's film prospects are not entirely bleak; productions like *En la puta vida* and *25 watts* have proved the receptiveness of the Uruguayan public to audiovisual renderings of national life that are well conceived and technically sound. Nevertheless, the very notion of Uruguayan film is being challenged by the increasing (and imperative) use of foreign resources in coproductions. The need remains, however, to produce films that not only reflect and interpret external circumstances in artistic terms, but that are also able to cope with the economic and logistical conditions governing production. For Uruguay's filmmakers, a tie with current realities would be a victory in itself.

Endnotes

1. See the discussion of Álvarez's work at: http://www.geocities.com/gonzamen/proley.html

2. Alberto Moreira, "The Order of Order: On the Culturalism of (Latin American) Anti-Cultural Studies," Projects on New York University Website, April 1998 (http://www.nyu.edu/projects/IACSN/order.htm).

3. Jesús Martín-Barbero, "Aventuras de un cartógrafo mestizo en el campo de la comunicación," *Revista Latina de Comunicación Social*, 19, La Laguna (Tenerife), July 1999. http://www.ull.es/publicaciones/latina.

4. Guillermo Zapiola, writing in *El País*, Montevideo, March 30, 1985, quoted in Eugenio Hintz, *Historia y filmografía del cine uruguayo* (Montevideo: Ediciones de la Plaza, 1988), p.29 (our translation).

5. Zapiola, *El País*, April 13, 1985. Ibid., p. 33 (our translation).

6. Zapiola, *El País*, May 18, 1985. Ibid., p. 46 (our translation).

7. Juan Rial, "The Social Imaginary: Utopian Political Myths in Uruguay (Change and Permanence during and after the Dictatorship)," in Saúl Sosnowski and Louise B. Popkin (eds.), *Repression, Exile, and Democracy: Uruguayan Culture* (Durham, NC: Duke University Press, 1993), pp. 59–82.

8. Hugo Achugar, "La nación entre el olvido y la memoria: hacia una narración democrática de la nación," in Alvaro Rico (ed.), *Cuentas pendientes: dictadura, memorias y desmemorias* (Montevideo: Ediciones Trilce, 1966), pp. 15–28 (our translation).

9. Ibid. and Jorge Ruffinelli, "Uruguay: dictadura y re-democratización. Un informe sobre la literatura 1973–1985," *Nuevo Texto Crítico*, 3: 5, semester 1 (1990): 37–61.

10. Homero Alsina Thevenet, "Dos palabras sobre Uruguay y cine," in Alsina Thevenet (ed.), *Después del cine* (Montevideo: Eds. Trilce/Buenos Aires: Eds. de la Flor, 1990), pp. 104–107.

11. Horacio Quiroga, "El cine nacional," in Horacio Quiroga (ed.), *Arte y lenguaje del cine* (Buenos Aires: Losada, 1997 [1928]), pp. 201–207 (our translation).

12. Manuel Martínez Carril, "De ayer y hoy," *Cinemateca Revista*, 49 (1995), p. 52.

13. Mario Handler, interview with César di Candia, *Uruguay en la coyuntura*, July 8, 1999, p. 46 (our translation).

14. Gabriel Peveroni, "El Chevrolé y los pasos del cine uruguayo: al rescate de beat criollo," *Revista Posdata* (Montevideo), October 1998 (our translation).

15. Quoted in Hintz, *Historia y filmografía del cine uruguayo*, p. 32 (our translation).

16. Ibid.

17. Silvio Waisbord, "Status of Media in Argentina, Uruguay and Paraguay," in *Encyclopedia of International Media and Communications Outline*, 2000. (http://www.scils.rutgers.edu/~waisbord/ENCYCLOP.html).

18. Mario Benedetti, "El Uruguay que queremos," *El País* (Montevideo), November 12, 1999 (our translation).

19. Ruffinelli, "Uruguay: dictadura y re-democratización," p. 42.

20. Mario Benedetti, interview with Luis Mendieta Asensio, *Cambiole, 16*, 1243, (1995), pp. 76–77 (our translation).

21. Rial, "The Social Imaginary: Utopian Political Myths in Uruguay," p. 76.

22. Carina Perelli, "The Power of Memory and the Memory of Power," in Saúl Sosnowski and Louise B. Popkin (eds.), *Repression, Exile, and Democracy*, pp. 147–159.

23. Rial, "The Social Imaginary: Utopian Political Myths in Uruguay," p. 73–76.

24. Jorge Abbondanza, "Para analizar el hoy entre ayer y mañana," *Cinemateca Revista*, 30: February (1982), pp. 20–21 (our translation).

25. Manuel Martínez Carril, "Los posibles caminos que se cierran (y los que se mantienen)," *Cinemateca Revista*, 34: September (1982), pp. 10–12.

26. Ibid. (our translation).

27. Personal communication with the author, January 1998.

28. Quintín, review of *Otario* in *El Amante Cine* (Buenos Aires), November (1997), p.27 (our translation).

29. Fernando Gago, "Pero, ¿y dónde están los demás?," *Otrocine* (Montevideo), September/October (1997), pp. 4–5 (our translation).

30. Ibid. (our translation).

31. Mónica Lettieri, "*La historia casi verdadera de Pepita la Pistolera*: Una mirada solidaria en la cinematografía uruguaya," Paper prepared for *XI Congreso Internacional de Literatura Femenina Hispánica*, Ontario, 2000 (our translation).

32. José Feliciano is the famous blind, Grammy-award winning guitarist from Puerto Rico.

33. Cristina Peri-Rossi, "Cita en Montevideo," *El País* (Madrid), November 1, 1998 (our translation).

34. Danubio Torres Fierro, "Juan Carlos Onetti (1909–1994): una visión del Uruguay," *Vuelta* (Mexico), 212: July (1994), pp. 44–45 (our translation).

35. Oribe Irigoyen, "Este fue el año de un dirigible al rescate de imágenes perdidas," *Cinemateca Revista*, 49: January (1995), p. 39 (our translation).

36. Gabriel Peveroni, "Al rescate del beat criollo," *Revista Posdata*, October (1988) (our translation).

37. Interview with Leonardo Ricagni, "En Perspectiva," Radio El Espectador (Uruguay), January 31, 1997 (our translation).

38. Mario Handler, "Individuell und solidarisch," interview in *Film und Fernsehen*, 5 (1990), pp. 38–40.

39. Victoria Ruétalo, "Staying Afloat with *The Lifejacket is Under Your Seat*: Uruguayan Cinema at the Turn of the Millennium," paper presented at conference *CineLit 2000*, Portland State University, February 19, 2000.

40. Guillermo Zapiola, "Una propuesta auspiciosa," review of *El viñedo* in *Pantalla*, May 5, 2000 (http://www.pantalla.info/pel/1290.html).

41. Álvaro Casal, "Más allá del video, un cine con vocación internacional," *Cuadernos Hispanoamericanos*, 632: February (2003) pp. 75–78.

42. Perelli, "The Power of Memory and the Memory of Power," p. 156.

43. Ibid., p. 157.

44. Benedetti, interview with Luis Mendieta Asensio (our translation), pp. 76–77.

8

Mulata Cubana: The Problematics of National Allegory

Alison Fraunhar

In the 1960s the filmmaking theory and practice known as *Third Cinema* captured the world's imagination with its radical formal strategies and ideological concerns. Throughout the "developing" world, and in some cases in the first world, filmmakers sought to foreground the struggles of indigenous people and the formerly colonized in terms of autonomy and agency. In postrevolutionary Cuba, filmmakers became famous for their remarkable and sophisticated anticolonial and antiimperial revisionist filmmaking. Using formal strategies, including textual openness and self-reflexivity, combined with the neorealist desire to portray the true conditions of people's lives, Cuban filmmakers struck out against the legacy of colonialism and contemporary imperialist political and economic domination. However, one arena in which these films by and large did not contest the status quo was in the representation of women and their agency (both in front of and behind the camera). This gap is even more pronounced with regard to the participation of women of color.

An examination of the roles and characterizations of mulatas (women of mixed African and European heritage) in Cuban Third Cinema raises questions such as these: What political and cultural meanings does the mulata body bear? How is the mulata body mobilized as the site of the construction of national identity? Is the mulata body charged with the burden of national allegory? In order to address these questions, this chapter will analyze films that exemplify certain tendencies in Cuban cultural production. *Lucía* (Humberto Solas, 1969), *El otro Francisco* (*The Other Francisco*, Sergio Giral, 1974), *De cierta manera* (*One Way or Another*, Sara Gomez, 1977), and *Cecilia* (Humberto Solas, 1982) are films that participate in different stylistic traditions, with the earlier two reflecting a more revolutionary formal and ideological position than the later ones. The later two do the work of historical revision by reinscribing antislavery narratives. In this chapter, I examine how representations of the mulata in these films map out complex and unstable relations of race and identity in Cuba throughout its history from its colonial past to the uncertain present. While much of the literature on Cuban Third Cinema relates this cinematic discourse to other filmmaking (and representational) traditions, I analyze these films through the lens of postcolonial theory, situating them at the intersection of cultural production and nationalism, race and gender.[1] I explore the ways in which representations of race and gender in Cuban cinema work to support and disrupt notions of Cuban identity across the colonial/republican/revolutionary divide, bringing up the problematics of national allegory.[2] While different political and social struggles were foregrounded in each of these three distinct periods in Cuban history, they shared certain deeply ingrained cultural values that continue to be reified in cultural production.

An understanding of the historical roots of representational codes in Cuba will help to clarify these issues and reveal complicity with and resistance to cultural stereotypes in filmic rhetoric. In the 19th century, the literary and artistic style known as *costumbrismo* was the dominant mode of cultural production in Cuba, and established a visual and rhetorical system whose codes continue to be recognizable. In poetry, fiction, journalism, painting, and graphic arts, costumbrismo depicted details of dress, occupation, setting, and lifestyle in Cuba. In doing so it served to interpellate[3] subjects into Cubanidad ("Cubanness"), providing Cubans with a blueprint for becoming Cuban, and also served to reflect "the Cuban image" for the benefit of the rest of the world (primarily Europe and North America).[4] Social, economic, and protonationalist discourse in Cuba in the 19th century produced tropic figures that both iterated and contested relations of power, fear, and desire, such as the guajiro (rural peasant), the criollo (those born in Cuba, particularly of Spanish heritage), the dandified calesero (coachman), and the tragic/erotic mulata.[5] It was through the literary and visual production of costumbrismo that tropes of Cuban identity were enacted and inscribed in the national imaginary. These tropes have tremendous power in articulating and maintaining the colonial order through an intricate system of social and economic valuation. Tropic figures such as the mulata and the calesero continue to be widely understood within Cuba, and to bear cultural signification that helps to construct the image of Cuba abroad. These meanings persist even as they are contested in Third Cinema film production. Indeed, it is the legibility of the tropes and their persistence that has made them function as a structuring absence or a zero point, even when they are not directly indexed in film or other cultural productions.[6]

While all the various tropes I have noted are bearers of Cubanidad, I am concerned in this chapter with the mulata. Images of mulatas were (and continue to be) a privileged site for the production and projection of both erotic and nationalist desire. Beginning in the colonial era, the mulata's desirability to men across race and class boundaries threatened the social order that sought to maintain strict hierarchies of race and class. Since Cuba gained independence from Spain in 1898, the mulata has embodied a variety of tropic positions in the national discourse. From eroticized hybrid to autochthonous earth spirit, nationalist symbol, patron saint, and jinetera (prostitute or hustler), representations of the mulata have circulated through a constantly shifting social framework, embodying the tensions and paradoxes inherent in both colonial and postcolonial states.

The Colonial Discourse

In colonial Cuba the mixed-race mulata, and not the black man or woman, was most often portrayed as the female other to the (male) colonial self, who is "like but not quite," to use Homi Bhabha's phrase.[7] In Bhabha's discussion of colonial mimicry, this "like but not quite" signifies a colonial difference that can never be "as good as" (the colonial self), and at the same time, always produces an excess of meaning that is deeply destabilizing to the colonial order. Thus, the subaltern is an agent acting both within the colonial order and beyond its control. As we shall see later in this chapter, the film *Cecilia* demonstrates the complexity and paradox of colonial mimicry.

Although mimicry describes the operation of colonial complicity and resistance, the theoretical model that describes the *mulata* most accurately is the concept of hybridity.[8] While hybridity is perhaps the single most pervasive feature of colonialism, present in every colonial setting worldwide, it is important to keep in mind that the term nevertheless bears the stigma of its 19th-century usage in biology to refer to the grafting of two different plant species. This concept also evokes the 19th-century pseudoscientific notion that different races belonged to different biological species. Thus, the colonialist racism inherent in the term *hybridity* invests it with asymmetrical power relations, and some contemporary theorists have voiced concerns that it cannot overcome this original association.[9] Hybridity is embedded in the very etymology of the word *mulata*, which comes from the Latin mulus, or mule, the sterile hybrid of a horse and a donkey. (In the face of overwhelming evidence to the contrary, mulatas were believed in colonial discourse to be similarly infertile.)[10] The notion that different races corresponded to different species whose sexual union would fail to produce offspring was apparently stronger than the evidence of legions of racially mixed people in Cuba. Furthermore, this belief masked the profound anxiety caused by these illegitimate children of the master and the slave, whose resemblance to the white father was often uncanny.

Roberto Retamar takes up the idea of hybridity in his famous essay "Caliban," to claim that the America mestiza (mixed-race America) is ontologically hybrid.[11] In accord with Bhabha's analysis of hybridity as an ever-present "disruption" affecting both colonizer and colonized, Retamar reclaims hybridity as a mechanism for postcolonial agency. Instead of situating hybridity as a derivative discourse dependent on Europe, he says that the tools and the language of the colonizer can be appropriated for the liberation of the subaltern. The idea of crossing, embodied by the mulata, is fundamental to an understanding of Cuba, a nation that is imagined at the crossroads of indigenous America, Europe, and Africa.

The mulata bears the trace of what Walter Mignolo calls "colonial semiosis," or the epistemological gap between the colonizer and the colonized in which new cultural forms are forged.[12] Because the life experiences of women of color and images of the mulata circulate through multiple social and political discourses, her *signifiance* (or power to signify) in these discourses is a crucial element in the space between signifier and signified. It is in this gap that recognition (and misrecognition) across ethnic, racial, and gender lines takes place. Mignolo's colonial semiosis shares qualities with Bhabha's mimicry, and Fernando Ortiz's transculturation,[13] although each theory takes on a slightly different aspect of colonial contact and each teases out different conclusions.

The 19th-century origins of the mulata as a trope of desire are both revisited and contested in 20th-century cultural production, as the mulata also comes to represent and be represented as Cubanidad through nationalist signification. That is, she serves as a symbol for the unique Creole identity of Cuba, so eloquently articulated by José Martí as "Nuestra America mestiza" (our mixed-race America).[14] While in the colonial and republican cultural contexts the mulata body signifies, in a variety of configurations, the erotic, spirituality, and commodification, in early Third Cinema, she stands for the revolutionary zeitgeist.

Third Cinema and the Mulata

Third Cinema was institutionalized in Cuba after the revolution, through the creation of the Instituto Cubano de Arte y Industria Cinematografico (the Cuban Film Institute; ICAIC). Stylistically, Third Cinema incorporates strategies of distantiation and dialectical editing along with Italian neorealism and documentary style to disrupt the passive viewing and consumption of film texts encouraged by the "Classic Hollywood" cinema model. Early Cuban Third Cinema tried to break away from the kind of formal narrative conventions associated with the "Classic Hollywood" style, choosing instead to promote a filmmaking theory and practice known as "Imperfect Cinema."[15] This concept, formulated by Cuban filmmaker and theorist Julio García Espinosa, foregrounds cinematic reflexivity and emphasizes the means of production, including limited access to the material and technological resources that give Hollywood film its "natural" and "smooth" style.

Lucía *and* De cierta manera: *Embodying the Revolution*

The film *Lucía* both fulfils and exceeds the parameters of Third Cinema. Although produced with a limited budget, it depicts three historical eras in three distinct film styles, as the three separate narratives each trace the life of a different woman named Lucía from a given period in Cuban history, each of whom participates in the events that lead inexorably to the revolution. The first section of the film, "Lucía 1895," deals with a bourgeois woman during the War of Independence, and is shot in a fragmented, highly formalist Brechtian style. "Lucía 1933" is set in the milieu of the anti–Batista movement of the 1930s, and brings together elements of neorealism and the conventions of the film noir genre. It is in "Lucía 196?" that the rough, documentary style of Third Cinema is used. In this section, a young mulata whose personal narrative mirrors the young revolutionary nation, is engaged in an ideological battle to overcome ignorance and reactionary bourgeois attitudes as she struggles with her patriarchal husband for the right to learn how to read and write and work outside the home. This allegorical female is not the mother of the nation, or the guerrilla warrior, or even a member of the bourgeoisie working for social justice, but an uneducated rural peasant, a guajira who embraces the principles of the revolution as an organic intellectual. Adela Legrá, the actress who plays the role of this third Lucía, was herself an uneducated worker in an agricultural brigade with no formal training as an actress,

Film poster for *Lucía* (Humberto Solas, 1969).

who taught herself to read much like the character that she portrays. This figuration of the nation/female as struggling to overcome ignorance and oppression (race is not addressed explicitly in this text) is a departure from other more widely disseminated symbolic associations. The powerful "reality effect" of Third Cinema is doubled by the credibility that Legrá brings to her performance as the third Lucía.

Lucía explicitly uses women as the raw material out of which the nation is imagined and constructed. Feminist film scholar Catherine Benamou argues that this identification in Cuban cinema rhetorically exhorts women across race and class lines to identify with the protagonist, who is invariably racially typecast as a white to light mulata.[16] As Chandra Talpade Mohanty has demonstrated, "woman" as a totalizing category tends to privilege the concerns and values of white women located in the first world, or middle-class women in the third world.[17] In other words, the term *woman* as deployed by Western feminists is a hegemonizing concept, which may or may not intersect with the needs of women of color and the stakes for women in the third world or other marginalized settings. While clearly there are many concerns that are shared by women across geohistorical lines, this asymmetrical relation of knowledge skewed toward first-world production and consumption often suppresses the conditions and concerns of those "other," or even doubly or triply "other-ed" women.[18] Gender relations cannot be easily extricated from questions of race.

In the Cuban context, the totalizing category of "woman" normalizes whiteness or light skin color as natural by providing no dark-skinned protagonists for either the purpose of audience identification or the production of a more inclusive presentation of Cuban culture. One of the consequences of this is the erasure of race from the problematic of Cuban identity formation, posing the question: does racial ambiguity "dissolve" the problems of racism and racial inequality? Not only are women inextricably identified and articulated in relation to men, they are also coded racially and figured as metonyms of the nation, struggling for self-definition and auton-

Adela Legrá in *Lucía* (Humberto Solas, 1969).

omy. In the film *Retrato de Teresa* (*Portrait of Teresa*, Pastor Vega, 1979), Daysi Granados (the same actress who plays a mulata in the title role in *Cecilia*) plays the part of Teresa and is coded not as a mulata, but as a *tipa criolla* (Creole type).[19]

If *Lucía* is a film that presents "woman" as "a cultural and ideological composite ... constructed through diverse representational discourses,"[20] Sara Gomez's 1972 film *De cierta manera* focuses on "women"—"real, material subjects of their collective histories."[21] While both *Lucía* and *De cierta manera* were produced during what I am calling the first phase of Cuban Third Cinema, they are distinguished by an important difference. *Lucía* is a film about women made by a man.[22] In contrast, *De cierta manera* is the only feature film released by ICAIC in this period directed by a woman, who also happened to be of Afro-Cuban heritage. ICAIC, such a powerful force in the theory and practice of Third Cinema, consisted almost exclusively of middle-class white men at this time (and for many years afterwards). There is thus a need to evaluate and critique the impressive accomplishments of this cultural institution by interrogating how its racial and class makeup contributes to the representation of race and gender on screen, and the relations of knowledge signaled by this formation.

Mario Balmaceda and Yolanda Cuellar in *De cierta manera* (Sara Gomez, 1977).

In *De cierta manera*, the powerful formal strategies of Third Cinema are directed toward revealing the complexities involved in the negotiation of daily life, and overcoming the kinds of stereotypical representations made explicit in other films. Through a combination of documentary and fiction film, it advances a critique of the *machista* attitudes portrayed more romantically (and more histrionically) as both the legacy of colonialism and the conditions of nation building in the film *Lucía*. *De cierta manera* is sophisticated in terms of its film style and in its dialectically structured and open-ended narrative. At the same time, it is aesthetically situated within the framework of Imperfect Cinema, in that it rejects a polished, transparent "Classic Hollywood" cinema style. Gomez had already made several highly regarded short films, and she would certainly have been capable of producing a film in a seamless, "smooth" style had she chosen to do so.[23] Her aesthetic choice in *De cierta manera* is therefore quite deliberate.

Yolanda, the mulata protagonist of *De cierta manera*, is neither an illiterate peasant nor a decadent aristocrat.[24] She is a modern, urban, working woman, an elementary school teacher whose consciousness raising takes place through her real, not symbolic life, which revolves around work, sexual relations, family, political consciousness, and community. Both her lower-middle-class family background and her profession situate her in a particular, relatively privileged position, even in revolutionary society. Yolanda struggles, both in her work as a teacher in a slum renovation housing project and in her budding relationship with Mario, a worker from the same project, to overcome bourgeois attitudes and to be a good revolutionary. But perhaps the most important contribution of this film to breaking stereotypes is that Yolanda's relationship with Mario is not the primary lens through which her story is told; instead, Yolanda is presented as a complex person whose efforts to achieve political and social awareness are highlighted. Other contemporary Cuban films, even such revolutionary films as *Lucía, El otro Francisco* and *Retrato de Teresa,* frame the female protagonists through their trials with men and romantic situations. Benamou has noted that in both "Lucía 196?" and the later *Retrato de Teresa* the otherwise independent and socially minded protagonists lean on strong men as they struggle to maintain their sense of purpose and identity through personal and social crises.[25]

Cecilia *and* El otro Francisco: *Embodying History*

It is against the accomplishments of such formally and ideologically revolutionary films as *De cierta manera* and *Lucía* that we may contrast the cinematic codes operating in *Cecilia* and *El otro Francisco*. Rather than directly addressing the issues inherent in the revolution, as the former films do, *Cecilia* and *El otro Francisco* rework abolitionist novels from the 19th-century Cuban literary canon, embedding a revolutionary critique within historical melodrama. While still structurally and stylistically dazzling, certain representational tendencies emerge that undermine some of the advances achieved in the earlier films. *Cecilia* and *El otro Francisco* were produced only a few years later than *Lucía* and *De cierta manera*, yet they seem to show pronounced signs of a retreat from the revolutionary deconstruction of sexist attitudes in early Third Cinema, reiterating patriarchal colonial tropes even as they are positioned as an explicit critique of imperialism and colonialism. It is striking that Solas, who was capable of visualizing various women as historical agents in *Lucía*, makes a film a decade later that reduces the female characters to mannerist *costumbrista* tropes.

Not all films from the 1970s and 1980s present women in essentialized roles, however. Films such as *Retrato de Teresa* and *¡Plaff! O, demasiado miedo a la vida* (*Plaff, or Too Afraid of Life*, Juan Carlos Tabio, 1988) feature more individualized female protagonists who negotiate contemporary social conditions. However, the genre of historical films to which *Cecilia*, *El otro Francisco*, and *La última cena* (*The Last Supper*, Tomas Gutiérrez Alea, 1976) belong has received more critical and popular attention internationally, and thus carries more representational validity than do more contemporary narratives.[26] The persistence of patriarchal tropes is most pronounced in the representation of mulatas in these films.[27] They do revisionist work in their representation of male characters, both white and black; they are individualized and three-dimensional. But the mulata character never strays from the tropic boundaries of her designation as tragic/erotic.

The change in narrative and representational codes in *Cecilia* and other historical films of the later phase of Cuban Third Cinema signals a dramatic move away from the earlier focus on the dialectics of revolutionary nation building. Narrative and stylistic concerns shift from the public, the political, and the symbolic toward the personal and the melodramatic. The historical conditions during which this shift takes place in part explain its occurrence. In the 1960s, when women of all racial and class backgrounds were dramatically underrepresented in the workforce in general and in the film industry in particular, Third Cinema took on the task of representing women's struggle for full citizenship, as discussed above in relation to *Lucía* and *De cierta manera*. There are other possible reasons for this shift, however. For one, although Third Cinema and other avant-garde or experimental film forms met with great critical acclaim in Cuba and abroad, they have never reached as large a market as, or captured the popular imaginary as much as more classic narrative cinema.[28] In addition, after 1980, Cuban filmmakers participated in a greater number of international coproductions and the demands of competing in a global market in all probability led them to seek a more popular, less stylistically rigorous form. At the same time, the nearly two decades of experience that Cuban directors had acquired by the early 1980s provided technical and narrative expertise, and there was a desire among them to expand their representational possibilities beyond the constraints of formally demanding and politically allegorical filmmaking. This was, after all, the time of the ascendancy of the postmodern aesthetic, and the potential of a plurality of approaches to film form, not least the creation of narrative pleasure, was not lost on these directors.

Julianne Burton-Carvajal has forwarded another interpretation of the move toward the melodramatic in Cuban film of the second era.[29] She argues that melodrama is a genre particularly well suited to the expression of social anxiety through its unique ability to enact larger social issues through the personal, as takes place in both *Retrato de Teresa* and *¡Plaff!*. Melodrama is also well suited to performing historical allegory for the same reasons. For example, in *Retrato de Teresa*, the eponymous heroine is a factory worker who organizes cultural activities among her fellow workers while she struggles to maintain her domestic responsibilities.[30] Although she is a model revolutionary worker, it is her struggle to integrate her home and professional lives with her inner self that forms the dramatic tension of the story, as a personal narrative and as a mirror of the conditions and issues facing society at large. In melodrama, the tensions and paradoxes of daily living through personal and public conflicts find expression, and a linear, narrative film form can effectively raise awareness of such experiences.

In *¡Plaff!* Clarita is a young engineer struggling against an overblown and counterproductive bureaucracy in order to produce a cheap, efficient polymer that she has invented; she is supported and abetted by her baseball player husband.[31] The film is set in the late 1980s and Clarita is a child of the revolution. Frustrated and demoralized, she is openly critical of the government's bureaucratic hypocrisy and inefficiency. She clashes constantly with her mother-in-law Concha, who never questions the unfortunate side-effects of the revolution, particularly rampant inefficiency and an oppressive bureaucracy, but instead takes the sacrifices she has had to make (necessitated in part by this inefficiency) as a badge of honor and moral authority. However, although Concha is a stalwart and unquestioning revolutionary, the plot mechanism upon which the narrative depends is her reliance on santería, the syncretic Afro-Cuban religious practice that was outlawed by the revolution. Thus, in this film, in the eyes of the regime, the model revolutionary subject depends on "backward," antiprogressive religious superstition. The generational and ideological clash between the two women can be read as a microcosm of the problems in Cuban society as a whole in the late 1980s. Marvin d'Lugo suggests that *¡Plaff!* should be read as a film in which "the tradition of allegorizing the nation through female characters is intentionally parodied."[32] Yet he goes on to claim that, nevertheless, "the comic reduction of recent Cuban history to the conflict between mothers and daughters-in-law clearly functions as a way of addressing and engaging a Cuban audience in serious national issues."[33] As has been widely argued, through melodrama, social and political opinions, and positions that would otherwise be unacceptable can be expressed.[34]

After the first decade of the revolution, the societal emphasis shifted from bringing about the revolution to managing it. That is, instead of the struggle to achieve revolutionary consciousness, films and other cultural productions turned to an examination of how people lived their daily lives in contemporary society. Issues such as women's employment and equal participation in public and private life, housing, literacy, racism, and labor became pressing concerns. The strides made by organizations such as the Federation of Cuban Women in the first decade of the revolution certainly led to more varied screen representations of women, who were no longer simply portrayed as fighters and nation builders.

Although the improved position of women in postrevolutionary Cuban society had opened the door to a wider range of portrayals by 1982, on one level *Cecilia* seems to invoke the traditional or stereotypical representation of the mulata. The eponymous protagonist is unable to overcome her identification with passion, romance, and desire for whiteness, and her tragic end (madness and death) fulfills the criteria for melodrama and the containment of the sexual woman. As what we might call a neo-costumbrista text, the film is more concerned with the presentation of tropes and stereotypes than with the nuances of individual lives. Yet in some ways *Cecilia* critiques the stereotypes as it represents them. For example, Daysi Granados is clearly too old for the role of Cecilia, suggesting perhaps an ironic critique of the myth of the lascivious mulata. Or is it, as it has been reported, that Solas said simply that the director was unable to find someone better suited to the part?[35] Other critical voices, however, have suggested that Solas deliberately "transgressed" the literary text in order to critique and deconstruct it.

Both the film and the 19th-century novel on which it was based, *Cecilia Valdez o La Loma del Angel* (Cecilia Valdez or Angel's Hill, Cirilio Villaverde, completed in 1838, published in 1879), map out colonial desire along the lines suggested by Frantz Fanon in *Black Skin, White Mask*.[36] The complexities of desire and race are enacted and discussed throughout the novel from a clearly elite point of view. The white men desire black women for their purported sensuality (and they fear black men for the same reason), and the black women want the agency and security that is the domain of white social and economic power. In addition to the tensions and psychoses produced by the racial inequities of the colonial system, the novel extends its cultural psychoanalysis to the domestic realm, by examining incestuous desire and relations between half-brother and half-sister, and between mother and son. The destabilizing effect on men of Cecilia's beauty and her sexual desirability reveals the danger of the erotic mulata; she threatens the always unstable colonial social order. The threat of this desire is central to a myth that forms a cautionary subtext to *Cecilia*, namely the possibility of incest.[37] The fear, not entirely unfounded, of incest between the unwitting illegitimate children and legitimate heirs of the colonial elite displaces the more epistemic fear engendered by the colonial system, namely fear of slave uprising and rebellion, such as occurred in 1802 in Haiti. It demonstrates powerfully how colonialism and slavery blurred familial lines, inflicting tragic psychic violence upon all concerned. Formally, *Cecilia Valdez o La Loma del Angel* skillfully blends the fictional with the real, by presenting a narrative interwoven with identifiable people and acutely observed historical events set in extremely detailed settings. This adds to the "authenticity" of the text, and partially explains why it is revered as the great novel of Cubanidad.

A comparison of the film and the novel reveals how narrative alterations reframe the film text in a different cultural moment. For example, in the film's prologue, a Yoruba procession segues into a Semana Santa (Catholic Holy Week) parade, with African drumming overlapping liturgical chanting. While the parade is passing, the camera goes to a closeup of a very old Afro-Cuban woman seated in a doorway. She is recounting the legend of the honey-skinned goddess Ochún to her young granddaughter, who is beautiful and much lighter-skinned than the old woman. Ochún is the Yoruba deity of sensuality and pleasure; her Catholic counterpart, the Virgin de la Caridad, is known in Cuba as the virgencita de bronce (little bronze virgin) because of her skin color (another powerful visual link to the mulata.) Serving as a foundational story for the myth of the irresistibility of the mulata, and mirroring the narrative of Cecilia, this legend inscribes the mulata body in the Afro-Cuban cultural context instead of merely as a liminal figure caught between the African and European colonial social orbits. Thus, the mulata indexes both the Catholic patron saint of Cuba and the Yoruba goddess of pleasure, framing both spirituality and carnal desire. In contrast to the film's foregrounding of the Afro-Cuban context of the story, the novel opens with the old woman, Cecilia's grandmother, Chepa, trying to frighten the young Cecilia into obedience, using a cautionary tale of evil spirits and saints taken directly from medieval European folktales.

Cecilia, the beautiful mulata protagonist of the novel spurns the affections of the sincere mulato activist José Pimienta in favor of the decadent Creole mama's boy Leonardo Gamboa, who only wants an amorous liaison with her. Cecilia's vanity, social climbing, and desire for whiteness cause her tragic downfall. To draw upon Bhabha's argument, Cecilia is a "bad" subaltern who uses mimicry to try to cross social boundaries.[38] This is where she is the greatest threat to the colonial order, and although the novel was abolitionist and proindependence, it never even questioned social boundaries. But, in truth, Cecilia is both a "good" and a "bad" colonial subaltern, and for the same reasons. Insofar as she seeks to operate within the colonial social framework, she is a "good" subaltern who does not subvert the existing order. At the same time, as she seeks to improve her status and gain entry into a "better" racial and economic class, she transgresses a crucial colonial boundary, which makes her "bad." As a colonial subject, Cecilia is "bad" because she is motivated by social ambition to choose Leonardo over the valiant Pimienta, but she is "redeemed" by her activism. Even Leonardo, a predictable elite lothario, has compassion for the suffering of the unfortunate members of society, and becomes a willing accomplice in Cecilia's plan to shelter a former slave. Although Cecilia wants Leonardo to marry her, and by doing so bestow legitimacy, economic security, and "whiteness" on her, she nevertheless acts as a resourceful participant in the clandestine Afro-Cuban insurgency. The demands of the melodramatic form are satisfied by Cecilia's self-sacrifice after Leonardo's assassination by José Pimienta. A closer look reveals a variety of kinds of colonial ambivalence and contradiction.

By emphasizing the Afro-Cuban context of the story, the film attempts to challenge the privileged position of European cultural practice that is normalized in the novel. In addition to the prologue, several other scenes also situate Afro-Cuban religion in a crucial space of identity and empowerment. In one such scene, when in a trance, possessed by the hypermacho Yoruba deity Changó, Cecilia's friend Nemesia swears that he or she will never let the "white boy" have Cecilia; it is the voice of the Yoruba deity who "speaks for those who cannot speak."[39] The film thus seeks to assert subaltern history and community, claiming the mulata as a member of that community and working to overcome the representation of her as a liminal colonial body. By contrast, in the novel the jealousy and treachery provoked by the patriarchal and skin-color-based colonial social order are shown as Nemesia seeks to undermine Cecilia's romance with Leonardo because she desires him for herself. We can see a critique of colonialism at work in both texts, each of which responds to the zeitgeist of its time.

Cecilia articulates an historical revision that fetishizes colonial relations of power and the kinds of values and survival strategies engendered by the always unstable and always unbalanced social order, the object of its critique. While the critique of historical forces is explicit, the film less successfully contests the stereotypes (decadent criollo, desirable mulata) produced by and productive of the colonial paradigm, allowing these tropes to narrate the struggle for identity with predictably problematic results.

Dorotea in *El otro Francisco* occupies the same social space as Cecilia, since both are beautiful mulatas desired by white and black men. In contrast to Cecilia, Dorotea does not seek the privilege afforded by whiteness, and prefers her Afro-Cuban lover Francisco to the young master who pursues her. Like *Cecilia*, *El otro Francisco* is loosely based on an antislavery novel, *Francisco*, written by Antonio Suarez y Romero in the 1830s and published in 1888. The novel is a melodrama concerning the human consequences of slavery and the plantation system of production. *El otro Francisco* cleverly deconstructs the novel by bracketing scenes drawn from it with a voice-over narration and inserting scenes that present a more accurate representation of what life would have been like for slaves in 19th-century Cuba. *El otro Francisco* dismantles the ideology of imperialism and colonial power relations, in addition to critiquing the motives and practice of the elite abolitionists in 19th-century Havana. It is an example of what Michael Chanan calls "*cine rescate,*" or cinema of historical retrieval, which foregrounds the context of the novel's production.[40] The novel was written within the *tertulia* (elite literary salon) of Domingo del Monte, the abolitionist scion of a wealthy plantation-owning family. As the film ironically shows, the young intelligentsia of the tertulia talked passionately about freedom and liberty, ignoring the African slaves dressed in livery serving them cakes and liqueurs.

In the fictional narrative of *El otro Francisco*, the beautiful mulata Dorotea is a stereotypical erotic/tragic figure, caught between her black lover Francisco and her abusive white owners. She is a "good" subaltern, to use Bhabha's term; one that has incorporated the values of Christianity, humility, and fidelity and wants only to marry Francisco, the father of her baby. Although she is "good," she must nevertheless be punished for the threat that her desirability represents to the male/colonial psyche. Dorotea's selfish mistress Sra. Mendizábal is threatened by the former's desire to marry Francisco because she does not want to lose her devoted and humble servant. Additionally, the lust felt by Sra. Mendizábal's son Ricardo for Dorotea is problematic from several standpoints. It is a problem for Sra. Mendizábal because her love for her son oversteps the purely maternal, and her motivation is jealousy as well as selfishness. Here we see a mother-son relationship that crosses the filial boundary just as does the relationship between Doña Rosa and Leonardo in *Cecilia*. Ricardo's lust for Dorotea overrides his sense of humanity and drives him to abuse her and Francisco (who was not only his slave but, as we are shown through flashbacks, formerly his childhood companion). All of these narrative strands passionately demonstrate the ways in which the institution of slavery degrades and oppresses all those concerned, not only its principal victims. While lust is a common *fabula* (story) element,[41] colonial psychosis, formed out of desire, fear, and asymmetrical power relations shifts the story from a personal tragedy to a larger social narrative space.

Francisco is the most complex and fascinating character in *El otro Francisco*, for although he is no less explicitly a colonial trope than the other characters, he maps out a greater range within colonial power relations. Francisco's narrative journey takes him from relative comfort (as a *calesero* or coachman, the most desirable household position and the least dangerous job for a slave) to the abjection of a stripped and broken sugar cane worker (the other extreme in the hierarchy of slave labor). Through this trajectory, Francisco traces both positions mapped out in Roberto Retamar's reading of the Caliban/Ariel dyad from Shakespeare's *The Tempest* through a Caribbean colonial lens.[42] Both are servants of Prospero, the Shakespearean colonizer. Ariel is the house-boy; spirit of the air (the intellectual or cultural producer, always working in the service of the elite) and Caliban is the "brutish" native whose wretched and oppressed existence is overdetermined by Prospero and the demands of the colonial machine. Writing against U.S. imperialism and in support of the Cuban Revolution, Retamar retrieves Caliban from the colonizer's vocabulary to embody, as the mulata does, the spirit of "*America mestiza.*"

Concluding Remarks: The Erotic Body and the Nation

Through the analysis of these different film texts we can see that the mulata body has been portrayed through different modes of cinematic representation to serve different ideological ends. Thus, she has served to confront prerevolutionary class-based and racial prejudices and embody the goals of the revolution, and to be both the tragic victim of the colonial system and the sly agent operating within that system. And finally, she has represented the nation struggling to maintain its revolutionary focus along with the demands of everyday life, as well as to self-reflexively critique this allegory.

Cuban Third Cinema greatly increased the range of representations available to women, and the eroticized mulata is by no means a mere mnemonic trace of the colonial past. In the two decades following the revolution, women were often portrayed in film as markers of the nation, both as metaphors for large social movements and as individuals making and responding to social change. However, since the fall of the Soviet Union forced new strategies for economic survival on Cubans both at home and in the global marketplace, the mulata body has been reinscribed as a libidinal zone. This body circulates in the neocolonial discourse of globalization as a signifier of desire in the burgeoning sex tourism industry of Cuba. In this discourse the mulata operates not as the colonial other, but as the embodiment of a tropical landscape constituted for neoimperial pleasure. No longer the plantation, Cuba becomes instead the playground for neocolonial leisure and fantasy, and race and desire are constructed along different but no less crucial lines. Perhaps *Cecilia* is, after all, prescient in its visual and textual fetishization of the mulata body.

Although the improvement in women's status in Cuba was one reason for the epistemological shift in cinematic representation away from national allegories to more complex negotiations of the personal and the political, other possible reasons for the endurance and appeal of characters like Cecilia and Dorotea call for further investigation. Cuba's relative prosperity in the 1980s led to the relaxation of revolutionary rhetorical and visual strategies, and the popular reception of different film styles has undoubtedly contributed to the prevalence of more conventional narrative forms. In addition to the economic constraints imposed as a result of the fall of the Soviet Union, this event marks another shift, from a modernist worldview to a postmodern one in which the idea of the nation is complicated by exile, diaspora, and a fragmented, heterogeneous sense of national identity. While the mulata body continues to operate as a signifier of "Cubanness," it has lost the universalizing allegorical power assigned to it in films made during the modernist heyday of Third Cinema.

Endnotes

1. See Jim Pines and Paul Willemen, *Questions of Third Cinema* (London: BFI, 1990), and Michael Chanan, *The Cuban Image: Cinema and Cultural Politics in Cuba* (London: BFI, 1985).

2. I refer to Frederic Jameson's famous essay "Third-World Literature in the Era of Multinational Capitalism," Aijaz Ahmad's response to Jameson, and Ismail Xavier's essay "Historical Allegory," in order to situate the relation between gendered and racialized bodies and third-world anticolonialist nationalism. Frederic Jameson, "Third-World Literature in the Era of Multinational Capitalism," in *Social Text*, 15 (1986), pp. 65–88; Aijaz Ahmad, *In Theory: Classes, Nations, Literatures* (London: Verso, 1994, see especially chapter 3, "Jameson's Rhetoric of Otherness and the 'National Allegory'"); Ismail Xavier, "Historical Allegory" in Robert Stam and Toby Miller (eds.), *A Companion to Film Theory* (London: Blackwell, 1999), pp. 34–50.

3. I use Louis Althusser's term to describe the process by which people are "hailed," called to believe and identify with the ideology of a particular national or cultural group. See his essay "Ideology and Ideological State Apparatuses (Notes towards an Investigation)" in Louis Althusser, *Essays on Ideology* (London: Verso, 1984).

4. I borrow the phrase "the Cuban image" from the title of Michael Chanan's book (see endnote 1), which is to date the most comprehensive and thoughtful analysis of the history of Cuban cinema.

5. The mulata is not of course unique to Cuba, and a comparative analysis of racial mixing and its cultural meaning in other Caribbean islands, Brazil, and the United States would prove useful and illuminating.

6. Noel Burch has advanced the concept of the "zero point" of cinema to discuss both the transparency of the "Classic Hollywood" cinema style, and its function as a standard against which all other cinematic production is measured. See Noel Burch, *Theory of Film Practice* (London: Routledge, 1973). Likewise, cultural norms, stereotypes, and tropes function as "zero points" for understanding cultural codes.

7. See Homi Bhabha, "Of Mimicry and Man," in *The Location of Culture* (London: Routledge, 1994), pp. 85–92.

8. Robert Young takes up the notion of hybridity in *Colonial Desire: Hybridity in Theory, Culture and Race* (London: Routledge, 1995). See also Ania Loomba, *Colonialism/Postcolonialism* (London: Routledge, 1998) and Bill Ashcroft, Gareth Griffiths, and Helen Tiffin, *Post-Colonial Studies: The Key Concepts* (London: Routledge, 2001).

9. See, for example, Ashcroft et al., *Post-Colonial Studies*; Ahmad, *In Theory: Classes, Nations, Literatures*; and Chandra Talpade Mohanty, "Under Western Eyes," in Chandra Talpade Mohanty, Ann Russo, and Lourdes Torres (eds.), *Third World Women and the Politics of Feminism* (Bloomington: University of Indiana Press, 1991), pp. 462–487.

10. An alternative etymology of the term comes from Ernesto Pichardo's 1854 *Diccionario Casi Rasonado*; in it he attributes the word *Muslim* or in Spanish *musulman* as the root of mulata, but this explanation is less than convincing.

11. Roberto Retamar, "Caliban" in *Caliban and Other Essays* (Minneapolis: University of Minnesota Press, 1989).

12. Walter Mignolo, *The Darker Side of the Renaissance* (Ann Arbor: University of Michigan Press, 1995), pp. 8–9.

13. See Fernando Ortiz, *Cuban Counterpoint* (Durham, NC and London: Duke University Press, 1995).

14. Martí published his famous declaration of American identity while in exile, in *La Revista Ilustrada de Nueva York*, January 10, 1891, p.

15. Julio García Espinosa's essay, "For an Imperfect Cinema," in Robert Stam and Toby Miller (eds.), *Film and Theory: An Anthology* (London: Routledge, 2000), pp. 287–299, remains one of the foundational texts of Third Cinema theory. Espinosa was a filmmaker as well as a theoretician, and also served as head of ICAIC in the 1980s.

16. Catherine Benamou, "Cuban Cinema: On the Threshold of Gender," *Frontiers*, 15: 1 (1994).

17. Mohanty, "Under Western Eyes."

18. A woman is a social "other," first as a result of her gender, but is doubly an other if she is from the low or working class. If she is located in a third world or southern hemi-

spheric position, she is "othered" once more, and yet again if she is from a minority or marginal social group or sexual identity within her country.

19. To the best of my knowledge, Daysi Granados does not speak publicly about whatever Afro-Cuban heritage she has. This is not entirely surprising, because most Cubans have some Afro-Cuban ancestry and therefore racial ambiguity is normalized and the issues associated with it are elided. Her role as Teresa, coded as a *tipa criolla*, further reinforces this ambiguity. Granados goes on to play Cecilia Valdez, and in playing a woman of mixed race, and such a memorable one as Cecilia, she is ever after explicitly associated with the trope of the eroticized mulata. Through this racial ambiguity, Granados represents the legacy of colonial fear and the contradictions of national identity.

20. Mohanty, "Under Western Eyes," p. 464.

21. Ibid.

22. Along with Pastor Vega, Humberto Solas, the director of both *Lucía* and *Cecilia*, is known as a director of "women's" films.

23. Chanan, *The Cuban Image*, p. 271.

24. We can question whether or not Yolanda can be considered the protagonist of *De cierta manera*; in the different vignettes that make up the film, we are also shown the point of view of the neighborhood association, the workers' meeting, and Mario.

25. Benamou, "Cuban Cinema."

26. There are several likely reasons for this. Both *¡Plaff!* and *Retrato de Teresa* were not as widely distributed internationally as *Lucía* and *El otro Francisco*, and have been seen less abroad. In addition, *¡Plaff!* and *Retrato de Teresa* can be seen as films that make a slightly awkward transition from the more explicitly formal style of *Lucía* and *El otro Francisco* to a more linear realist style. This shift is evident in several other films of the period, including Tomás Gutiérrez Alea's follow-up to Gomez's *De cierta manera*, *Hasta cierto punto* (Up to a Certain Point, 1983).

27. The exception is *La última cena*, an exemplary text of cinematic historical revision and postcolonial critique, but which has very few female characters.

28. The most telling illustration of the poor popular reception of formalist or avant-garde films may be the case of Sergei Eisenstein. After producing the most rigorous and memorable film texts of Russian formalism, his work and theory underwent an epistemological shift toward socialist realism, with its proletariat heroes and linear, teleological narratives, at least partially in response to the lack of popular success (and strong official criticism) of his earlier films.

29. See Julianne Burton-Carvajal, "Portrait(s) of Teresa: Gender Politics and the Reluctant Revival of Melodrama in Cuban Film," in Diane Carson, Linda Ditmar, and Janice R. Welch (eds.), *Multiple Voices in Feminist Film Criticism* (Minneapolis: University of Minnesota Press, 1994), pp. 305–317.

30. Teresa is characterized as a *tipa criolla* or typical Creole beauty (a term borrowed from costumbrismo), and yet is played by Daysi Granados, wearing a scarf on her head in an Afro-Cuban fashion. Seven years after she played Cecilia, Granados is still clearly associated in the popular imaginary with the figure of the mulata.

31. Clarita's mother-in-law is played by the ubiquitous Daysi Granados, who once again blurs racial certainties not only is she darker than her fair daughter-in-law, she is also involved in Afro-Cuban religious practices.

32. Marvin d'Lugo, "Transparent Women: Gender and Nation in Cuban Cinema," in John King, Ana M. López, and Manuel Alvarado (eds.), *Mediating Two Worlds: Cinematic Encounters in the Americas* (London: BFI, 1993), pp. 279–290, (p. 287).

33. Ibid.

34. See, for example, Marcia Landy (ed.), *Imitations of Life: A Reader on Film and Television Melodrama* (Detroit: Wayne State University Press, 1991) and Christine Gledhill (ed.), *Home is Where the Heart is: Studies in Melodrama and the Women's Film* (London: BFI, 1987).

35. Francisco Rey Alfonso, personal communication, July 2001.

36. Frantz Fanon, *Black Skin, White Mask*, trans. Charles Lam Markham (New York: Grove Press, 1967).

37. There is a significant body of literature on the subject of interracial incest, which is a recurrent theme in abolitionist literature, and forms a subtext or undercurrent to colonial racial anxiety. See Verena Martinez-Alier, *Marriage, Class and Color in Nineteenth-Century Cuba: A Study of Racial Attitudes and Sexual Values in a Slave Society* (Ann Arbor: University of Michigan Press, 1988), and Vera Kutzinski, *Sugar's Secrets: Race and the Erotics of Nationalism* (Charlottesville and London: University of Virginia Press, 1992).

38. Bhabha, "Of Mimicry and Man."

39. Gayatri Spivak, "Can the Subaltern Speak?," *Wedge*, 7/8 (1985), reprinted in Cary Nelson and Lawrence Grossberg (eds.), *Marxism and the Interpretation of Culture* (Urbana: University of Illinois Press, 1988), pp. 271–310.

40. Chanan, *The Cuban Image*, p. 165.

41. The idea of fabula or story works with *syuzhet* or plot to allow the viewer to construct a narrative. These notions, crucial to film analysis, are derived from Russian formalism, and were originally used to theorize literature. Fabula deals with character and motivation, the engine that drives the plot forward.

42. Retamar, *Caliban*.

9

Brazil through Hollywood's Gaze: From the Silent Screen to the Good Neighbor Policy Era

Lisa Shaw and Maite Conde

The cinema often permits us to see how a nation and its people are perceived through the eyes of another, but the impact of external forces, such as political motivations and economic strategies, on the representation of the "other" on screen is sometimes far from obvious. Less obvious still are the effects of screen images from abroad on a given country's sense of self. Various important studies have been carried out on Hollywood's depiction of Latin America,[1] and more specifically, on the image of the Latina.[2] Naturally, in this context the celluloid persona of Carmen Miranda has been a recurrent concern, but specific analyses of the portrayal of Brazil are few in number.[3] Sérgio Augusto provides an overview of Hollywood's vision of Brazil since the 1930s, paying particular attention to geographical and ethnic blunders,[4] and there has been considerable interest in the consequences of this vision in terms of the way in which Brazilians have seen and depicted themselves.[5] The aim of this chapter is to trace the evolution of Brazil's cinematic image in order to illustrate how the stock motifs and trite themes associated with Hollywood's "Brazil" as far back as the silent era were later appropriated as a pivotal element of the U.S. courting of Brazil and other Latin American nations during the "Good Neighbor Policy" years. The ways in which Brazilians reworked Hollywood images of themselves as emblems of national self-definition and for commercial ends will also be considered.

Ignoble Savages and Spanish Accents in Silent Films and Talkies

In the silent era, the jungles of Brazil and their "cut-throat savages" were a common motif in Hollywood, and featured in Pathe's *The Brazilian Ring* of 1909 and Selig's *In the Amazon Jungle* of 1915. The latter is probably best remembered for its "Spanish" characters, who were placed in the depths of the Brazilian Amazon in search of rubber. Although some of their names were Portuguese, they were apparently not: Characters include "Silva, a young Spaniard" and Arrival, "a Spanish half-breed."[6] In *The Jungle Child* (Triangle, 1916) both the savagery of tribal peoples in Brazil and the country's supposed "Spanish" heritage are reiterated; a villain from the United States discovers a winsome woman in charge of an Amazonian village. On discovering that she is in fact the lost heiress of a wealthy Spanish family, he marries her for her inheritance. When she overhears his motivation for their marriage she reverts to her tribal ways and violently chokes him to death with her bare hands. In the face of such clichés and inaccuracies, a North American of Brazilian descent, one Francisco Silva Jr., was prompted to send the following letter of complaint to the *New York Times* in 1925, published on March 17:

> Some months ago I saw a motion picture supposed to have been taken in Rio de Janeiro, Brazil. However, the "Rio" shown in it was like a Spanish village some centuries ago, with a Spanish aspect in everything — even Spanish names and phrases were used in it.... I feel greatly surprised at this ignorance of geography when I remember that any seven-year-old child in Brazil knows that in the United States English is spoken, that New York is not a Federal Capital and that New England is not a British State.... Spanish is not even spoken in Brazil.

These geographical and ethnic blunders would resurface in Hollywood film well into the 1940s, as will be discussed later.

The equation of all things Brazilian with barbarous behavior even found its way into documentary shorts in the pretalkie era. Powers's *In Monkey Land* of 1917 centered on the rare saki monkey of Brazil, and declared that "the tiny Brazilian marmoset has a savage countenance." In the same vein, Educational Films Corp's *The Living Book of Nature* (1917) dedicated two episodes to the "wild dogs" of Brazil, Argentina, and the Andes, namely the vicuña, the llama, and the alpaca, which were given the following description: "Their grotesque forms cause them to look more like animated caricatures than wild animals."[7]

With the arrival and consolidation of the talking cinema in the late

1920s and early 1930s, Hollywood's version of the Amazon rainforest continued to be as dangerous and uninviting as ever. *Matto Grosso* (Principle Adventure Pictures, 1933) depicted the area as follows:

> Nature in this strange region is revealed at her most fantastic in the gargoyle features and twisted bodies of the native fauna. Some of the animals must be seen to be believed. The company includes the tapir, half horse and half rhinoceros; the jabiru, a huge stork with a bright scarlet collar [a native legend told that a company of jabiru, approaching a Spanish encampment at night put the invaders to rout by their resemblance to uniformed soldiers] a hideous fish called the piranha, with a bull dog face and jaws that can bite a man's foot off, boot and all; a giant bat with vampirish tendencies and extraordinary [*sic*] repulsive features and tiny armadillos which become quite spheroid like baseballs at the approach of an enemy. The natives, an ugly and malformed race are the least interesting of the jungle sights.[8]

Law of the Tropics (Warner, 1941) combined a rather trite love story, involving two Anglo characters, one a rubber company representative and the other a tarnished lady, with a tropical location in the rainforest. The Technicolor travel short, *A Hunter's Paradise* (Sports Parade/Warners, 1942) took its audience back to the Mato Grosso in search of the South American tiger, and "we are privileged to get glimpses of the many strange beasts and birds that inhabit this unusual country."[9] Both comical and fearsome creatures are the stars of *Jacare* (United Artists-Mayfair, 1942), an expeditionary picture filmed in Brazil, described by *Variety* as a "typical 'bring-'em-back-alive' jungle thriller," which centers on a series of adventures and struggles to capture a range of extraordinary beasts.[10] Hollywood's penchant for the mysterious and often terrifying inhabitants of Brazil's rainforests continued into the late 1940s and early 1950s: *Urubu* (United Artists–World Adventures, 1948) took the form of a photographic record of an expedition through the Mato Grosso *selva* (jungle), which culminates in an encounter with the Urubu tribe, an allegedly murderous indigenous group which has kidnapped a white girl;[11] *Amazon Quest* (Film Classics-Agay [Max Alexander], 1949) was described as "a routine jungle actioner ... replete with tropical safaris, savages, tom-toms and wild life, all tied together by a strained adventure yarn"[12]; *Jungle Headhunters* (RKO, 1951) was yet another account of an expedition into remote South American rainforests, which focused on the head shrinking practiced by the feared Jivaro tribe of Brazil and the deadliness of the piranha fish.[13]

Rio de Janeiro as City of Desire

Counter to Hollywood's predilection for Brazilian bandits and savages, the city of Rio de Janeiro emerged in the silent era as a trope of sophistication and exotic natural beauty, a trend that would reach its apogee in the Good Neighbor Policy A-movies, both musical spectaculars and melodramas. The U.S. Navy Department's thinly veiled recruitment film, *Rolling Down to Rio* (1922), made only passing reference to points of interest in the city of Rio, but traded on the breathtaking backdrop of the Guanabara bay during the hundredth anniversary celebrations of Brazilian independence. Pathe's *Below the Equator*, a Fox Variety travelogue made in 1927, depicted the Brazilian capital as "not only a thoroughly modern city in every respect, but a veritable fairyland when it comes to scenic beauty. The towering mountains and hills in and around the city offer vistas of unusual magnificence. In fact this is a regular dream city that is unique among the world capitals."[14] In the 1930s, Rio de Janeiro retained its iconic status as city of wonder, as in MGM's *Rio the Magnificent*, a James Fitzpatrick "Traveltalk," released in 1934. Similarly, Twentieth Century Fox's *Touring Brazil* (Magic Carpet Movietone, 1936), the release of which conveniently coincided with President Roosevelt's trip to Rio as part of his Pan-American tour, "featured Rio's magnificent harbor" and "the most celebrated carnival in the world," as well as religious shrines, spectacular views of tropical scenery, and the ubiquitous "warfare with alligators."[15] This trend would reach its peak during the Second World War, as Hollywood was mobilized in support of the Good Neighbor Policy. *Over the Andes* (FitzPatrick Traveltalk/ MGM, 1943) took its audience over the mountain range by air, beginning in Valparaiso and ending in Rio de Janeiro, with views of the airliner's route in glorious Technicolor. "Unfolded is scenery made to order for the color camera. Glimpses of life in Rio add to the film's interest."[16]

Although Rio's charms helped to remedy Brazil's dark and menacing cinematic image on the silver screen, it remained a land peopled by male thugs and lascivious women of loose morality. The city of Rio was established as a place where sexual license and transgression were virtually inevitable, particularly for Anglo visitors, a further theme that would characterize many of the Good Neighbor productions. In Gotham's *The Girl from Rio* (1927), for example, a young English gent played by Walter Pidgeon succumbs to the charms of a Brazilian woman named Lola. She is described in the titles as "a skilled coquette" and a "professional breaker of hearts," who just happens to be the mistress of the richest man in Brazil. The latter at one stage plots to eliminate his rival with the help of a gang of local ruffians. In the silent movie *A Girl in Every Port* (Fox, 1928), Rio is just one of many seaports where two sailors enjoy shore leave to the full. The lady who is loved and left in Rio goes by the Spanish name of Chiquita, played by Maria Casajuana, in yet another case of linguistic confusion. As early as 1930 Rio was synonymous with illicit trysts and the chosen destination for runaway lovers. In the melodrama *Derelict* (Paramount, 1930) two sailors fall for the same cabaret singer whom they see perform in Havana (in the film there are identification shots of the Cuban capital, as well as of Rio). To win her over, one of them offers to take her to Rio with him, but later he spurns her advances. The lovers are finally reunited on the seas off Rio, having survived a collision with another ship and a tropical storm, a fitting metaphor for the turbulent passions that the locale awakens.

The advent of sound did little if anything to dispel the myth of carnal temptations lying in wait for foreign visitors. In MGM's *Strangers May Kiss* of 1931, a worldly international newsman is called away to Rio de Janeiro, leaving his common-law wife behind in Mexico, and it is then all too apparent that he intends to continue to enjoy his bachelor lifestyle in Brazil's then capital. Hollywood characterized male members of Brazil's elite as inveterate womanizers, such as the catalogue of unscrupulous coffee millionaires who pursue the alluring Anglo woman in the Paramount melodrama *Fatal Lady* of 1936.

Flying Down to Rio *with a Pan-American Crew*

The Brazilian actor Raul Roulien starred in a variety of Hollywood movies in the 1930s, but usually played a Spanish American.[17] The most notable exception was his portrayal of a rich Brazilian in RKO's expensively staged *Flying Down to Rio* of 1933, the first U.S. musical comedy set in Brazil, which paved the way for the Good Neighbor musicals produced by Twentieth Century Fox in the 1940s. As Alfred Charles Richard Jr. writes, "the scenario reflected twenty years of accepted stereotyping blended with Hollywood's bizarre conception of upper class Brazilian café society life."[18] The year 1933 marked the beginning of the Good Neighbor Policy era, and according to Catherine Benamou, the purpose of *Flying Down to Rio* was, "to create an impression of *latinidad* that would be acceptable to both North and Latin American audiences while loosely enacting the diplomatic gestures towards Latin Americans mandated by the new foreign policy."[19] It therefore did not matter that actors of other nationalities played the "Brazilian" characters. In *Flying Down to Rio* the

Mexican actress Dolores Del Río played Belinha Rezende, a member of Brazil's elite, who is courted by both a North American band leader and aviator named Roger Bond (played by the very blond Jean Raymond) and a wealthy Brazilian playboy, Julio (played by the dark-haired Roulien). In true Hollywood tradition, the inhabitants of Brazil, with the exception of high society, are portrayed as buffoons with white skin, and the Latin beauty rejects the amorous advances of her fellow countryman in favor of the charms of her Anglo suitor. As a review of the movie in *Variety* says, "Miss Del Rio looks well, as also Mr. Raymond. But both seem in just for their looks, a blonde boy against a dark girl."[20] Brazilian women are once again synonymous with powers of seduction and lascivious ways, and when Belinha first dances with Bond one of her blonde-haired female companions from the United States suggestively complains: "What have the South Americans got below the Equator that we haven't?"

An advertisement for the movie, which appeared in *Variety*, declared:

> For the first time north of the equator ... they're doing the Carioca, the tantalizing, mesmerizing Brazilian Dance Sensation that soon will be driving America Melody Mad! See it! ... And a thousand other wonders in a spectacle set to rhythm, that fills the earth with beauty, laughter, song and dance ... and sweeps to eye-staggering sensation as the Flying Armada of Beauty soars on wings of giant planes down heaven's twinkling pathway! Nothing like it has ever been done! It makes your fondest dreams of musical romance come true![21]

The "carioca" dance was invented for the film, and its somewhat eclectic choreography centered on the male and female dance partners pressing their foreheads together. Audiences in Rio de Janeiro were left with bemused smiles on their faces when the film premiered in the then capital, but the screen audience is delighted by the performance, and Fred Astaire and Ginger Rogers, starring opposite each other for the first time and in supporting roles, are inspired to join in, although even they cannot master the delicate forehead move.[22] The dances that featured in this film and other Good Neighbor productions were often synthetic amalgams of Latin American popular forms to which various "national" origins were attributed ex post facto.[23]

The city of Rio was depicted in a most flattering light in *Flying Down to Rio*, as a review in the *New York Times* attests: "The settings are very striking and there are several clever process scenes which help to reveal that those responsible for the film have succeeded in giving an unusually good impression of Rio de Janeiro, for the actual photographs of that city are blended with those of studio structures."[24] All of the action was shot on studio sets, with picturesque views of Rio inserted into the background by way of the matte process. As the action moves to Brazil's capital, several shots of Rio are shown in quick succession: Guanabara bay, Santos Dumont airport, modern buildings in the affluent Zona Sul beachside districts, well-dressed crowds in the city center, the Municipal Theater, the Jockey Club, Sugar Loaf Mountain, the Botanical Gardens, and various views of the coastline. Most of the activity in Rio centers on the luxurious Hotel Atlantico, the exterior of which bears a distinct resemblance to the Copacabana Palace hotel, and the urbane sophistication of the city is similarly evoked in the elitist café from which Fred Astaire's character is forcibly ejected by the attentive staff.

The emphasis in the title of the film on airline travel (and implicitly on the proximity of Rio to the United States) is reinforced via the repeated appearance of aircraft, particularly in the opening credits and in the spectacular finale, in which planes soar over the city with young women performing acrobatic acts on their wings. Travel themes are also reflected in the set designs and choreography of the production numbers. The titles of Twentieth Century Fox's Good Neighbor musicals starring Carmen Miranda would take up this idea again, in an effort to foster closer links between the two Americas and to promote tourism in Latin America by stressing the ease with which U.S. citizens could travel to these exotic locations. South American nations were "civilized" and blessed with modern communications, such as frequent air and sea connections, telegraph services (Belinha sends two telegrams from the U.S. to Brazil in *Flying Down to Rio*), and sophisticated diplomatic representation.[25] It is no coincidence that in 1933, the year in which *Flying Down to Rio* was released, Pan-American Airlines expanded its routes to include South America, with Rio as its most popular destination. (This direct link between film and travel was to continue well into the 1940s and early 1950s and was exploited during the war years in particular, as discussed later with reference to the film *Now Voyager*.)

Black actors appear only in the minority in certain production numbers in *Flying Down to Rio*, and when Bond lands his plane in Haiti. There Belinha spies a group of bare-chested black men and exclaims "wild men, cannibals," mistaking the tourist resort for an island inhabited by savages, who turn out to be bellboys from an adjacent hotel and a well-spoken golfer who is out for a little practice at Port-au-Prince golf club. The previous Hollywood image of Brazil as one great uncivilized and inhospitable jungle is here transposed to the island of Belinha's "white" imagination, and in contrast Rio is packaged as a less "ethnic" and thus "safe" destination for Anglo travelers.[26]

The War Years and the Intensification of the Good Neighbor Policy

The fascination with Latin America evidenced in *Flying Down to Rio* heightened during the late 1930s and the 1940s. Between 1939 and 1947, Hollywood films featuring Latin American stars, music, locations, and stories flooded U.S. and international markets. By 1943, for example, 30 films with Latin American themes or locales had been released and 25 more were in production, and by 1945 84 films with Latin American subjects had been produced.[27] The dominance of Latin America within Hollywood movies during these years was a direct consequence of the vigorous implementation of the Good Neighbor Policy.

During the Second World War, Latin America was the only market available for exploitation, and the continent thus became a key focus for the exportation of U.S. consumer goods and for the importation of cheaper raw materials. Many of the South American countries, however, held dubious political positions with regard to the Axis powers. Argentina, Paraguay, Uruguay, and Brazil had all revealed enthusiasm for the recently emerged fascist regimes in Europe. Their significant Italian and German immigrant populations added to concerns over the political allegiances of these nations. Brazil was a focus for U.S. interest in light of both the economic and the political contexts, and the Good Neighbor Policy was implemented just three years after the coup that brought Getúlio Vargas to power in 1930. The Vargas regime (1930–1945) strengthened Brazil's commercial potential via rapid industrialization and the reorganization of the agricultural economy. In the run-up to the Second World War, Vargas openly sided with the fascist dictators of Germany and Italy, maintaining strong links with Germany in particular. With the outbreak of the war in Europe, the State Department focused its sights on Brazil, with its fascist-style Estado Novo or (New State), established in 1937, its trade links with Germany, its Italian and German populations in the south of the country, and its strategic location.

Central to Franklin D. Roosevelt's Good Neighbor Policy were ideas of harmony, hemispheric unity, and cooperation with Latin America, summed up in one word, *Pan-Americanism*. Film was central in fostering a spirit of Pan-Americanism that worked toward bridging the distance between the U.S. and Latin America. Indeed film titles from the period (*Down Argentine way*, *That Night in Rio*, *Weekend in Havana*) emphasize proximity rather than distance, and the accessibility of the new neighbors. To implement this policy the U.S. government established the Office of the Co-ordinator of Inter-American Affairs (CIAA) in 1940. Headed by Nelson Rockefeller, the CIAA sponsored newsreels and documentaries for Latin American distribution and, along with the Hays Office, pressed studios to make films with Latin American themes. It also set up a motion picture section, with John Hay Whitney as its director, designed to ensure that North Americans developed a better understanding of Latin America and to avoid causing any offense to the neighbors to the south. Hollywood thus began exercising more care when depicting the continent's cultural and geographical characteristics, incorporating authentic location shots, iconographic sites (especially Rio's Corcovado and Sugar Loaf Mountains), and explanations of the cultural practices of the inhabitants. (Walt Disney's Good Neighbor projects, discussed in more detail below, typified this last element of Hollywood's strategy.) Thus when the film *Down Argentine Way*, which featured "Argentines" dancing and singing the Mexican mariachi, was deemed offensive to Argentine audiences, the CIAA gave Darryl Zanuck $40,000 to reshoot portions of the film. In order to avoid similar episodes, in 1941 the CIAA appointed Addison Durland as its Latin American advisor. Hollywood was now conscious of avoiding the distortions and misrepresentations that had previously characterized the portrayal of Spanish America and Brazil on the big screen. With this in mind, Durland employed native Latin Americans to advise on the cinematic representation of their own countries. Ronald Smondak and Dr. Assis Figueiredo assisted Durland in projects involving Brazil.

Carmen Miranda as Tropical "Other"

Ana M. López identifies three basic kinds of Good Neighbor Policy film:

> First, there were a number of standard, classic Hollywood genre films, with American protagonists set in Latin America with some location shooting, for example, Irving Rapper's *Now Voyager* [1942], with extensive footage shot in Rio de Janeiro; Edward Dmytryk's *Cornered* [1945], shot totally on location in Buenos Aires; and Alfred Hitchcock's *Notorious* [1946], with second-unit location shots of Rio de Janeiro. Then there were B-productions set and often shot in Latin America that featured mediocre US actors and Latin entertainers in either musicals or pseudo-musical formats.... Finally, the most successful and most self-consciously good-neighborly films were the mid to big-budget musical comedies set either in Latin America or in the USA but featuring, in addition to recognizable US stars, fairly well-known Latin American actors and entertainers.[28]

Almost every Hollywood studio produced one or more of these types of pictures during this period. It was Twentieth Century Fox, however, that specialized in the mid to big-budget musical comedies. For these films Fox used well-known Latin American artists, the most famous being Carmen Miranda. By the mid–1930s Miranda was well established as a singer and performer in Brazil. In 1936, she was one of the many Brazilian stars to appear in the film *Alô. Alô. Carnaval!* (Hello, Hello, Carnival!). Whilst successful in Brazil, the film achieved no critical or popular attention when exhibited in the United States. A review from *Variety*, however, singles out Carmen Miranda along with her sister Aurora and Dirce Baptista as among the few features of note in the film: "The Miranda sisters and Miss Baptista, long local radio and vaude favorites are best in the show."[29] In the years that followed the image of Carmen Miranda became central to both Hollywood's Good Neighbor films and Pan-Americanism itself. She made nine films with Fox between the 1940 and 1946, and became the highest paid female star in Hollywood in 1946. Miranda was also a key figure in advertising campaigns of the time, promoting clothing based on her own exotic style for Saks Fifth Avenue and various beauty products. However, her cinematic image was far from a simple case of assimilation into Hollywood's new, ostensibly friendly regime.

The figure of Carmen Miranda reveals a partial appeasement on Hollywood's part toward Brazil. In reference to this, López states: "it is difficult to describe Hollywood's position with regard to these suddenly welcomed 'others' as respectful or reverent."[30] She adds:

> Hollywood [and the United States] needed to posit a complex "otherness" as the flip side of wartime patriotism and nationalism and in order to assert and protect its economic interests. A special kind of "other" was needed to reinforce the wartime national self, one that — unlike the German or Japanese "other" — was non-threatening, potentially but not practically assimilable [that is, non-polluting to the purity of the race], friendly, fun-loving, and not deemed insulting to Latin American eyes and ears. Ultimately, Hollywood succeeded in all except, perhaps, the last category.[31]

For López the figure of Carmen Miranda embodies this complex "other," who is privileged cinematically but simultaneously marginalized. This marginalization is represented textually in the films that Miranda made for Fox, in which she is incorporated as an "exotic" entertainer and is thus denied a valid narrative function. Due to her excessive work schedule in New York, where she was appearing in the Broadway show *The Streets of Paris*, Miranda was unable to travel to Hollywood to film her scenes for *Down Argentine Way* so Fox sent a crew to New York to film her. In the film she therefore appears strictly as a performer and her presence in no way impedes the narrative proper. This is emphasized when the film's principal characters, played by Betty Grable and Don Ameche, are told to stop talking whilst Carmen Miranda performs. The importance of Miranda within the film is therefore visual and musical rather than one that legitimizes the narrative order. Indeed in this film the Brazilian performer is not included as a fictional character but simply plays herself.

As an "exotic" performer for whom the narrative pauses, Miranda is held as an object and is endowed with an aura of what Laura Mulvey has termed "to-be-looked-at-ness," embodying the pleasures of the voyeuristic gaze, and provoking a regime of spectacle and "specularity."[32] This is exaggerated in Busby Berkeley's musical and dance extravaganza *The Gang's All Here* (1943) where Miranda is literally transformed into a crowning centerpiece of the performance. Central to the regime of specularity attributed to Carmen Miranda is her identification as tropical "other" through her costumes, which were based on those of the Afro-Brazilian women, known as *baianas*, who sold food in the streets of Salvador in the state of Bahia. Miranda's exuberant, and often apparently edible turbans represented the baskets of produce that these women carried on their heads. Referring to her outlandish outfits, the Brazilian musicologist José Ramos Tinhorão states: "The exporting of Brazil's image ... that Carmen Miranda balanced on her head, on her stylized tray, in the form of bananas and other tropical products, corresponded to a need for propaganda for the recently installed dictatorship."[33]

When the Vargas regime initially came into existence with the coup of 1930, the Wall Street crash of 1929 and the ensuing Great Depression had reduced the spending power of the United States, which was the chief market for Brazilian exports. This led to a surge in industrial output in Brazil, as a result of government policy and the collapse of competition from abroad. Once the effects of the Wall Street crash had dissipated, Vargas restructured the economy to incorporate exports of raw materials to the United States. This was extremely important for Brazil, as Tinhorão highlights: "coffee, threatened by the closure of European markets, needed an increase in its export quota that only the North Americans could provide."[34] The war years offered the possibility for Latin America and particularly Brazil to redefine themselves, and there can be no doubt that the Hollywood stereotype of excessive tropicality was exploited by Brazil in order to promote exports of its primary products to the United States.

At the 1939 World's Fair, held in New York, Brazil capitalized on its cinematic image as exotic land of plenty, boasting of an abundance of coffee, rubber, cocoa, cotton, and other agricultural products, in addition

Carmen Miranda in Twentieth Century–Fox's *That Night in Rio* (Irving Cummings, 1941) (courtesy of the Academy of Motion Picture Arts and Sciences).

to a vast range of mineral deposits and types of wood. In the *Official Guide Book* to the event, Brazil was described as "endowed with a wealth of natural resources," and Carmen Miranda, clad in her baiana costume, performed typical Brazilian songs in the restaurant of the Brazilian pavilion, where *feijoada* (black bean stew) and *vatapá* (a spicy seafood dish), both of Afro-Brazilian origin, were served.[35] Appropriately, the Pavilion also housed lavish displays of Brazilian fruit, "especially oranges, that today are the national product that offers the greatest possibilities for increasing exports abroad."[36] Tourism was also central to Brazil's marketing of itself at the World's Fair, and a huge display entitled "Travel in Brazil" graced the nation's pavilion. The Good Neighbor Policy, its ideology of mutual exchange, and this international event provided an ideal vehicle for the Vargas regime's promotion of Brazilian exports, and Brazil thus drew on Hollywood stereotypes of tropical excess to bolster its image abroad and to attract foreign visitors.

The Brazilian musical comedy *Banana da terra* (Banana of the Land, 1939), set in the fictitious Pacific island of Bananolândia, the plot of which centers on the banana trade, is a clear reflection of Brazil's willingness to be portrayed and subsequently to portray itself as an exotic land of plenty. It was in this film that Carmen Miranda first appeared dressed as a baiana. It was "Miranda the baiana" who arrived on Broadway in 1939 and went on to star in a host of hugely successful Hollywood musicals. Although the baiana costume was traditionally worn chiefly by the Afro-Brazilian lower classes in carnival celebrations in Brazil, and had in fact first appeared in Hollywood in a musical sequence in *Flying Down to Rio* in 1933, it was the exaggerated Broadway/Hollywood version of the outfit as created by Miranda that reappeared in Brazil. The stylized creations by Travis Banton that she wore in *That Night in Rio* (1941) made such an impact in the Brazilian press that organizers of the Rio carnival celebrations requested replicas from the Twentieth Century Fox wardrobe department, which were used as the inspiration for the parade costumes in 1941.[37]

López sees the self-conscious appropriation of the Hollywood image of Brazil/Latin America operating within the figure of Carmen Miranda herself during her screen performances in Hollywood.[38] Whilst her inclusion as a performer freezes the narrative, openly displaying her as an object of a voyeuristic gaze, Miranda herself undermines the passivity inherent in this role by aggressively returning the gaze of the camera and the spectator. As a result, she is seen to acknowledge and openly participate in her representation as tropical "other." Her aural register also marks her accent and frequent malapropisms as blatant pretense in "a nod to the requirements of a conception of foreignness and 'otherness' necessary to maintain the validity of the text in question as well as her persona as a gesture of good neighborliness."[39] There is in Miranda's own performance a sense of self-conscious representation and mimicry of the stereotype of the exotic Latina. This corresponds to the self-awareness of the musicals themselves, which contain blatant references to "good-neighborliness." At the beginning

Poster advertising *That Night in Rio* (Irving Cummings, 1941) (courtesy of the Academy of Motion Picture Arts and Sciences).

of *That Night in Rio*, for example, Don Ameche's character sings the following message:

> My friends I send felicitations
> To our South American relations
> May we never leave behind us
> All those common ties that bind us

This opening points directly to the strategic production of the ideology of hemispheric unity and mutual exchange. The United States and Hollywood are not the only participants in this creative process, however, and both Miranda and Brazil can be seen as willingly assisting in the construction of these self-referential texts.

Brazil and Its Thrills in Musical Features

Alongside the Technicolor musical extravaganzas produced at Fox during the Good Neighbor Policy era, musical comedies with "Latin" themes or settings were being released by most of the other large studios. Republic's *Brazil* (1944) incorporated the hit songs of the Brazilian popular composer, Ari Barroso, such as "Brazil" and "Rio de Janeiro," some of which were performed solely in Portuguese in the film. The plot finds Virginia Bruce playing Nicky Henderson, the author of *Why Marry a Latin?*, who is in Rio to collect material for another book on Brazil. Romance is typically in the air in Rio, even for this skeptical foreigner, who keeps encountering the handsome "Latin" songwriter Miguel Soares, played by the Mexican Tito Guizar, in a series of swanky night spots. Offended by her book he sets out to prove to her that Latin men make good lovers, and spends time with her by pretending to be a tourist guide. Once again the contrasting physical coloring of the romantic couple underlines their ethnic differences sufficiently, but both are white-skinned and therefore their union is permissible in the eyes of Hollywood. As a review of the film in *Variety* states, "Miss Bruce makes an excellent contrast to Guizar with her blonde beauty."[40] Rio is depicted as a city of irresistible charms where tourists would delight in the rich musical and dance traditions (Roy Rogers, in a cameo role, plays a Western film star visiting Rio for the carnival, for example). A review in *Film Daily* declares: "Romance and music are wedded in *Brazil* to create a show that is easily the worthiest of its kind to come from Republic.... The picture is prodigally endowed with Ari Barroso numbers among them the one bearing the title of the film. Those who relish South American music will revel in *Brazil*."[41] The movie acknowledges Brazil's commercial clout in the form of its most elaborate production number, entitled "Café" (Coffee), which depicts how this most Brazilian of commodities is produced. The studios evidently took great pains to create as authentic an impression of Brazil as possible, and the movie carried one of the highest budgets in the history of the Republic studios. In addition to commissioning Barroso to compose music for the production, the studios chose Aurora Miranda, Carmen's sister, to perform in the film, and a special camera crew was sent to Rio for background shots, the most important of which were those of the annual carnival celebrations. The Motion Picture Society for the Americas assisted Republic in producing one of the most successful and the least offensive of the "South American" musicals by sponsoring the flight which took film crews to Brazil for the location shots.[42]

Columbia's musical comedy *The Thrill of Brazil* (1946) also starred Tito Guizar, but in spite of Ann Miller's hip-shaking dance routines in what was supposed to be a Rio nightclub, and the presence of the famous Latin dance duo, Veloz and Yolanda, who performed a stylized creation called the "Silhouette Samba," this film received some lukewarm reviews. The story revolved around an American theatrical impresario working in Brazil and his efforts to win back his almost-divorced wife. According to *Newsweek*, "There isn't much to be said about an ingenuous effort like *The Thrill of Brazil* except that it's harmless if you want to kill time, and Brazil is friendly enough not to take offense. As a matter of fact, pictorially, and in song and dance, the nation comes off very well indeed. But the plot is strictly from Hollywood and hardly worth Pan-American examination."[43] The picture played on the more mysterious aspects of Brazil's Hollywood image in one of the production numbers, "a Brazilian macumba or voodoo dance performed to the savage rhythms of tom-toms."[44] The "Latin" music included Guizar's rendition of "Linda Mujer" by Raphael Duchesne, and performances of "Minute Samba" and "Mucho Dinero" by Enric Madriguera's orchestra.[45] The rendition of the song "Man is Brother to a Mule" by Ann Miller is most notable for the lapses into Spanish (not Portuguese) in the lyrics, which feature occasional references to "muchachos." Columbia did in fact take the trouble to hire a Brazilian by the name of Louis Oliveira as technical advisor, who was said to have wide-ranging film experience in both the United States and his native land.[46] Furthermore, the studios claimed to have checked as much of the factual content of the movie as possible with the Brazilian consul in Los Angeles, who read the script and visited the set at the invitation of the producer Sidney Biddell. The musical evidently aimed to attract audiences by calling on

Poster advertising Republic's *Brazil* (Joseph Santley, 1944) (courtesy of the Academy of Motion Picture Arts and Sciences).

Rio's cinematic image as city of infectious melodies and passionate encounters, and appealing to North Americans' desire to be armchair travelers. A general advance story released by the studios to promote the movie began: "Exciting Rio de Janeiro, city of romance, adventure and torrid Latin rhythms, is the setting for *The Thrill of Brazil*, Columbia's lavish South American musical.... Advance reports on the picture say that moviegoers are going to be treated to a real tour of the capital of Brazil — its gay night life, exotic customs and colorful scenic beauty."

War-Time Romance in Rio

During the war years, Brazil featured as a setting not only for musicals but also for melodramas, most significantly, Irving Rapper's *Now Voyager* (1942) starring Bette Davis and Paul Henried. The narrative of *Now Voyager* revolves around the therapeutic treatment of an intelligent but highly repressed woman, Charlotte Vale (played by Davis). Part of her cure involves a cruise that takes her to South America, and during which she is slowly seen to transform herself from a dowdy spinster into an elegant, alluring woman. The mise-en-scène emphasizes this transformation, with long and lingering shots of the new and improved Charlotte. The apotheosis of this transformation is a trip to Rio de Janeiro, one of the ports of call. In Rio, Charlotte encounters romance (with Jerry, who meets her on the cruise) and she dances, drinks, and smokes to her heart's content. This film would therefore appear to reinstate the typical exotic and sensual representation of Brazil, and more specifically, its then capital city.

The economic motivations for the Good Neighbor Policy are also evidenced in *Now Voyager*. As the pleasure cruiser approaches Rio, Charlotte Vale gives a brief guide to the city: "Rio's harbor, one of the few sites that doesn't disappoint you after the picture postcards. There's the famous Sugarloaf Mountain and to its left the beautiful beaches of Copacabana." This blatant discourse of tourism overlays picture postcard shots of Sugarloaf and Corcovado. Later on a montage of shots shows Charlotte and Jerry indulging themselves in Rio, including scenes of them in a horse drawn carriage on Avenida Central, and in various cafés and bars. Ana López refers to the visual representation of travel in many of the films from this period. For her such travelogue sections serve to justify the authenticity of the locales and are proof of Hollywood's attempt to display and fix the "other" through the mastery of the gaze.[47] Here Latin America is passively displayed for the spectator's voyeuristic eyes.

At the time of the production of *Now Voyager*, however, Rio had already become a popular destination for both cruise liners and airlines. Just before the film's release, Pan-American Airways announced the confirmation of new air connections to South America, which included daily flights to Rio and Buenos Aires. There was a direct link between Pan-American Airways and Hollywood, in that RKO boss Mervyn Cooper was on the airline's board of directors, and John Hay Whitney was also a major shareholder. The promotion of tourism and travel in Latin America in these Good Neighbor era films could thus be read simply as an instance of marketing and product placement, rather than pointing to the sense of colonial mastery. Indeed films from this period are careful to include not just travelogue sections but drawn-out shots of airplanes where the Pan-American logo was proudly displayed. The expansion of air travel was marketed with recourse to the Good Neighbor Policy in daily newspapers in the United States, and tourism south of the border clearly benefited U.S. commercial interests. In Brazil, foreign tourists were equally seen as an important source of revenue and foreign currency by the Vargas regime, as discussed earlier.[48] In the war years commercial and political interests converged, and in *Now Voyager* Rio is not merely a romantic backdrop but forms part of the discourse of consumerism dominant in both the United States and Brazil. Indeed *Now Voyager* had two Brazilian advisors, Raul Smondak and Dr. Assis de Figuereido, who actively participated in the attempt to portray Brazil as a modern and attractive city that North Americans would want to visit.

Espionage South of the Border

Hollywood film production of the Good Neighbor Policy era also embraced a number of thrillers with plots that hinged on espionage in South America, particularly in Argentina and Brazil. The best known and critically acclaimed is Alfred Hitchcock's *Notorious*, a project that commenced in 1939, at the height of Pan-American fervor, and ended in 1946. The film tells the story of Alicia Huberman, played by Ingrid Bergman, whose father is a convicted Nazi collaborator. Cary Grant's character, an agent for the U.S. State Department, decides to enlist Huberman as a spy for the United States and she is sent to Rio to uncover the secrets of a Nazi group operating there, headed by an old friend of her father's named Alex Sebastian, played by Claude Rains. At the time of the film's production there was general concern in the United States over the infiltration of Nazi ideology into South American countries, particularly in Brazil, with its sizeable German immigrant population. This was exacerbated by President

Vargas's dubious political allegiances: for as late as 1940, he praised the fascist regimes in Europe. Newspaper headlines in the United States reflected anxieties over Brazil's enthusiasm for Hitler's Germany and over the influence of Nazi ideology in the Southern hemisphere.[49] Coverage of this issue in the U.S. press, however, did not condemn Brazil itself; indeed the Good Neighbor was depicted as an innocent party being invaded by unwelcome outsiders and their political ideas. A report for the *New York Times* on June 9, 1940, for example, is titled, "Latin America is in Fear of Blow at Democracy." The American press sought to transmit a sense of solidarity between Brazil and its democratic neighbor north of the border, itself a means of courting cooperation. Such positive collaboration is seen in *Notorious* as Brazilian officials work with the U.S. State Department in combating the Nazis. Brazil is thus portrayed as an ally in spite of the fact that the nation's position remained ambiguous until 1942, the year in which Vargas finally declared war on Germany after the bombing of ships off the coast of Pernambuco in the northeast of the country. The declaration brought with it the establishment of a U.S. naval base in the northeastern town of Natal and the enlistment of Brazilian soldiers in the war effort. The geographical setting of *Notorious* is therefore one that is historically pertinent to the spy story in question, and the city of Rio is far from merely an exotic backdrop.

Disney's Joe Carioca

Walt Disney chose to embody Brazil in the figure of Joe (José or Zé) Carioca, the streetwise parrot who appeared in *Saludos Amigos* (RKO-Disney, 1943) and *The Three Caballeros* (RKO-Disney, 1945).[50] On returning from his fact-finding trip to South America in 1941, Disney emphasized that attention to authentic detail would be a principal feature of his Good Neighborly projects. In an article he wrote for *Variety* he stated:

> The most important result of our trip, to me, was the fact that we learned a great deal of what not to do. From talking to people of every country— from government officials to fruit peddlers— we think we found out what the composite Brazilian, Argentine, Uruguayan, Chilean or Peruvian citizen likes about his own country, and also what he wouldn't like to see on the screen.
>
> For instance, Brazilians know that a lot of Americans have the erroneous notion that their beautiful and progressive country is one big jungle. Naturally, they are proud of their artists and their music and the beauty of the country itself, as well as cities like Rio or the modern, strapping industrial city of Sao Paulo.[51]

Saludos Amigos was a combination of a travelogue documenting the trip carried out by the Disney team and an animated cartoon, the latter divided into four discrete shorts, the first set in Bolivia, the second in Chile, the third in Argentina, and the fourth in Brazil. Critics tend to agree that the Brazil sequence, entitled "Aquarela do Brasil" (Watercolor of Brazil), was the most technically and aesthetically rewarding of the four.[52] In it Joe Carioca, "the fast-talking, cigar-smoking, umbrella-toting parrot from Rio,"[53] introduces Donald Duck, the self-parodic U.S. tourist, to the wonders of Rio, more specifically samba, *cachaça* (local rum), and the nightspots of the Urca casino and Copacabana. As the sequence opens, Disney uses a flowing paintbrush technique, dipping a brush into a pot of color and moving it across the screen to first form a waterfall and then to depict an array of extravagantly plumaged birds. Disney's Brazil combines natural and exotic treasures with cosmopolitan sophistication, and the foreign tourist (Donald) is made most welcome.[54]

The Hollywood image of Rio as a free-and-easy location conducive to abandoning one's inhibitions is clearly emphasized in this movie, as an advertisement for it in *Variety* suggests: "Sway to the Samba's tantalizing tropic rhythms! Marvel at the land of exciting Senoritas, comic Llamas, the colorful Pampas, the snow-capped Andes, festive Rio with its nights of love! A new world of Disney wonders awaits you in this sun-kissed Paradise of laughter and romance!"[55] The colorful parrot physically connotes Brazil's tropicality, his consummate dancing to the samba rhythm represents the mythical vitality and sensuality of the country's inhabitants, and his wily personality and dapper appearance establish Brazilians as urbane and streetwise, but also evoke the "playboy" cliché. As Disney wrote: "we've got one short in work that takes Donald Duck to Rio, where he's shown around to all the gay spots by a raffish sophisticated papagaio that turns out to be a little sharper than D. Duck."[56] The documentary footage that precedes this fourth animated segment opens with shots of Sugar Loaf and Corcovado mountains, and Copacabana beach, as Disney narrates: "This time we planned to stay a little longer and get a better look at some of the famous sights, such as Sugarloaf overlooking the bay, and Copacabana beach, the playground of Rio, and Corcovado overlooking Rio itself. This is the kind of city that always appeals to artists, picturesque little outdoor cafes, colorful mosaic sidewalks." These same images appear at the end of the animated sequence in a cartoon vista.

The Three Caballeros mixes live action with animation and it was viewed in the motion picture press as a remarkable technical achievement. Aurora Miranda, Carmen's younger sister, appears dancing alongside Joe Carioca,[57] (see page 201). Beautiful young girls such as Miranda, the Mex-

Aurora Miranda, Carmen's sister, with Donald Duck in Disney's *The Three Caballeros* (Norman Ferguson, 1945) (courtesy of the Academy of Motion Picture Arts and Sciences).

ican singer Dora Luz, and dancer Carmen Molina feature prominently in this Technicolor visit by Donald Duck to Mexico and Brazil, prompting Julianne Burton-Carvajal to argue that "*The Three Caballeros* parades rampant (masculine) desire and the explosive results of its repeated frustration."[58] The Brazilian section is once again authenticated by the incorporation of songs by Ari Barroso.[59] Promotional material for the picture describes it as "a miracle-world of rhythm and fun!"[60] an epithet that encapsulates Disney's view of Brazil. In this film the spectator visits Salvador da Bahia (usually referred to as simply Bahia), not Rio, but the two cities are barely distinguishable and the choice of Bahia would appear to stem, in part at least, from the themes of Barroso's two songs, "Bahia," a hyperbolic anthem to the city of Salvador, and "Os quindins de Iaiá" (Missy's Coconut Cakes), a tribute to the Afro-Brazilian food sellers of the city (represented on screen by the very white Aurora Miranda in the traditional dress of the Afro-Brazilian baiana). In both *Saludos Amigos* and *The Three Caballeros* Brazil represents, more than any other nation depicted, the essence of Hollywood's vision of Latin America as a source of pure spectacle, rhythmic exuberance, and carnal spontaneity. As Julianne Burton-Carvajal writes in relation to the second film:

> In the sections depicting Brazil and Mexico, reason gives way to passion, order to disorder and incoherence, the logic of experience to the chaos of nightmare. It is this impression/projection of Latinness which unleashes both Donald's and Disney's libido. The Latin is rendered synonymous with license and licentiousness. The tendency to project onto the other what we most assiduously suppress within ourselves lies at the root of the film's indulgence in excess—an excess which is specifically, relentlessly sexual.[61]

Brazil's Adoption of Hollywood Motifs

There is much evidence that Hollywood's vision of Brazil was exploited by the Vargas regime to promote the nation's economic riches and commercial potential abroad. Carmen Miranda's success in the Broadway show *The Streets of Paris* in 1939 was proudly reported in the Brazilian press. A review of the show in a Brazilian newspaper described how she appeared at the top of a flight of stairs resplendent in an exaggerated and embellished version of the baiana costume and proceeded to perform the samba "O que é que a baiana tem?" (What is it about the baiana?), albeit to a modified rhythm. It added: "And other songs follow to the delight of the audience. And the act ends with the Brazilian totally winning over Broadway."[62] It is no coincidence that white Brazilian women dressed as baianas worked as hatcheck girls at the Brazilian restaurant at the World's Fair in 1939. Similarly, at the Golden Gate Exposition in San Francisco the following year a pale-skinned Carmen Miranda clone performed in the Brazilian pavilion, whilst the real Miranda was photographed next to a display of Brazilian cotton.

Having taken Manhattan by storm (her face was soon plastered all over billboards and magazines), Miranda as baiana became a template for recreations of a manufactured Brazilian identity in Brazil itself, particularly those destined for consumption by tourists. The song "O que é que a baiana tem?" that Carmen turned into a huge hit, introduced the Bahian word *balangandan* (metal ornamental amulets worn by baianas) into the Brazilian vocabulary.[63] The term became synonymous with Carmen's screen/stage baiana in Brazil, and was incorporated into the title of a stage production designed to raise funds for the charitable works of Brazil's First Lady, Darcy Vargas, entitled *Joujoux e balangandans* (Trinkets and Amulets) and performed in August 1939 at Rio's Municipal Theater. The show consisted of a series of acts, and culminated in the performance of a song entitled "Nós temos balangandans" (We have amulets) by a group of white baianas, clearly inspired by Miranda's appearance on Broadway (tellingly the penultimate show number was called "Hallo Manhattan"). Just a matter of weeks later the Brazilian press was advertising a forthcoming show to be held at Rio's Urca Casino, *Urca's Balangandans*, and billed as "The voice and the music of Brazil for tourists."[64]

The Brazilian film industry's vernacular variant of the musical comedy, the low-budget *chanchada*, focused on Afro-Brazilian cultural production, chiefly samba, but was characterized by the structuring absence of black performers. As Robert Stam writes, "the musicals do manifest the strong presence of black cultural forms, as if Brazilian producers, not unlike their Hollywood counterparts, wanted to have black culture without dealing with the people who produced it."[65] Looking to Hollywood for emblematic motifs of national self-definition, the chanchadas reworked the baiana persona, and just as Carmen Miranda had done in Hollywood, they whitened her skin. The white Brazilian actress Eliana Macedo starred in countless chanchadas as the *mocinha* or (girl next door), and often donned an ornate version of the baiana costume in the musical sequences, such as in *Carnaval Atlântida* (Atlântida Carnival, 1952). The reappropriation of the white stylized baiana in the chanchadas of the 1950s signified a creative challenge to Hollywood's hegemony. If we accept that nonnarrative interludes allow for negotiated or subversive readings by spectators, it is important to note that the baianas of these Brazilian films of the 1950s always appear in the musical/dance sequences, when the narrative simply pauses. Thus, these Carmen Miranda "wannabes" are instantly marked as synthetic constructs, totally separated from the "reality" of the story line. The diegetic audiences, made up of members of Brazil's white elite or foreign tourists, do not identify with the baianas on stage. They are mere diversion, to be looked at by both the screen audience and its real-life counterpart. No intimacy is permitted between the baiana and the real-life spectator, whereas Brazilian audiences were clearly intended to identify with the characters of the narrative proper, particularly the lowly migrants and marginalized urban dwellers. Shari Roberts contends that Miranda's appeal and fame resided in the audience's perception of her as producer of her own star text and as being in control of her own self-parody.[66] The Miranda lookalikes that we see in the chanchadas of the 1950s similarly reveal Brazil's acknowledgment of its stereotypical Hollywood representation and can therefore be interpreted as an ironic comment on the U.S. film industry's falsification and homogenization of Latin identity in the Good Neighbor years and beyond.

Conclusions

With the advent of sound, Rio de Janeiro, with its associations with music, dance, and carnival, became the perfect stage for the musical extravaganza, and although the misnomers, inaccuracies, and clichés of the silent era reappeared, Brazil's image in Hollywood was tamed and civilized. Hollywood diluted Brazil's ethnic mix, and Carmen Miranda became the perfect embodiment of the nonthreatening, exotic "other," her white European complexion sufficiently sanitizing the Afro-Brazilian origins of her costumes. Rio de Janeiro's promotion by Hollywood in the Good Neighbor Policy era as a sophisticated, quasi–European capital, built on the visions of earlier travelogues, and was clearly a consequence of U.S. pragmatism. But this flattery of Rio/Brazil on screen, irrespective of the State Department's geostrategic and economic preoccupations, was not as exploitative as is often thought. Indeed, the Vargas regime had much to gain from Hollywood's promotion of Brazil, however stereotypical, to boost commercial interests, particularly tourism, and to exploit the economic and political vacuum created by the war in Europe. Both Brazil and its most famous "export," Carmen Miranda, adopted the discourse of the Hollywood "other" for their own ends. Nowhere is this more striking than in the Brazilian chanchada's appropriation of the stylized Hollywood baiana, introduced to the United States by Miranda.

Endnotes

1. See Allen Woll, *The Latin Image in American Film* (Los Angeles: UCLA Latin American Center Publication, 1977); Robert Beverley Ray, *A Certain Tendency of the Hollywood Cinema: 1930–1980* (Princeton, NJ: Princeton University Press, 1985); Antonio José Ríos-Bustamante, *Latinos in Hollywood* (Encino, CA: Floricanto Press, 1991); Alfred Charles Richard Jr., *The Hispanic Image on the Silver Screen: An Interpretive Filmography from Silents into Sound, 1898–1935* (New York, Westport, CT and London: Greenwood Press, 1992); Alfred Charles Richard Jr., *Censorship and Hollywood's Hispanic Image: An Interpretive Filmography, 1936–1955* (Westport, CT and London: Greenwood Press, 1993).

2. See Ana M. López, "Are All Latins From Manhattan?: Hollywood, Ethnography and Cultural Colonialism," in John King, Ana M. López, and Manuel Alvarado (eds.), *Mediating Two Worlds: Cinematic Encounters in the Americas* (London: BFI, 1993), pp. 67–80; Frank Javier García Berumen, *The Chicano/Hispanic Image in American Film* (New York: Vantage Press, 1995); Carlos E. Cortés, "Chicanas in Film: History of an Image," in Clara E. Rodríguez (ed.), *Latin Looks: Images of Latinas and Latinos in the U.S. Media* (Boulder, CO and Oxford: Westview Press, 1998), pp. 121–141.

3. A notable exception is Tunico Amancio's book, *O Brasil dos gringos: imagens no cinema* (Sao Paulo: Intertexto, 2000), which traces the evolution of Brazil's depiction in foreign movies.

4. Sérgio Augusto, "Hollywood Looks at Brazil: From Carmen Miranda to *Moonraker*," in Randal Johnson and Robert Stam (eds.), *Brazilian Cinema* (New York: Columbia University Press, 1995), pp. 351–611.

5. See Cláudio de Cicco, *Hollywood na cultura brasileira: o cinema americano na mudança da cultura brasileira na década de 40* (São Paulo: Convívio, 1979); Nicolau Sevcenko, "Brazilian Follies: The Casting, Broadcasting and Consumption of Images of Brazil on Both Sides of the Continent, 1930–50," paper given at the *Ways of Working in Latin American Cultural Studies* conference, King's College, London, April 1995; Cristina Meneguello, *Poeira de estrelas: O cinema Hollywoodiano na mídia brasileira das décadas de 40 e 50* (Campinas: Editora da Unicamp, 1996).

6. Richard Jr., *The Hispanic Image on the Silver Screen*, p.150.

7. Ibid., pp. 201–202.

8. Ibid., p.468.

9. *Film Daily*, July 6, 1942.

10. *Variety*, December 23, 1942.

11. *Variety* (August 18, 1948) exposed the hackneyed nature of this film's principal motifs, saying: "Pic offers the usual pegs for sensational ballyhoo in its lurid yarns, shots of prehistoric monsters and flock of primitive Indians, including an average quota of undraped native females."

12. *Variety*, May 11, 1949.

13. See also *Strange World* (United Artists, 1952), a semidocumentary shot for the most part in the wilds of Brazil, Bolivia, and Peru, which exposes the dangers of the jungles of South America, and *The Naked Jungle* (Paramount, 1954), a romantic drama which mixes jungle adventure with science-fiction thriller.

14. Richard Jr., *The Hispanic Image on the Silver Screen*, p. 343.

15. Richard Jr., *Censorship and Hollywood's Hispanic Image*, p. 28.

16. *Film Daily*, October 8, 1943.

17. In *Granderos del Amor* (1934), a Spanish language version of *Grenadiers of Love*, produced by Twentieth Century Fox, Roulien even played a Viennese composer. In 1935 he starred alongside Antonio Moreno and Conchita Montenegro as an insurance company boss in Fox's *Asegure a su mujer/Insure Your Wife*, written by the Argentine writer Julio Escobar.

18. Richard Jr., *The Hispanic Image on the Silver Screen*, p. 464.

19. Catherine Benamou, "Orson Welles's Transcultural Cinema: An Historical/Textual Reconstruction of the Suspended Film, *It's All True*, 1941–1993," Ph.D. dissertation, New York University, 1997, p. 326.

20. *Variety*, December 26, 1933.

Rick Altman explores the conventions of the Hollywood film musical, which include the union of the male and female leads. Each partner is seen as potentially complete, but needs the perfect mate in order to awaken a specific facet of his or her personality. He writes: "Until boy meets girl, an important aspect of human experience is lost for each character. When two lovers meet, however, each sees his/her repressed self in the other as if he/she were looking in a psychic mirror," and cites the scene from *Flying Down to Rio* in which Gene Raymond and Dolores Del Río find themselves listening to an alter ego as a classic example of this tradition. The images on screen suggest that to fall in love is to listen to one's other self or hidden personality. Rick Altman, *The American Film Musical* (Bloomington: Indiana University Press, 1987), pp. 82–83.

21. *Variety*, December 19, 1933.

22. According to Douglas McVay, "The 'Carioca' also contains a stunning crane-shot gradually revealing the entire whirling ballroom, together with an exciting low-angle view of dancers sweeping past the camera, and a climactic burst of quick cutting from pair to pair." Douglas McVay, *The Musical Film* (London: A. Zwemmer Ltd; New York: A.S. Barnes & Co., 1967), pp. 17–18.

23. Benamou, "Orson Welles's Transcultural Cinema," p. 326.

24. *New York Times*, December 22, 1933.

25. In the movie *Brazil* Virginia Bruce's character is escorted around Rio by her friend Rod Walker, played by Robert Livingstone, who happens to be an employee of the U.S. consulate. Also in *Charlie Chan in Rio* (1941), one of the detective's suspects asks to see the

U.S. ambassador, and another character refers to seeking the consul's help in solving a crime.

26. Orson Welles, as U.S. cultural ambassador to Latin America, visited Brazil in 1942 to begin work on *It's All True*, the ill-fated film project. The Vargas regime (1930–1945) clearly saw this as an opportunity to attract North American tourists to Brazil with dollars to spend. For the Carnival section of the film Welles's team was strongly discouraged from filming in the favelas or shantytowns of Rio by the Brazilian secret police; and elements of the conservative press, as well as RKO executives, objected to Welles's foregrounding of black and mixed-race Brazil in his re-creation of carnival. Benamou, "Orson Welles's Transcultural Cinema," pp. 612–619.

27. López, "Are All Latins from Manhattan?," p. 70.

28. Ibid., p. 70.

29. *Variety*, February 12, 1936.

30. López, "Are All Latins From Manhattan?" p. 70.

31. Ibid., p. 70.

32. Mulvey, Laura, *Visual and Other Pleasures* (Bloomington: Indiana University Press, 1989).

33. José Ramos Tinhorão, *O samba agora vai: A farsa da música popular no exterior* (Rio de Janeiro: JCM Editores, 1969), p. 46 (our translation).

34. Ibid., p. 55 (our translation).

35. *World's Fair 1939, Official Guide Book*, p.8.

36. *Correio da manhã*, May 9, 1939 (our translation).

37. For more detail on the origins of Miranda's baiana costume and the relationship between her performance and Afro-Brazilian culture, see José Ligeiro Coelho, "Carmen Miranda: An Afro-Brazilian Paradox," Ph.D. dissertation, New York University, 1998.

38. López, "Are All Latins From Manhattan?"

39. Ibid., p. 77.

40. *Variety*, October 25, 1944.

41. *Film Daily*, October 27, 1944.

42. Critics saw this musical as portraying Latin America with tact and accuracy. An advertisement for it that appeared in *Film Daily* (November 6, 1944) quoted the following comments from a review in *Hollywood Reporter*: "Head and shoulders above any other picture Hollywood has made to date in the matters of authenticity and the capable handling of the delicate problem of depicting our South American neighbors to the world."

43. *Newsweek*, September 16, 1946.

44. *The Thrill of Brazil* official press book (consulted at the Margaret Herrick Library, Los Angeles).

45. Enric Madriguera, decorated in Washington as the "Ambassador of Music to all the Americas" by the ambassadors of all the South American republics and the U.S. State Department, was the subject of various musical shorts in the 1940s. In *Enric Madriguera and His Orchestra* (Jamboree/RKO, 1943) he performed the samba "Brazil" and the rhumba "Bim, Bam, Bum," and accompanied Patricia Gilmore in her rendition of a conga called "Pan-American Way" and an unidentified samba allegedly of Portuguese origin. In *Enric Madriguera and Orchestra* (Melody Master/Warners, 1946) Patricia Gilmore performs a song called "Maria from Bahia" to the band's accompaniment. A review of this short in *Film Daily* (March 8, 1943) is indicative of the role of popular music within the Good Neighbor Policy: "Enric Madriguera adds to the appreciation of Latin-American music by offering a number of items that reflect the warmth of our neighbors to the South." In the 1940s, musical shorts proved the ideal vehicle for the promotion of Latin music, the specific origin of which was often undetermined and largely immaterial. Warner Brothers's *Carioca Serenaders* (1941) featured Humberto Herrera "and his South American band," the vocalist Dinora Rego who performed several numbers including "Chick-Qui-Boom," and "some flippant torso tossing so characteristic of Latin-American dances contributed by good looking dancers" (*Film Daily*, October 31, 1941). Paramount's *Carnival in Brazil* (1942) com-

bined newsreel shots of the Rio festival with production material, and paraded a host of Latin American artists, including the Brazilian soprano Elsie Houston, before the cameras. According to *Variety* (March 11, 1942), this 10-minute short was "Exciting enough to make one want to visit Rio at carnival time." This fascination with Latin music and dance continued well beyond the end of the Second World War; 1948 saw the release of the shorts *Samba Mania* from Paramount, and *Copa Carnival* from U-I. The former rehashed the clichés of the fiery but ultimately submissive Latina and philandering macho, as the following synopsis reveals (*Film Daily*, March 30, 1948): "Latin lovely, Isabelita, stars in this tale of a jealous dancing star who traps her night club owner boy friend when his roving eye falls on a red-headed boogie-woogie doll. He pours on the masterfulness and she agrees to love, honor and obey. Done in Technicolor, it's gay, musical and lots of fun." Of *Copa Carnival*, *Film Daily* (July 15, 1948) wrote: "Many points of interest are covered in this excellent short on Brazil. Ben Grauer's narration and the skillful photography enhance the interest of people frolicking at the Mardi Gras, perambulating market places, cadets on review, civic beauty of Rio and nearby beaches."

46. Very probably Aloísio Oliveira, a member of Carmen Miranda's support band, who traveled with the star to the United States. See endnote 52.

47. López, "Are All Latins From Manhattan?"

48. See endnote 26.

49. Headlines, for example, read: "Reich's Air Potential Holds Real Threat to the Americas" (*New York Times*, June 29, 1940); "German Colonizers in Brazil Taught to Resist Assimilation" (*New York Times*, June 29, 1940); "Nazi Threats Growing in Brazil" (*New York Times*, June 26, 1940). In addition, RKO-Pathé released a short film entitled *Eyes on Brazil* in 1941, which dealt specifically with the German population in Brazil. According to a review in *Film Daily* (March 4, 1941): "The film should be an eye-opener for the average U.S. audience, showing as it does a predominant German population in the Southern district of Brazil, with 1,200 German schools functioning and German industrial works and airlines booming."

50. The character made his first appearance as a series of two-color sketches, with no background and only briefly animated, in the documentary *South of the Border with Disney* (1941). See Julianne Burton-Carvajal, "'Surprise Package': Looking Southward with Disney," in Eric Smoodin (ed.), *Disney Discourse: Producing the Magic Kingdom* (New York and London: Routledge, 1994), pp.131–147 (pp. 134–136).

51. Walt Disney, "Getting Hep on Latins," *Variety*, January 7, 1942, p. 7.

52. The title "Aquarela do Brasil" was taken from the original Portuguese name of the patriotic samba "Brazil" by Ari Barroso, which provided part of the soundtrack, along with the more percussive samba "Tico, Tico, no Fubá" (Tico-tico Bird in the Cornmeal) by Zequinha de Abreu. Aloísio Oliveira, a member of Carmen Miranda's Brazilian band, the Bando da Lua, who performed "Brazil" in the picture, provided the narration. Disney was clearly anxious to harness the potential of true Brazilian music in his film. He wrote (*Variety*, January 7, 1942, p. 7): "And in Brazil we were all so hypnotized by the spell of samba music — which has the Brazilians just as hypnotized."

53. Burton-Carvajal, "Surprise Package," p. 134.

54. Both a Spanish- and a Portuguese-language version of this film were made for the Latin American market, and both were well received. Special premieres were held in Latin American capitals.

55. *Variety*, January 6, 1943.

56. *Variety*, January 7, 1942, p. 7. In this article Disney claims that people he met in Brazil were continually asking him to create a parrot character, and that he was told lots of jokes which began: "Did you hear the one about the *papagaio* that...?" He makes no reference to any encounter with such birds, although various books about the composer Ari Barroso tell the following story: During his visit to Brazil, Disney stayed at the Grande Hotel, Belém, where he heard North American music being played by a quartet. He asked his host, Celestino Silveira, if he could hear some Brazilian music and the band began to play

"Aquarela do Brasil." The following day the two of them caught a plane to Rio and the scenery transfixed Disney as they flew over Amazonia. During a stop in Barreiro, in the *sertão* or interior of the state of Bahia, Disney saw a collection of brightly colored birds, including parrots, in the airport, and started to play with them as he hummed the tune he had heard the night before. When the time came to select the music for the film he was to make about Brazil, Disney remembered the tune he had heard in Belém and Silveira tried to track Ari Barroso down as soon as they arrived in Rio, without success. The two finally met for the first time at a cocktail party given by Disney in the Hotel Glória during that same visit.

57. Joe Carioca and the Aracuan Bird of Brazil also appear in "Blame It on the Samba," one of seven stories told in the film *Melody Time* (RKO-Disney, 1948).

58. Burton-Carvajal, "Surprise Package," p. 132.

59. As Julianne Burton-Carvajal writes: "To its enduring credit, *The Three Caballeros* does utilize Latin American music, accents, performers, locales, artifacts, and modes of cultural expression more extensively than any previous Hollywood film." Ibid., p. 147.

60. *Variety*, January 3, 1945.

61. Burton-Carvajal, "Surprise Package," p. 141.

62. *Correio da manhã*, July 1, 1939 (our translation).

63. When Carmen Miranda created her own version of the baiana costume she added different kinds of bracelets, armlets, earrings, and necklaces.

64. *Correio da manhã*, August 13, 1939 (our translation).

65. Robert Stam, *Tropical Multiculturalism: A Comparative History of Race in Brazilian Cinema and Culture* (Durham, NC and London: Duke University Press, 1997), p. 102.

66. Shari Roberts, "'The Lady in the Tutti-Frutti Hat': Carmen Miranda, a Spectacle of Ethnicity," *Cinema Journal*, 32: 3, (1993), pp. 3–23.

About the Contributors

Sarah Barrow is senior lecturer in the Department of Communication Studies at Anglia Polytechnic University (APU), Cambridge. There she is Pathway Leader for the degree program in film studies. She is currently working on her Ph.D. thesis on Peruvian cinema and has published a number of papers on this topic. Research interests also include the relationship between cinema, memory, and trauma, as well as the role of national cinema within the context of globalization.

Maite Conde was awarded a Ph.D. in Brazilian Culture from the University of California–Los Angeles in 2004. She is currently a visiting research associate at the University of Oxford's Centre for Brazilian Studies, and visiting lecturer in Portugese at the University of Liverpool.

Stephanie Dennison is a lecturer in Portuguese and Brazilian studies at the University of Leeds, England, where she also devised and coordinates the master's program on world cinemas. She has published a number of articles on Brazilian cinema and is coauthor of *Popular Cinema in Brazil* (Manchester University Press, 2004) and coeditor of *Remapping World Cinema: Identity, Culture and Politics on Film* (forthcoming with Wallflower Press).

Alison Fraunhar is a doctoral candidate in the Department of the History of Art and Architecture at the University of California, Santa Barbara, where she teaches in the Film Studies Department.

Randal Johnson is professor and chair of Spanish and Portuguese at the University of California, Los Angeles. He has published widely on Brazilian culture and film, and is coeditor of *Brazilian Cinema* (University of Columbia Press, 1995).

Robert J. Miles is a fellow in Hispanic studies at the University of Leeds. His areas of research interest include 20th century Hispanic literature (particularly post–civil war prose fiction and exile writing), Spain under Franco, art history and aesthetics, Hispanic cinema, and contemporary visual cultures.

Keith Richards has taught in several universities in Britain and the United States. He has published widely on Latin American cinema and Andean literature. His book *Lo Imaginario Mestizo* (The Mestizo Imaginary) was published in 1999 by Plural, La Paz; a critical study of contemporary writing and popular culture in Bolivia and an anthology of fiction from eastern Bolivia are in preparation.

Lisa Shaw is senior lecturer in Portuguese and Brazilian studies at the University of Leeds. In the fall term of 1999 she was visiting professor in Brazilian culture and civilization at the University of California, Los Angeles. She is author of *The Social History of Brazilian Samba* (Ashgate, 1999) and a range of articles on Brazilian and Portuguese popular music and film, and coauthor of *Popular Cinema in Brazil* (Manchester University Press, 2004).

Claire Taylor is lecturer in Hispanic Studies at the University of Liverpool, where she currently teaches a variety of courses on Latin American literature, art, and film. Her research interests cover broadly three areas: contemporary Latin American women's writing; Latin American cinema; and Latin American popular culture. She has published articles on a variety of women writers, and is author of the book *Bodies and Texts: Configurations of Identities in the Works of Griselda Gambaro, Albalucía Angel and Laura Esquivel* (MHRA, 2003).

Ismail Xavier is titular professor of cinema at the Escola de Comunicações e Artes (ECA) of the University of São Paulo, Brazil. He is the author of a number of important monographs on Brazilian cinema, including *Allegories of Underdevelopment: Aesthetics and Politics in Modern Brazilian Cinema* (University of Minnesota Press, 1997).

Index